October Baseball

For Gail, Amy and Valentino.
All good things in life begin with a dream.

October Baseball

*Ballplayers Discuss
Postseason Play*

DAN ZACHOFSKY

foreword by Mike Lowell

McFarland & Company, Inc., Publishers
Jefferson, North Carolina, and London

ALSO BY DAN ZACHOFSKY
AND FROM MCFARLAND

*Idols of the Spring: Baseball Interviews
About Preseason Training* (2001)

*Collecting Baseball Memorabilia:
A Handbook* (2000)

LIBRARY OF CONGRESS CATALOGUING-IN-PUBLICATION DATA

Zachofsky, Dan, 1951–
  October baseball : ballplayers discuss postseason play / Dan Zachofsky ; foreword by Mike Lowell.
    p.   cm.
  Includes bibliographical references and index.

  ISBN 0-7864-2181-9 (softcover : 50# alkaline paper)

  World Series (Baseball)—History. 2. Baseball—United States—History. 3. Baseball players—United States—Interviews. 4. Baseball managers—United States—Interviews. I. Title.
GV878.4.Z33   2005
796.357'645—dc22   2004030524

British Library cataloguing data are available

©2005 Dan Zachofsky. All rights reserved

No part of this book may be reproduced or transmitted in any form or by any means, electronic or mechanical, including photocopying or recording, or by any information storage and retrieval system, without permission in writing from the publisher.

Cover: The Florida Marlins celebrate their 2003 World Series win *(Online Sports)*

Manufactured in the United States of America

*McFarland & Company, Inc., Publishers
  Box 611, Jefferson, North Carolina 28640
  www.mcfarlandpub.com*

Acknowledgments

It took me many years to realize that a star is born in the postseason, from an unheralded player. In the 1959 World Series a relief pitcher delivered for the Los Angeles Dodgers in all four games that the team won. Larry Sherry won two games in relief and saved two games, pitching over 12 innings, which is unheard of today. In the 1997 postseason, an unknown Craig Counsell, with practically no major league experience, was born in the Series and knocked in the tying run and scored the winning run for the Florida Marlins in Game 7 of the World Series.

As an eight year old, I experienced my first postseason series in 1959, watching the Dodgers defeat the Braves by winning two games in the playoffs to win the National League pennant. Then in the World Series the unexpected happened, as it does from time to time. The Dodgers had no really great players, no one of superstar caliber at that particular time — Snider was near the end of a Hall of Fame career and Koufax and Drysdale were just beginning to come of age. After being clobbered 11–0 in Game 1, the Dodgers found a way to win the World Series in six games against the favored Chicago White Sox.

Nobody saw the Marlins matching up with the Yankees in the World Series in 2003, but a young Florida Marlin team that was fearless and inexperienced found a way to defeat a talented and experienced Yankees team in six games. Josh Beckett, the 2003 World Series MVP, was outstanding in his performances against the Cubs and the Yankees.

I began to conduct my interviews during spring training in 2004 and continued throughout the season. Since the Marlins World Series championship was the end to an amazing storybook season, and since the Marlins had won two World Series championships as a wild card team, I felt I had to begin the process and conduct interviews with Jack McKeon, the taskmaster and "old geezer," who turned the season around when most thought he was too old to manage again. Along the way I sought out Mike Lowell, Josh Becket, Dontrelle Willis, Juan Pierre and the new pitching coach, Wayne Rosenthal, who butted heads with the young arms, but in the end, helped them improve their pitching approach to win a championship. In particular, I want to thank Mike Lowell for writing the foreword to this book and reflecting upon the 2003 championship season.

The players I conducted interviews with were all enthusiastic and provided personal postseason experiences and interesting comments. Thank you Tony Perez, Robin Yount, Luis Gonzalez, Mark Grace, Craig Counsell, Tom Glavine, Javy Lopez, Chipper Jones, John Smoltz, Craig Biggio, Jeff Bagwell, Jim Edmonds, Jim Thome, Alfonso Soriano, Jeff Nelson, Don Baylor, Burt Hooton, Steve Blass, Tommy Hutton, Lou Piniella, Larry Bowa, Jim Leyland, Jack McKeon, Wayne Rosenthal and Steve Blass. Each player gave me a different perspective about postseason play and they are the reason that baseball reaches its glory in October to even the casual fan.

A heartfelt appreciation is given to Steve Copses, the Marlins' media relations director, who provided me access to the clubhouse, field and press box to conduct my interviews. I want to thank Andrew Feirstein, Alex Horowitz and Maria Armella from the Marlins' media relations offiice. Andy provided me player information and postseason game notes; Alex provided me team media guides and daily notes to conduct my research; and Maria provided me field credentials and was personable throughout the season.

I would also like to thank the other media relations directors who allowed me to interview the players: Bill Stetka of the Orioles, Lisa Ramsperger of the Astros, Mike Swanson of the Diamondbacks, Brad Hainje of the Braves, John Olguin of the Dodgers, Leigh Tobin of the Phillies, Jim Trdinich of the Pirates and Brian Bartow of the Cardinals.

I want to thank Oscar Huete, a freelance photographer, who contributed some of the photographs while I interviewed the players at Pro Player Stadium, and became my friend, mi amigo.

My biggest fan, my wife, Gail, has provided support and has endured my passion for the game for over 30 years. My beautiful daughter Amy, who is a graduate student pursuing her own career, will one day realize that her dreams will come true too.

My parents, Adele and Morris Zachofsky, provided support and love throughout my life, and have always been an inspiration for all of my accomplishments. They would definitely have enjoyed this book.

For the following fans who've experienced the thrill of victory and the disappointment of postseasons past, and still believe that next season will be their World Series championship, this one is for you: John Henry Ledwith (Giants fan), Dr. Martin Marenus (will never forgive the 1964

Phillies and later became a Marlins fan), Ira Berkowitz (lifelong Phillies fan), Raymond Batt (great Dodger fan who tells everybody to "Wait till next year"), Rick Thompson (a starved Orioles fan), Lori Cobb (Marlins fan from their inaugural season and looking forward to another championship season), Vicki Deater (Mariners and especially an "Ichiro" fan), Gail Tanner (loyal Marlins fan), RJ Timmens (Marlin season ticket holder from the beginning and hardcore Yankees fan), Joe Alfonso (Marlins and Yankees fan), Russel Bleiler (happy about the Red Sox championship—no more curse!—and dedicated Phillies fan), Judy Champagne (born a Red Sox fan, and became a great Marlins fan while living in Florida—Judy realized her dream of a championship season in back to back years, first in 2003 with the Marlins and experiencing it again in 2004 with the Red Sox championship) and Heather Richards (a disappointed and obsessed Yankees fan). I want to thank Marla Press (Mets fan), a colleague at Horizon Elementary School, who provided good suggestions while reading my introductory chapter.

Finally, after 86 years, a lifetime of waiting for Red Sox fans, the Boston Red Sox are the 2004 World Champions. A colorful sign displayed by Red Sox faithful at Busch Stadium summed up their remarkable championship season: "From cursed to first." Will the loveable Cubbies emerge in 2005 and have their goat reverse the curse? For even casual baseball fans, nothing compares to baseball in October.

Table of Contents

Acknowledgments   v
Foreword by Mike Lowell   1
Introduction   3

Jack McKeon • *Trader Jack, the Donald Rumsfeld of Baseball*   15
Jim Leyland • *The Skipper*   26
Mike Lowell • *Marlins Hometown Hero*   37
Josh Beckett • *World Series Most Valuable Player*   47
Wayne Rosenthal • *Pitching Coach and Guru*   54
Dontrelle Willis • *The Journey of the D Train*   64
Tony Perez • *The Heart and Soul of The Big Red Machine*   70
Robin Yount • *The Brew Crew's Most Valuable Player*   78
Luis Gonzalez • *Gonzo's Championship Season*   89
Mark Grace • *Professional Hitter and Gold Glove Winner*   98
Tommy Hutton • *The Phillies' Steady Pinch-Hitter and Commentator*   105
Juan Pierre • *Team Leader and Master of the Small Game*   114
Chipper Jones • *Baseball's Best Run Producer and Switch-Hitter*   122
John Smoltz • *Braves Top Gun Turned Closer*   132
Javier Lopez • *Quiet Superstar*   141
Tom Glavine • *Braves Pitching Great, Future Hall of Famer*   148
Burt Hooton • *Mr. Happy, 1981 Championship Season*   157
Lou Piniella • *Sweet Lou, Clutch World Series Performer and Manager*   167

Don Baylor • *Manager, 1987 Championship Season*	177
Steve Blass • *1971 Pirates World Series Hero*	185
Jeff Bagwell • *Superstar, Future Hall of Famer*	193
Jim Thome • *Phillies' Winning Slugger*	199
Craig Biggio • *Astros Leader and Gold Glove Winner*	206
Larry Bowa • *The Phillies Fanatic—Manager, 1980 Championship Season*	212
Alfonso Soriano • *All-Star, Superstar and Future Hall of Famer*	220
Jeff Nelson • *The Set-up Man in Pinstripes*	226
Jim Edmonds • *Clutch Hitting Slugger and Defensive Anchor*	239
Craig Counsell • *The Grinder and Winner*	246
Bibliography	255
Index	257

Foreword
by Mike Lowell

The 2003 season was the realization of a dream come true. Twenty-five guys coming together to attain a world championship when no one thought it was possible. We were young and inexperienced, yet fearless and confident.

Our playoff run actually began in September, chasing a wild-card berth with as many as six teams still in the hunt. The final week of the season clinched our playoff spot with a sweep of the talented Phillies and a victory over the Mets with two games left in the regular season.

The division series began in San Francisco and we managed to split the first two games. We came home to a crowd of over 70,000, which provided a baseball atmosphere never before seen to support this Marlin team. The series featured Marlins victories with a two-out game-winning single and a collision at the plate to secure a spot in the league championship series. That throw from Jeff Conine to Pudge Rodriguez was definitely one of the most exciting plays to end a playoff round in post-season history.

We headed to Chicago to face the Cubs in the league championship series. This was finally my chance to prove I was healthy enough to contribute after my hand was fractured when it was hit by a pitch in late August. Fortunately, I hit the biggest home run of my career, a pinch-hit game-winner in the 11th inning to put us ahead 1 game to 0. After falling behind 3 games to 1, our guys regrouped and were able to win the series in seven games, taking Games 6 and 7 in an electrifying atmosphere at Wrigley Field. What another amazing series!

In the World Series our young arms took over, bolstered by timely hitting, to take the series in six games and win the title in Yankee Stadium. We overcame a team that had more playoff experience, more world titles, and a historic tradition that is second to none in baseball. Yankee

Stadium seemed silent as Josh Beckett tagged out Jorge Posada for the final out.

All in all, enjoying a career year, winning a World Series, proving the experts wrong with the closest group of teammates I have ever played with, and doing it all in the city I grew up in was nothing short of a dream coming true.

Introduction

When Jack McKeon became the Marlins' new manager in 2003, he had no idea that the dream of a championship season would be realized after 50 years in baseball. And who would believe that dream would culminate in a celebration at Yankee Stadium where the heart and soul of Ruth, Gehrig, DiMaggio and Mantle pass from one generation of champions to another? For the Florida Marlins to rise from mediocrity to surprise the Giants, to make an amazing comeback against the Cubs and then suck the life out of the Yankees, is the dream of a championship team. That dream took place in 2003.

Some would tell you it was surreal, a dream come true, the unbelievable ending to a season of unexpected accomplishment—one of baseball's most amazing feats in recent years. The 2003 postseason script called for a young, brash and confident player to pitch his team to a World Series title. What kind of personality did it take to pitch a shutout in the World Series and at Yankee Stadium? It took a confident and arrogant sort of thrower who wasn't intimidated by the ghosts of series past in Yankee Stadium.

In the eighth inning of Game 6, he came to the plate with a runner on base, the tying run at the plate. He asked for time, adjusted the top part of his helmet, and grabbed his inner thigh, placing his bat between his legs, pulling on each glove and finally grasping the end of the bat. There was electricity in the stadium, the realization that the game was on the line. He froze and looked at a called strike one. The crowd made a collective gasp to distract the pitcher, but Jeter swung and missed for strike two on that cold October night. Jeter flied out and a double play ended the eighth inning.

Josh Beckett realized he was one inning away from the Marlins winning their second world championship. With the Marlins leading 2–0, the Yankees went down 1, 2, 3 in the bottom half of the ninth inning; the exclamation point was Beckett fielding a slow hit ball toward first base and tagging Jorge Posada firmly on his chest to end the game. This was no fluke. Beckett and the Marlins quietly and decisively shut down the Yankees to win the title. The team played flawless, perfect baseball, in the fashion of former Yankee teams. The New York fans sat in their seats in disbelief, in shock at the unexpected loss. The silence was deafening; it became so quiet that evening that you could hear the sound of the Yankees dynasty crashing.

Spring Training

The dream of a championship season takes shape as the players report for spring training and get into their fresh, new uniforms to start working on fundamentals. They work as hard as anybody else, learning a new position or developing a new pitch, but practicing the only job they've been trained to perform. The veterans come into camp in good physical condition, getting ready for the season at their own pace, not too quickly; they want to peak over the six weeks of training. Some veterans are ready after four weeks and seem to drag over the last couple.

The daily preparation includes a stretching session on the outfield grass, running sprints at half speed, bunting drills, pitchers fielding practice, infielders bonding with each other and turning double plays in rapid succession, catchers fielding pop-ups shot out of a cannon-like machine and overrunning wind-blown balls or making spectacular diving catches. Many players believe the practicing of drills over and over again and being fundamentally sound are what it takes to get to the postseason.

It's the beginning of a new baseball season. The veteran players have reported to their spring training camps in Florida and Arizona to work out the winter stiffness at their leisure, with patience that is one of the rites of spring and a sign of experience. Most of the veterans will make the squad, but refining their skills and having fun for six weeks is their main objective. Spring training also brings anticipation, hope, high expectations and lofty goals, and for the injured prospect, the older veteran or the older rookie with too many years in the minor leagues, the unlucky and the defeated, the either comforting or terrifying prospect of closure.

At Roger Dean Stadium, in Jupiter, Florida, where the Cardinals and Marlins conduct spring training, the teams have their own practice fields, outdoor batting cages, several pitching mounds, and state-of-the-art conditioning rooms. They share the main stadium where the games are played every day. The instructors for the Cardinals include Hall of Fame inductees

Introduction 5

2003 World Champs running sprints at spring training.

like Bob Gibson, Lou Brock and Red Schoendienst, who has spent over 60 years in baseball. He is a special assistant to the general manager.

Schoendienst, a spry 81 year old, provides infield work by hitting ground balls to the infielders on a daily basis. He provides a vast amount of baseball knowledge and experience to those players hungry to learn and gain an edge. He experienced the dream of a world championship season as a player in 1946, along with teammates Stan Musial, Enos "Country" Slaughter, Terry Moore, Marty Marion, Joe Garagiola and World Series star Harry "The Cat" Brecheen (who earned three wins in the 1946 World Series).

In 1965 he began a 12-year stint as Cardinals manager, the longest tenure in club history. He managed the Cardinals to a World Series championship in 1967 and the National League pennant in 1968. His 1967 championship team was comprised of talented players and future Hall of Fame inductees Lou Brock, Orlando Cepeda, Bob Gibson and Steve Carlton. In addition, that Cardinals team had well-known names, players who've significantly contributed to the game: Roger Maris, Curt Flood and Tim McCarver.

Jim Leyland, a Cardinals spring training coach and scout during the season and 1997 manager of the world champion Marlins, went out on the

Red Schoendienst, Cardinals spring training instructor, at Roger Dean Stadium in Jupiter, Florida.

field to greet his former players, embracing Edgar Renteria and Luis Castillo, members of the 1997 world championship team. Renteria (now with the Red Sox) and Castillo (playing for the Marlins) solidified the middle part of the infield defensively, and were one of the best double-play combinations in baseball. Leyland made comparisons to the great 1991-92 Pirate teams he managed in the postseason with his 1997 championship team and indicated the teams were similar, except the '97 Marlins had better pitching, with Kevin Brown, Al Leiter, Alex Fernandez, Livan Hernandez and closer Robb Nen.

Talk to any player and ask about what he hopes to accomplish this season, he talks about good health, contributing to their team and being able to play in October—to get to the postseason. Even baseball lifer Jack McKeon reflected on his recurring dream to play the New York Yankees in the World Series and to defeat them at Yankee Stadium. It took him over 50 years in baseball to accomplish the big dream, when the Florida

Jim Leyland greets former teammates Edgar Renteria and Luis Castillo, members of the '97 championship team.

Marlins became the 2003 world champs and he was named National League Manager of the Year.

As I sat with McKeon in his office, his explanation of the team's plan to reach the postseason again sounded so simple and so achievable. He told his players last season that winning a game over .500 every week for 20 weeks (when he was hired on May 11, 2003) ought to get them to the postseason. He told his team they were capable of going 4–3 and making 5–2 runs or better. The Marlins were 10 games under [.500] and he said, "Let's take our time and pick up one game a week, and it worked. We used that philosophy last season and we've told the guys this season, let's not try to do it all at once."

When McKeon took his team to the White House to meet the president in January 2004, George W. Bush called him the Donald Rumsfeld of baseball. The players responded to his approach and discipline by working hard and developing a winning attitude. McKeon believed that unlike most teams he managed, this group had chemistry among the 25 guys in the clubhouse.

Unlike the fire sale of 1997, the club made some moves and parted ways with some key players, including catcher and postseason hero Ivan Rodriguez, Juan Encarnacion, Gold Glove first baseman Derek Lee, pitcher Mark Redman and closers Ugueth Urbina and Braden Looper. When I spoke to Jack McKeon I learned there was competition for a few jobs on the team; however, the loss of Pudge Rodriguez could be a major concern for playing in the postseason again.

McKeon, a no-nonsense and to-the-point baseball veteran, talked about what it takes to experience a championship season. "I told the guys what we do on the field is going to make us a good team. There's no pressure on us. They don't think we're good; nobody thinks we can get to the playoffs. Just play hard and have fun." When the subject of a repeat of the world championship was brought up, he reiterated, "It's going to be a *challenge.*"

McKeon told his young team to perform at a higher level to get to the postseason again. "It's tougher to play on a winner than a loser. The players have to work a little harder." The way you become good is to be consistent.

Watching the workouts, the players appeared to be more serious under McKeon than they were last year under former manager Jeff Torborg. You saw a more businesslike approach to preparation with pitchers Beckett, Penny, Willis and Pavano. The players seemed to know what they had to do to win another world championship.

When Wayne Rosenthal, the new pitching coach, was promoted from the minor league to the Marlins on May 11, 2003, he spoke about the conversation with McKeon and the pitching staff during his first meeting with them. McKeon told the players, "If you don't want to pitch, we're going to get players up here who do." A new attitude emerged. The manager likes to call it tough love.

Wayne Rosenthal, the unknown Marlins pitching coach and new guru in baseball, he believes it's all about mechanics in baseball today. He adjusted Josh Beckett's delivery during the 2003 season. He encouraged Beckett to use his legs more and slowed his pitcher's windup. He believes the reason a pitcher will break down is related to mechanical problems. It's more important how a pitcher throws than how much—pitch counts and innings.

The evolution of the game in the last 10 years with free agency and arbitration has meant that the chemistry of every team has been changing. Just look at the teams that won the last three world championships—the Diamondbacks, Angels and Marlins. Coincidentally, only the 1999 and 2000 Yankees have consecutively repeated in the last 10 years. In reality, die-hard baseball fans in Pittsburgh, Seattle, Tampa, Milwaukee and Montreal have to accept that they have little or no chance of competing to play in the postseason.

As I traveled to spring training camps in Florida in early March, I reflected upon the 2003 season as a renaissance for the game of baseball since the season had been called one of the greatest in baseball history. It was highlighted by remarkable individual accomplishments from players like Eric Gagne, who successfully converted all 55 of his save opportunities (a new major league record) and in a dominating manner to earn the Cy Young Award. Albert Pujols became the National League batting champion with a .359 average, 212 hits, 43 home runs and 124 RBI. And it can be argued that Pujols deserved the Most Valuable Player Award. Alex Rodriguez had another great season with 47 home runs and 118 RBI. In fact, during his three seasons with the Rangers, A-Rod has batted .305, averaged 52 home runs, drove in 132 runs and scored 127 runs. Baseball purists talk about great pitching, but it's the potent individual batting accomplishments that make baseball our national as well international game.

Baseball fans witnessed dramatic pennant races during the 2003 season. There were 17 teams in contention at the beginning of the season's final month. A magnificent postseason with a wild-card team playing against the goliath of baseball teams—defeating the Giants, the Cubs and the heavily favored New York Yankees, and amazingly winning the World Series at Yankee Stadium with the confidence of a champion. It's interesting to note that the Florida Marlins have become the only major league team to win two world championships as a wild-card team, and despite the fact that the Atlanta Braves have garnered 13 consecutive division titles, they've earned one less world championship than the Marlins. Go back a few seasons and think about the suggestion of Commissioner Bud Selig to contract the Florida Marlins. Winning the 2003 World Series was remarkable for the Marlins and one that has captivated fans around the world.

Traveling to interview players at the beginning of a new season is an exciting experience. Interviewing managerial greats Jim Leyland and Jack McKeon and listening to them talk about their postseason experiences was a dream for me as well. And interviewing baseball's greats like Jeff Bagwell, Javier Lopez, Luis Gonzalez, Jim Edmonds, Chipper Jones and Tom Glavine—these players are winners and future Hall of Fame inductees. Jones and Glavine talk about what it takes to win in the postseason. The postseason is short, and it takes talent, getting hot at the right time, good pitching, good defense, a little bit of luck to be successful in the postseason. There's little room for mistakes.

Javy Lopez talked about the letdown with the Braves over his eight years with the team. He seemed to believe that clinching the division so early and having a long layoff prior to the postseason play affected his team and maybe their motivation level. Another factor in postseason success according to Lopez was the fact that the postseason is a short series—anybody can get hot during the playoffs and World Series. In terms of great pitching, Glavine, Smoltz and Maddux are great pitchers with power, great control and off-speed stuff; that has made Lopez more patient and a better hitter. As far as having a career year in 2003, Lopez batted .328 with 43 homers (a new record for a catcher), and 109 runs batted in. He attributed his great numbers to hard work and motivation because he played poorly in the 2002 season. He indicated that his great season had nothing to do with renegotiating a new contract with the Braves.

I also caught up with several stars-to-be—Juan Pierre, Alfonso Soriano, Mike Lowell, Dontrelle Willis and Josh Beckett—talented players with leadership qualities and great work ethics. Pierre, a throwback to the days of Pete Rose, Maury Wills and Rickey Henderson, was always working on improving his game—despite having 204 hits, 100 runs, 65 stolen bases, a .305 batting average and making only three errors the entire 2003 season. He still felt he needed to work harder to become an accomplished ballplayer. His teammates and manager recognized his leadership qualities in some of the little things he did: He got to the ballpark early to work on his lead (off first base and second base), and he tossed balls off the outfield wall at other stadiums to study the movement and angle of hit balls against the wall to properly position himself.

Dontrelle Willis brought to his team a high level of energy and enthusiasm the players fed off of. He was called up to the big leagues from Double-A in early May 2003 and piled up 14 wins, making the National League All-Star team and being selected the Rookie of the Year. He attributed much of his success to his teammates, specifically his catcher, Pudge Rodriguez. In our conversations, he stated, "It's a blessing and a challenge to be able to compete mentally and physically with players I grew up watching and admiring." He realizes he had a remarkable rookie season and wouldn't change the success, or the struggles, he experienced. He reflected that he was throwing great early in the season but at one point couldn't get anybody out. Willis said, "I'm a guy that likes to put everything in perspective and I try to be positive, even when I do well or struggle. I realize now you have to grow up, be a man, and take responsibility."

I cannot forget my interview with Tony Perez, an outstanding player and a member of the 1975-76 Big Red Machine (championship team), who spoke about his teammates—Concepcion, Rose, Morgan, Bench, Griffey

Introduction   11

Sr., Foster, Geronimo—and the impact they made. He told me, "In 1975-76, we had the best team in baseball, and we dominated." Perez remembered a home run he hit in Game 7 of the 1975 World Series against the Red Sox that provided a 4–3 game and series win. He spoke with tearful enthusiasm and pride about his induction into the Hall of Fame in 2000 and what the honor meant, to be included with the greatest players—Ernie Banks, Frank Robinson, Roberto Clemente and Willie Mays. He also indicated that upon his demise, his Hall of Fame plaque will be an eternal fixture in the Cooperstown museum.

When I arrived at the baseball camps I observed the Dodgers, Cardinals, Marlins and Orioles clubhouses and noticed that each was similar in how the players were approaching the new season. After reporting around eight o'clock and getting into uniform, some players immediately reported to the weight room for strengthening exercises. Jim Edmonds, who was recovering from off-season shoulder surgery, spent the early morning working in the weight room. He was a vocal clubhouse leader and a hard-working player who had to stay healthy for the Cardinals to get to the postseason. Watching him participate in batting practice and fielding drills, you knew you were seeing a unique and talented ballplayer. He's a great hitter with exceptional defensive skills and a leader by example. In the clubhouse you quickly noticed ballplayers like Scott Rolen, Reggie Sanders and Ray Lankford standing by his locker and talking hitting with Edmonds.

Mike Lowell, who grew up in Miami and had an outstanding season in 2003, reflected upon the fact that the championship team was young and inexperienced, yet fearless and confident. Hitting the biggest home run of his career, a pinch-hit game-winner in the 11th inning of Game 1 against the Cubs in the 2003 league championship series provided the confidence his team needed to continue on to the World Series. It was a young team coming together to win a world championship when no one thought it possible.

Luis Gonzalez, the Diamondbacks' left fielder, spoke about his childhood dream to hit a game-winning home run in Game 7 of the World Series with the bases loaded, two outs and the game on the line. You act out that scenario over and over as a child, but that dream came to fruition for Gonzalez in Arizona's win over the Yankees in Game 7 of the 2001 World Series. He was facing Mariano Rivera with the bases loaded and two outs in the bottom of the ninth inning and hit a bloop single over Jeter's head to win the World Series.

The players are extremely optimistic and have dreams about the new season. When the season begins the players become more serious, and getting off to a good start is essential. The baseball season is very demanding, and the good teams will establish an identity while the mediocre teams will struggle without hope and drop out of contention early in the season. The good teams that get to the postseason find ways to win. Clutch hits, great defensive plays, stealing bases, solid pitching and the fundamentals they've practiced over and over again have given them an edge.

Teams that get to the postseason are also more dependent on players called specialists. Managers want six to seven quality innings from their starters, then an inning or two from the set-up man; the key guy, the closer, has to shut the door on the other teams accumulating 40 to 50 saves in a season. It comes down to pitching in the postseason to win it all. The more successful pitchers know that pitching in the ninth inning is more about a player's mind and less about his arm. The closer has one inning to get it done and the successful throwers become intimidating.

Eric Gagne has been the most dominant closer in the game today. He had 84 consecutive saves (a record that dates from August 26, 2002, to July 5, 2004). I met up with him in the Dodgers dugout before the game and he told me, "Every time I step on the mound, you have to be a good liar and an idiot. You got to be able to lie to yourself and be an idiot to believe your lies. You got to go out there and know you're going to be the best. Just think it." The mental aspect of closing is vital to Gagne—he sees those final three outs while he is getting ready to close it out. He would surrender his awards and accomplishments to get the opportunity to be called upon in Game 7 of the World Series.

John Smoltz was a dominating starting pitcher throughout the 1990s and became a closer in 2001 to save his career from shoulder injuries. In 2002 he closed out 55 games and in 2003 he saved 45 games. Talking to me about his role as a closer, he stated, "The last three outs are the hardest thing to get. You face failure every single time and it's a mental challenge, as well as a physical challenge because you can potentially pitch in 80–84 baseball games a year, and the pressure mounts." Closing out 95 to 98 percent of the games is what it's going to take to get a team to the postseason.

The game hasn't changed. In fact, baseball today seems to be more exciting with the addition of interleague play, pitting teams from the American and National League, and the addition of a wild-card team that will need to win 11 games to become world champs. With this system in place, the season is longer; generates more excitement for the fans, and adds more revenue for the teams and Major League Baseball. It gives some teams the chance to compete as a wild card to get to the postseason (Twins, Diamondbacks, Angels and Marlins).

Introduction

The great baseball franchises are rich in tradition. Talk about the Yankees, the Red Sox and the Cubs, and the conversation centers on a championship season for these storied teams with a great history. The question asked every season is will this be the year the curse finally ends for the Boston Red Sox and the Chicago Cubs? It did end for the Red Sox in 2004 and despite the fact that the Red Sox and Cubs have been called loveable losers, you would never know that when you go to Fenway Park or Wrigley Field. The enthusiasm and excitement of a sold-out crowd of baseball fans exudes the feeling of a championship team.

The fans know that baseball is a team game played with 25 players, and each player has an important role in a long season of 162 games. Players talk about respect and leading by example. Most will tell you that it's about earning the respect of your teammates and becoming a leader. Still individual statistics is the prevailing theme among the truest purist. Will Bonds break Aaron's home-run record? Will Maddux and Johnson win 300 games? And in a season of records, what about Sheffield batting .330 with 190 hits, 39 home runs, 132 runs batted in and an amazingly low 55 strikeouts in the 2003 season? But, the prevailing question I keep hearing over and over is, how has the game of baseball changed? How has the game changed?

Have the Yankees created what the media calls an evil empire, which may be bad for baseball, with the acquisitions of Alex Rodriguez, Jason Giambi, Gary Sheffield, Kevin Brown, Kenny Lofton and Javier Vazquez? Listening to the scribes covering the Florida teams for their local newspapers and the beat writers with the Orioles, Marlins, Mets and Dodgers, the general consensus is the Yankees are not bad for baseball, and neither is their trade for Alex Rodriguez. While it seems the Yankees have historically had a stronghold over and dominated their opposition with the acquisition of players each season, one would dispute this rational thinking by just looking at the outcomes of the past three World Series. The Yankees lost the series to the Diamondbacks, Angels and Marlins, three teams that had payrolls significantly less than the Yankees. So, this argument leads to the next question that I've heard over and over from a fan's perspective: what about a salary cap like the National Football League?

Ken Rosenthal, in the *Sporting News*, wrote that Major League Baseball has had three different champions the past three years, which has created more than the parity-crazed, salary cap–diluted National Football League can say. A middle class in baseball is emerging because of the recent labor agreement which provides money from the high-revenue teams like the Yankees, Dodgers and Mets, that is redistributed to low-revenue teams like the Marlins, Twins and Royals (who made a playoff run in their 2003 campaign). Ultimately, higher payrolls do not automatically equate to success, as evidenced by the recent lavish spending of the Dodgers and Mets.

The hot topic in baseball today is the talk and media coverage about the use of steroids. A recent polling of the players found that 5 to 7 percent of them use steroids. Both the owners and the players union realize the daily talk about steroids isn't good for the game. The players union has the power, responsibility and duty to rid the game of illegal drugs. It has become very clear that baseball has been too slow to deal with this problem. And some players using performance-enhancing drugs compromise the playing field, while others don't.

The interviews in the following chapters have been conducted with Major League Baseball players, managers and pitching coaches. Many have played on championship teams and expect to again; others like Jeff Bagwell and Craig Biggio, have done nearly everything in the careers that ballplayers dream about—winning Gold Gloves and MVPs, playing in the All-Star Game, reaching the playoffs—but haven't yet celebrated a World Series title.

The players share their thoughts and feelings about their accomplishments, about hitting and pitching, what it takes to become a champion and the conversation about leadership qualities on a winning team. Each player talks about his dreams, about people who've provided the motivation and encouragement to become a better ballplayer, and what goes on in a winning major league clubhouse.

Imagine what it's like for young pitchers when a baseball great like Sandy Koufax comes into a back room in your clubhouse to talk about baseball and a lesson in being a professional. The young pitchers become the students of the game discussing pitch selection, grips, attitude, and technical aspects of pitching with the master, who accomplished the same dream a half century ago.

October Baseball is about playing in the postseason; many players go home for the winter, while some get the opportunity to continue to play. Will the ghosts of Yankees past reappear this season? Will the goat leave the loveable Cubbies or will the young Marlins repeat again?

Jack McKeon
TRADER JACK, THE DONALD RUMSFELD OF BASEBALL
2003 National League Manager of the Year

"The first thing I said, hey fellas, I don't need this job. I'm down here to win. I'm going to show you there's enough talent in this room to get to the playoffs. We can play in October if you all want to pay the price." —Jack McKeon

John Aloysius McKeon, better known as Jack McKeon, has been involved in Major League Baseball for the past 55 seasons as a player and manager and he has worked in the front office as a senior advisor for the Reds. He was signed in the Pirates organization as a catcher in 1949. In 1950, he played at Burlington where he caught 139 of the club's 140 games. He played 10 seasons in the minors with the exception of the 1951 season, when he served in the military.

He became the catcher-manager for Missoula of the Pioneer League from 1956 to 1958 and had his best offensive season in 1958, when he hit .263. In addition to playing, he developed young players with talent and recognized Jim Kaat, who became a 283-game winner in the majors. Many people in baseball believe that Kaat is deserving of the call from the Veterans Committee for induction into the Hall of Fame. McKeon believed Kaat would be a successful big-league pitcher when few others did. Kaat spoke about McKeon and said, "Encouragement was his greatest contribution to my career."

McKeon served as the vice president of baseball operations with the San Diego Padres from 1980 to 90, where he earned the nickname "Trader Jack" for his penchant for multiplayer trades. He made 45 trades during his tenure in the Padres front office. He joined the Reds organization in 1993 and served as senior advisor for player personnel, consulting with the general manager on trades, player evaluations and special assignments.

He began his managerial career in 1972 with the Kansas City Royals and led the Royals to an 88–74 record and a second-place finish in the AL West. He managed in Oakland in 1977 and 1978 and was named the Padres' skipper in 1988. He spent parts of three seasons with the Padres posting a 193–164 record in his 357 games while at San Diego. In 1999 he led the Reds to a 96–67 record and became the National League Manager of the Year.

He was named the seventh manager in Marlins history on May 11, 2003, replacing Jeff Torborg, and posted a 75–49 record (.605) in his 124 games with the team. He became the oldest major league manager to reach the postseason for the first time—was 72 years old. In the 2003 World Series, he led the Marlins to their second world championship, defeating the Yankees in six games and winning the World Series at Yankee Stadium. McKeon was named National League Manager of the Year by the Baseball Writers Association of America in 2003, his second award (the first coming in 1999 with the Reds).

I conducted an interview with the enthusiastic McKeon in his office

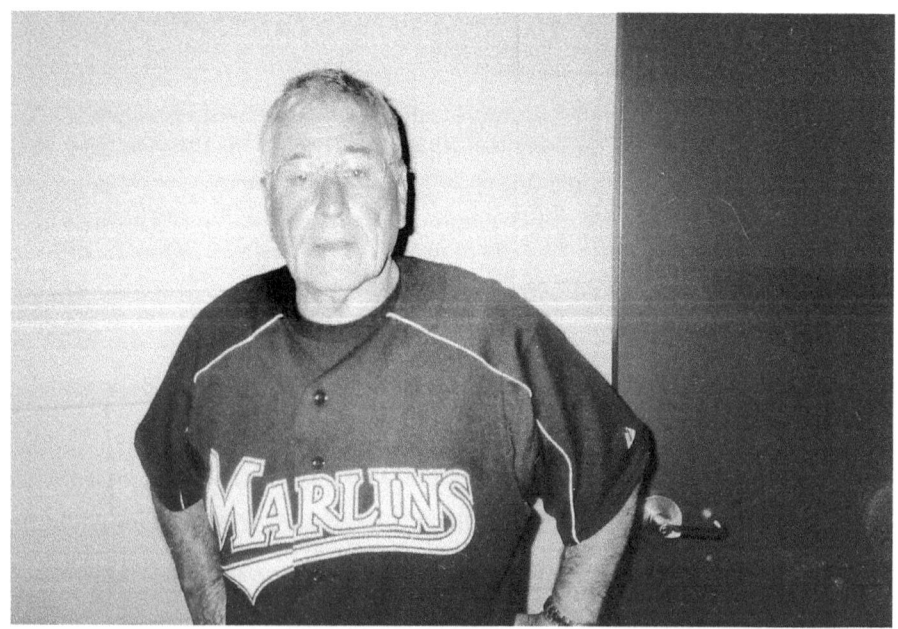

Jack McKeon at spring training at Roger Dean Stadium in Jupiter, Florida.

at Roger Dean Stadium in Jupiter, Florida, at the end of spring training. He spoke about what it would take to defend the championship, while holding his trademark cigar in his hand.

Conversation with Jack McKeon

You've been described as a baseball lifer with over 55 years of experience. How do you relate to the players today?
    I've had a lot of opportunities to help young players reach the major leagues. My main objective [as a manager] is to try to provide them knowledge from my years of experience and help them become better players.

To players like Dontrelle Willis, Josh Beckett, and Miguel Cabrera, you're like a grandfather. Do you feel you can relate to these guys with little big league experience?
    Actually, they're no different than my own youngsters growing up, and I treat them like my sons. I give them tough love when I have to; I have to discipline them at times. I try to encourage these players to dedicate themselves to hard work to become better players and All-Stars. They need to be better prepared and stay on the right path to be successful players.

When you received the call from Larry Beinfest about a managerial change, what did he tell you?
    He said, "We're making a change in managers and we want you to come down and manage the club. Do you want the job?" I said, "Yes." [Laughs.] It took me about 15 seconds because this is what I love. I love teaching kids; I love being around young kids; I love being able to put my mark on helping them become good major league players.

What did you tell the players during your first team meeting when you became the new manager on May 11, 2003?
    The first thing I said, "Hey fellas, look, I don't need this job; I'm down here to win. I'm going to show you there's enough talent in this room to get to the playoffs. We can play in October if you all want to pay the price; it's all up to you. Some of you guys have got to change your ways. Here's what we have to do: We're going to dedicate ourselves a little bit better; we're going to have to improve our work habits; we're going to have

to become more focused. We have to have a little bit of pride, work together as a unit and be unselfish. And the main thing, I want you to go out there and have fun. I want you to play relaxed, have fun, enjoy coming to the ballpark, and if everybody wants to pay the price, [do those things] we can play in October."

What did you observe about the team when you arrived early in the season?

I found out a lot of youngsters didn't know how to prepare themselves. They didn't know it took a lot of dedication and hard work to achieve the goals that they've achieved. I think it was a constant riding them to get better, to get better, push, push yourself, [push, push]. I kept pushing them and pushing them and getting on them to work harder. [Basically,] I kept on encouraging them because they had a tremendous amount of ability—a God-given ability and they're not going to get to the top unless they work for it.

So, when you took control of the team, you gave the players a kind of kick in the butt?

[Absolutely.] I had to help the young players. I can't blame the youngsters because they came into a situation—that's the way it was in the past. These young guys followed the pattern of the other guys—hey, you know, I don't have to work hard, I don't have to run, I don't have to do this—why should I have to do it? I don't think they knew any better. When I came in I said, "No, this is not the way it's going to be. You want to be successful; this is what you have to do." This was a case where they had to stay focused. I wanted them to pay attention every day, and sit on the bench and learn. Watch the opposition, become better focused on your job, try to learn something new every day, and don't take anything for granted.

Who were some of the players you had to talk to?

I spoke to the young pitchers—Beckett, Penny, Willis and Pavano. I said, "If you don't want to pitch, we're going to get players up here who do." We talked about pitching and mechanics. I told them, "It's more important how a pitcher throws than how much he throws. Poor mechanics is the reason why players hurt themselves." Those young guys ended up becoming pretty good pitchers.

Prior to joining the Marlins in 2003, how were you spending your retirement away from baseball?

Well, I was basically working with my grandson and his high school baseball team. I have a grandson that was a junior in high school, so I had two years to help develop him—polish up his baseball skills and hope he would get a college scholarship. Well, he received a scholarship to the University of North Carolina at Wilmington. I kept involved with the American Legion in high school teams by helping the youngsters, giving them some of my knowledge and helping them become better ballplayers.

What was your initial goal when you became the new manager?

My initial goal was to turn this club around into a winning club. Did I know we would win the World Series? No, but I knew we were going to win. I knew there was too much talent on this team and my job was to provide them a new direction, and [basically] they needed a little discipline.

As a young 73-year-old manager, what is it about this game that still gets you excited?

Well, it's something I grew up in; I've been in the game for a number of years [55 years]. This is what I love. I don't know anything else but baseball. I think I have a tremendous amount of experience to give to these youngsters.

Did you ever dream you would play in the World Series and defeat the Yankees in six games?

No, I didn't. [Laughs.] After being out of baseball for two years and at the age of 72, I didn't think there would be anybody that would be willing to give me a chance again because of the age factor. Larry Beinfest and Jeffey Loria had the courage to take a chance on a 72-year-old guy.

Talk about the 2003 world champion Marlins.

This was a special team. I managed 14 years in the big leagues and I've never had a group of players that were so unselfish, so dedicated, had tremendous chemistry, and had a tremendous desire to win. It's unique to find 25 guys that bonded together so well. And I think I'll probably never have it happen again.

Who were some of the leaders on that club?

Well, we had a number of leaders on that club. Pudge Rodriguez, Mike Lowell, Jeff Conine came in late and gave us a little spurt in leadership. You look at a number of players—Castillo and Gonzalez. But I think a lot of guys didn't recognize the fact that my extra players were some very important key leaders on this club. They were unselfish, dedicated guys that had every right to gripe and complain about not playing, but they were encouraging their teammates on the field [playing] every day. Many times I apologized to the players at a meeting, [that] I didn't give them enough playing time and to a man they would come up to me and say, "Don't worry about it, Skip, we're only concerned about winning. Don't worry about us."

What can you say about Pudge [Rodriguez] and what he meant to this club?
Oh, Pudge is going to be in the Hall of Fame. There's no question about that. He's an outstanding player and I had a tremendous relationship with him. I love him. He's a guy that really came through big time in the playoffs and World Series with his leadership skills. And he led by example—he did the job. Like I've said, he will definitely be in the Hall of Fame one day. Anybody that loses a player of that caliber is going to be missed.

When did you notice the team was beginning to click—to play winning baseball?
Well, I thought after 10 days I saw a big improvement in the way we were going about our work. When did it really sink in? When we got 10 games under .500, I told them this is a marathon, not a sprint. I said, "Let's not try to do it all at once. Let's pick up a game a week. If we can pick up a game a week, we can be 20 games over [.500] by the end of the year, and we'll be in the playoffs." [Basically,] we would be playing seven games in a week and I was preaching, "Let's be 4–3." And there was 20 weeks left and it was only two weeks that we didn't pick up a game a week. And some weeks we picked up two [games]. It was a case of seeing these guys start to pull together and everything started to click about the middle of August. I knew at that point we're going to the playoffs.

Once you get to the playoffs as a wild-card team, you realize you need to win 11 games to be the world champs. What did you tell your players?
Well, the biggest thing ... there was no pressure on us. I told the guys my philosophy is to go out and have some fun, so we play with less pressure. I want my players to have fun; I want them to enjoy coming to the park. If they have fun coming to the ballpark and they enjoy their work, they're going to play with no pressure. All through the playoffs I kept telling them, "Look guys, let's go out and do our thing, let's play our regular

game. What we do on the field is going to make us a good team. Why should we worry about it? No one has picked us to win, and let's show the world what kind of team we are. Let's go out there, just play hard and have fun."

What is it going to take to repeat again?

Well, it's going to take the same kind of dedication; it's going to take improvement on our pitching. We have a young staff that everybody wants to rank up as one of the better ones. This staff has the potential to be great; this is going to be an outstanding staff in another year or two, but we must continue to improve. We cannot rest on our laurels. Yesterday is history—last year's World Series is history. The major league is a pretty good league and you can't get by on what you did last year. Some of the clubs in our division made significant improvement and what we're hoping is that our players continue to improve. If the players continue to improve, we'll be right up there again.

Talk about the core of your pitching staff.

We have a great young staff with Beckett, Penny, Willis and Pavano. You have four guys right there that are potentially 20-game winners. We have a sleeper in the hole, hopefully, if he gets back in the middle of May, and that's A.J. [Burnett]. He is probably the best pitcher on the staff, but he's been out with arm injuries. When he returns healthy, this is like picking up a player in a trade. So you put him in the mix and I don't think he can win 20 games this year because he doesn't have enough time. In the long run, I have four or five guys that have the potential to win 20 games, but they're not there yet. It's going to take a year or two to get there with their stuff and ability.

Does adding Darren Oliver to your staff make up for the loss of Burnett?

Darren Oliver is a great acquisition. He knows how to pitch. I think he's been a blessing for us. To be able to pick up a fifth starter like that while Burnett has been out, and who knows when he will come back. In the mean time, Oliver has certainly showed us he is very capable of winning 15 or 16 games.

While Pudge [Rodriguez] is a huge loss, what can you say about Ramon Castro?

He is a youngster with great potential and we have high hopes for him. He hasn't had an opportunity to play on a regular basis. Last year he was slated to be in there, but all of a sudden we got Pudge. That bumped him down to third string again. We know he has good power; we know he's a pretty good catcher and it's a question if he can do it on a consistent basis. We all believe that give him 120 games behind the plate, he will put up pretty good numbers and solidify himself as a number-one catcher.

Describe a typical day for Jack McKeon.

During spring training I get up at five in the morning and get to the ballpark around five thirty. I do running, or jogging in the outfield, or doing three or four miles on the treadmill. I try to take care of business, smoke a couple of cigars and get ready for the game. During the season I get up at seven thirty and get to church at eight thirty and at nine thirty I'm at the ballpark. At 10 o'clock I walk and jog about five miles a day. After showering, I sit in the bullpen with the newspapers and a couple of cigars for a couple of hours. I relax with the beautiful weather here in Florida and wait for the players to show up.

Do you ever wake up and think the 2003 season was a dream?

Many times ... many times. I wake up and tell myself, "I can't believe it happened." You come to spring training and see the words "world champions" and I still can't believe it. The good Lord has been looking after me for a number of years. I think he decided that I was a pretty good guy and he was going to give me one more chance to hit the pot of gold at the end of the rainbow.

Do you still have dreams?

Oh yeah, yeah. I got dreams of winning another World Series. You know, when you get that first one, you get kind of greedy. [Basically,] it was a long time coming and one of the nicest things that was said to me at the final press conference in the World Series in New York, when Joe Torre came up and shook my hand, and said, "Congratulations, you deserved it, enjoy it, and I had to wait a long time too." Torre knew what I went through and he'd been through it before, and I think he was happy for me. I said, "Thanks Joe. I hope I can do it as many times as you did."

What did President Bush tell you when the team visited the White House?

He congratulated us on our great season and world championship. We were going back and forth with banter; he loves baseball, and was so impressed with our team. When he introduced Congressman Cole and me from North Carolina, he told the audience that two old geezers know how to get the job done. He called me the Donald Rumsfeld of baseball.

During your great career in baseball, who were some of the phenoms you developed?

I was privileged to have Harmon Killebrew, Jim Kaat, Tony Oliva, George Brett, Tony Gwynn, Joe Carter and Frank White.

What can you say about those players?

Outstanding. Every one of those guys was something special. [Laughs.] You always remember the guys that were special. I mean, every one of those guys was All-Stars and Hall of Famers, and I'm probably missing some guys in that group. Those guys were just super individuals. The guys played the game the way it should be played. They had tremendous dedication, unselfishness, tremendous focus and great work habits [every one of them]. You know, I often tell this story here—of all my years in managing the guys that had the greatest work habits that I've ever been associated with have been Tony Gwynn and Juan Pierre.

Why is Juan Pierre special?

He's like Tony Gwynn; he's a specialist. He wants to succeed; he has a tremendous amount of pride and wants to be perfect in his game. And Pierre gets to the ballpark at one o'clock and he's practicing his leads and breaks off first base, off second base. He's running in the outfield; he's checking the walls—he throws balls against the walls to get the rebounds. He is practicing to see how the ball caroms off the walls. He always looking for the little edge that you wish every player would have the dedication and desire to succeed and be prepared as this guy does.

As a manager of major league players, is your role that of a teacher?

I'm a teacher, no question about it. I told the players, "Anybody that looks back and says, hey, here's a guy that's been in the game over 50 years—you can learn something from him." I want to give all the knowledge I have to these young guys. Sure, maybe some of it is going to work, and some of it is not. I'll give you the advantage of all 50 years of experience. All the mistakes I've made, I'm trying to help the players to not make those mistakes again. And this is where some of the guys are great. I had a great rapport with some of our young guys last year, even though I give them tough love once in a while. I sit in the dugout and they come up and they pound me for information day after day: "What do you do, Skip—what about this situation, what about that situation?" [which is great] I sit on the bench and go through situations with the young guys, hoping that during the course of a season some of this stuff will sink in and help them become better players. Basically, it is all teaching.

Which players talk baseball with you?

[Many of the players.] Penny is always sitting by me in the dugout talking pitching and stuff like that. These guys want to learn. Pavano and Beckett like to sit around talking about certain situations, asking questions and learning too. Beckett, Pavano, Penny and Willis want to be good pitchers.

Do you see this season as a challenge?

It's definitely going to be a challenge. Like I've said, there's so many clubs that have improved and we've improved. When you look at this team, we have Conine and Cabrera who will be here for a full year. And look at our young pitchers who have great potential. It's just a question if they continue to improve and hopefully they will. It's going to be a great challenge. I mean, everyone is shooting for us; we're the world champs. The biggest thing is going to be the motivation factor—get these guys to realize they can't sit back and rest on their laurels. They have to work a little bit harder. You can have a fun-filled season with hard work and dedication, and it will pay off. The woods are filled with one-year phenoms, and let's go out and prove to the world that we're consistent.

How do you feel starting the new season and defending the world championship?

I'm excited. I'm excited for our team because I think we have a good team. We still have a hole or two in our bullpen. Right now, at the end of spring training, I'm happy with the nine I could put on the field. The thing that most impressed me coming into spring training was the way these guys came into spring training in a very business-like manner. I never saw that in other guys that have been around here. They came here prepared and there's no messing around. These players are professionals and leaders. Our workouts have been precise; no one messes around and screws up. The veterans will not tolerate the young kids not being focused. This team has amazing chemistry and everyone seems to be on the same page.

Which veterans are more focused?

Well, Jeff Conine and Mike Lowell are two professionals [all the way] on this club. The players look up to these guys and they lead by example. They are very, very dedicated to their work. They're prepared and there's no messing around with these guys. They're not afraid to get on somebody if other guys are not pulling their weight and if anybody needs advice, they're there to help them. You couldn't ask for two better veterans to have on your ballclub.

What about Castillo and Gonzalez?
 Oh, shit. These guys are magicians out there. They just go about their job, there's nothing loud about them—they have that charisma because of their defensive wizardry, but they're just quiet leaders out there, without the reputation of Conine and Lowell at this stage. They're darlings and I love them.

Talk about Miguel Cabrera and what he means to your club.
 Well, [laughs] here's a kid with unlimited ability. This is a fun-loving kid that you rarely see come into the big leagues and perform with such confidence that this guy has. He's an intimidating player and he doesn't fear anything—no fear in this guy. Like I've said, he's a super kid willing to learn and he's going to be a great one.

What about your rookie sensation—Dontrelle Willis?
 Willis is a character. He's a fun-loving kid with charisma because of his high leg kick. He came in here early last season and did an outstanding job for us, and he became the Rookie of the Year. He's got a lot to learn, he's improving, and I can see this kid being a pretty good pitcher for a long time in the major leagues.

What about a healthy A.J. Burnett?
 Well, from what I've heard, he has the best stuff on our club. It's just a question of bringing him back slowly and hopefully he will return to our club in the middle of May. When he returns we'll be in pretty good shape.

You often talk about "leading by example." What does that mean?
 Leading by example means running out all base hits, breaking up double plays, executing in bunt situations, being tough in the clutch and getting a key base hit when you need it. Pudge did it a lot of times and Cabrera did it quite often too. Mike Lowell [outstanding defense] making the defensive plays when you need it. That's leading by example.

Jim Leyland
THE SKIPPER
1988, 1990, 1992 NL Manager of the Year

"You always start with talent, and I think the key is to get that talent all on the same page. You work within the team concept and have that goal of being a championship team—knowing how to go about it."—Jim Leyland

James Richard Leyland, a catcher during his playing days, signed his first professional contract with the Detroit Tigers in 1963. After six seasons as a minor league player, he was appointed as a coach at Double-A Montgomery in the Southern League in 1970. He became a manager at the age of 26 in 1971, taking over the Tigers Bristol club in the Appalachian Rookie League.

Leyland won league championships with Lakeland (Single-A) in 1977 and 1978 and was named Manager of the Year in the Florida State League both years. He was also American Association Manager of the Year in 1979 after leading Evansville (Triple-A) to the league title. Prior to joining the Pirates, he served as a coach under Tony LaRussa, with the Chicago White Sox and managed for two games while LaRussa was suspended.

Leyland managed the Pittsburgh Pirates for 11 seasons (1986–1996) where he steered the team to first place in the National League's Eastern Division three consecutive years (1990–1992). He led the Pirates in 1990 to their first division title in 11 years. He was named the National League Manager of the Year three times by the *Sporting News* (1988, 1990, 1992).

He was named the third manager in Florida Marlins club history on October 4, 1996, and guided the Marlins to their first World Series championship in 1997 (his first season with the Marlins). He managed the Marlins in 1998 when the team was dismantled—a fire sale–type situation. He retired as a major league manager following the 1999 season (with the Rockies), his 14th year as a big-league skipper.

Leyland joined the Cardinals staff in 2000 as a major league scout. From his primary base in Pittsburgh, he scouts National League teams that visit PNC Park and travels to Cleveland's Jacobs Field to evaluate American League clubs. He reports directly to Senior Vice President–General Manager Walt Jockerty

CONVERSATION WITH JIM LEYLAND

Describe your present role as a scout in the Cardinals organization?

During spring training I work as an instructor for the Cardinals. I throw batting practice, I hit fungoes, and I listen to Tony [LaRussa]. I'm kind of a sounding board for Tony. I give Walt Jocketty my opinion on players if he asks for it (sometimes he does, sometimes he doesn't). Then I go back to Pittsburgh and scout the National League when other teams come through Pittsburgh. I don't travel anymore, except on a rare occasion. When Walt has a deal going or a trade, he'll call me for my opinion (see if I've scouted a player) and he basically does what he wants to do. I try to find players that I think fit into the scheme of things for the Cardinals. There are certain players you know you're not going to get (I can't use names), so you're really looking for certain pieces to the puzzle, to try to complete the puzzle. When you have Jim Edmonds in center field, you're not looking for a center fielder, so it's what your needs are and what players on other teams might fit those needs. You need the best available players to fill out the 25-player roster—complete the puzzle—and I find this job very interesting.

What can you say about the Cardinals, the team you're scouting?

This team has the potential to win its division. Everybody is talking about Chicago; everybody is talking about Houston (they should be) and I think they're probably also talking about the Cardinals. This is going to be a very competitive team that has a chance to win. People always say you have to play good to win. Well, this is one of my pet peeves when people say that. You have to play good to win—this is the major leagues. The competition is supposed to be good. I think it's more satisfying when you do win—nobody goes into the season saying it's going to be easy; it's never going to be easy and it's not supposed to be easy. I think the St.

Jim Leyland, Cardinals spring training instructor and scout.

Louis Cardinals will make a lot of noise and if they grind it out, and go about their business, then I think, come September 1st they'll be playing for something.

Managers and players often talk about leadership qualities that develop on winning teams. What is your feeling about leadership?

Well, I think you really have to be careful when you start emphasizing too much about leadership with your players. I think it's a manager's responsibility to get his team ready to play and everything. I think it's great when you have leadership in the clubhouse amongst the players. Tony LaRussa and I talk about this all the time. I think you have to have more than one leader because there's too many times when you have one so-called leader and things aren't going good for him—that can change things a little bit. I think it's necessary to get four or five guys in that clubhouse that people really look up to and you know, they lead through example and that type of thing. I think that's very important, but I'm not a believer in like a captain; I just don't think that works too well.

Through your experience as a manager, who were some of your leaders?
[It's funny.] I always thought the leaders were the guys that went out and performed. I like to lead by example. You can have guys in the clubhouse that maybe try to lead or make an effort to lead, but really they don't get as much respect from me as the silent leader—the guy who just grinds it out every day, plays every day and produces. I think those are the guys—so I think of Sheffield, I think of Bonds, I think of Jay Bell and Andy Van Slyke, and guys like that. They were all good players and it's easy to lead when you're a good player. It's like anything else—it's easier to come to the clubhouse when you're hitting .300 than when you're hitting .200. So I think you need a combination of the manager and a group of players that take the bull by the horn and know what it takes to win. I think that's leadership to me.

You talk about players that are grinders. In 1997 you had a player like Craig Counsell. Would you call him a grinder?
I don't think there's any question when you talk about Craig Counsell. He's one of those guys if you grade him out, the grades might not be that high, but to me Craig Counsell is a baseball player. Many people emphasize athletes and I always try to emphasize baseball players, and to me, Craig Counsell is a perfect example. He might not be one of the best athletes on the team, but to me he's one of the best baseball players because he knows what to do in all situations. He knows how to get it done. I've always liked baseball players first, athletes second. Most people like it just the opposite.

Who would you consider the baseball players?
Craig Counsell was one of them; Jay Bell was one of them. I think Donny Slaught was one of them. They were good athletes, but they weren't your prototype tremendous athletes; they were baseball players. Doug Drabek and John Smiley were tremendous baseball players, but not necessarily what you would call a tremendous athlete.

From your experience as a manager of good teams like the Pirates and Marlins, what do you need to do to become a championship team?

Number one, you always start with talent and I think the key is to get that talent on the same page. You work within the team concept and have that goal of being a championship team—knowing how to go about it. I think one of the biggest things is preparation, being able to grind it out. Baseball is a grueling sport; you're talking about 162 games—you can grind it out for three-fourths of the season and if you don't take it all the way out, you lose [in September]. I think one of the things is the ability to be steady, the ability to take care of yourself, so you can make that run late in September. I never really believed in a clubhouse atmosphere being a big thing. Everybody says they have a great clubhouse, well, I never believed in that. I don't believe all the players have to get along with all the players on a team to be a good team. The good teams to me are the ones that go out between the white lines to beat someone's ass. If the players get along with each other that's a bonus, not a necessity. When the players go out on the field they separate all other issues and play like a team to win.

What can you say about the 1997 championship team you managed?

First of all, we had talent. We pretty much had all the ingredients that it takes to win a championship. We had good starting pitching, we had pretty good defense, a good bullpen and good offense. You start with all that. I think this was a team that got on a roll and wasn't going to be denied. Early in the season till the All-Star break, we were okay. Afterwards, we started a little slow, but then we picked up on it and they smelt it. You can see it as we kept getting into the season. I actually thought we wouldn't win till 1998. I thought it would take everybody a year to get on the same page, but after the All-Star break for some reason—when Charles Johnson started hitting three home runs, Livan Hernandez came up and gave us a big shot in the arm, and we had good success against the Braves that year [the entire season]. I think the Braves were the pinnacle of success. So, once we were having success against them throughout the entire year, I think our guys believed more and if you get on a roll at the right time, and you're a pretty good team, then you have a chance to win it all. That's what we did.

Who were the players that contributed on the '97 world championship team?

Well, I think Moises Alou had a big year. He was tremendous that year. Edgar Renteria had a big year—clutch hit after clutch hit. Everybody talks about Game 7, but he won two games in the playoffs with base hits. He won several games in the course of the season. Gary Sheffield led the league in on-base percentage; Kevin Brown was just a horse; every time he pitched, he took us into the seventh inning. Al Leiter came up big and we got a shot in the arm with Livan Hernandez [an unknown] that particular year. Jeff Conine was like an old shoe; he was just steady every day. He would come to the park to beat the other team. Was he a great, great player? He probably wasn't, but was he a real, real good player? He definitely was a real good player. I think he proved that again last year. He was probably one of the guys who got them over the hump again last year when the Marlins won it in 2003. We had lots of nice ingredients: Bobby Bonilla was a good player on that team; Charles Johnson contributed and we had a combination of good players. Darren Daulton was the frosting on the cake; he put us over the hump.

What did you talk about in the postseason?
　　I remember in the 1997 playoffs I told the guys it's a little different than it used to be. You know, to be the world champions you have to win 11 games — that's a lot of games to win; it used to be four. Get your thought process right and when you look at me every day, know that the magic number is 11 games. I entered the World Series talking about it — it really doesn't matter what you've done up to this point. We've won seven games, but people only remember if you've won or lost. I focused on telling the guys, "People will only remember who won the World Series; they're not going to remember what happened in Game 1 or Game 2; they're going to remember who was the winning team." They will remember that Beckett won Game 6 in 2003.

You see any similarities between the 1997 and 2003 championship teams?
　　I think there are many similarities between those two teams. We knew in '97 we could beat the Braves because we had success against them during the regular season. Obviously, we had respect for them; they had been to the postseason many times and were a great team. In 1997 we knew we could beat the Braves and they knew we could beat them. And I think the 2003 Marlins had the same attitude. They knew they could beat the Cubs and the Yankees. They went into the playoffs with the attitude we have nothing to lose. Inside their clubhouse they knew how good they were. Maybe other people didn't [know], but Jack McKeon and Josh Beckett knew how good this team performed. Basically, we did the same thing in '97. Atlanta was a big hump to get over and we performed.

In the previous question you talk about respect for teams and players. What is respect?

When the players get a manager they feel goes about his business the same way they go about theirs, I think you've earned the players' respect. It's more difficult for a manager to earn the players' respect than for the players to earn the manager's respect. It's an issue a manager can't force; it happens over time. In the big leagues you establish yourself and gain that credibility, but I think it's important not to push yourself onto your players—not to hope for their respect, but to earn it with your performance as a manager.

You consider yourself a player's manager, a teacher, or a disciplinarian?

I consider myself a manager. I love the players because one thing that helped me throughout my career, being such a lousy player—I think it helped me as a manager. I realized what a tough game it was to play. Consequently, I thought I had pretty good patience with players for that reason—when you're not a very good player yourself, you have a tendency to understand how tough the game is to play. I just considered myself, basically, a manager that tried to do whatever I thought it took to win each game and to me that was my job. My job was to put my team in the best position to win. That's the way I tried to manage. I tried to support the players; I tried to be up-front with them; I tried to have a good time with them in the clubhouse, but like I've said, I followed the concept that my job allowed me to do whatever I thought it took to give our team a chance to win that particular game.

After winning the 1997 World Series, how did you deal with the letdown [dismantling the team] in 1998?

Well, actually, to be honest with you, as tough as it was, it was one of my most rewarding seasons because we had something like 36 rookies. We had 36 rookies on the roster that year. Everybody thought they played poorly, but we weren't good enough at that particular time. We were young and you could see the potential was there. Actually, many of the players held their head above water as individuals, but we weren't ready as a team yet. They were young; they were babies and you could see the potential. It paid off for some of the players last year when they became a world championship team. You could see the talent was there, but when you play that many rookies in the big leagues, you're going to get your brains beat out. They played good baseball at times; they hit the cutoff man; they knew how to bunt and hit and run. They could do lots of things, but as a team they weren't ready to compete. It was too tough for the amount of young players we had that season.

Talk about the 2003 team. You managed some of the players and no one expected this team to make it to the postseason. How did they win a World Series?

Well, number one, it starts with talent. This was a young club that came of age. Luis Castillo had played five or six years; Alex Gonzalez had experience with five or six years; they added Conine—a tremendous veteran player—and Mike Lowell was clutch. They had pitching; they had great young arms and I thought Jack McKeon came in just at the right time. He pushed the right buttons; he knew how to relax them and he let them play. He knew when to step on them a little bit, and he knew when to back off. I think the main thing—from June to the end of the season they had the best record in baseball [75–49]. So, they weren't really a secret to the baseball people; they were a little bit of a secret to the fans. The fact that they weren't drawing many people down there, you didn't hear much about that franchise. Here's a franchise that won two World Series in the past 10 years and it's amazing to me that the Florida Marlins have more world championships than the Atlanta Braves.

Describe a typical day when you managed.

Well, when you get to the ballpark, you usually relax a little bit. Then you start getting into your routine—you make out the lineup and check with the trainers to find out if everyone is all right, see if everyone is healthy. You begin checking on your pitching to see which pitchers you have available. The pitching coach always brings something in—tells me how many pitches a guy has thrown the day before [talking about relief pitchers]. Then you look at your matchups; you study it and you get the lineup ready. I go out for batting practice—maybe hit some fungoes, walk around and talk to some of the players—make sure everyone is all right. You have infield practice, obviously you talk to the media at some point during those hours, and then you get ready for the game. After the game you talk to the media again and you take some time to relax before you go home—particularly if you lost, so you don't take that game home with you. That was pretty much how I went about my day.

What did you expect from your players?

Basically, all I expected my players to do was be prepared to give their best effort. I never asked my players to win; I very rarely mentioned winning. I mentioned preparation to win, but not so much winning. There's many games you're prepared, you go out, you don't win. You've got to tip your hat to the other team. In the famous words of Lou Holtz, "The other side gives scholarships too." There's days you play your ass off, but that's not good enough. I think the main thing is to know how to go about it for 162 games. I mean, you're obviously going to have some days when you don't feel as good as others, and you're not going to be at your peak performance every day. You have to understand that. The teams that learn how to grind it out, I think those are the teams that come out on top in the end. Obviously, talent is important as well.

You talk about peak performance, but how did you deal with slumps and poor performance on your 1997 championship season?

You have to have several leaders on a team because when two or three guys go down [not hitting], you need somebody to pick them up. When you have guys like Jeff Conine and Gary Sheffield, you know you have professionals. They know they're going to have those ups and downs, but you have to be there for them. I need to encourage them. They know they're going to get through it, you know they're going to get through it, but at the same time it's tough for them; there's a lot of spotlight on them. They don't need the manager when they're doing well; they need the manager when they're not doing well. Everybody is in their corner when they're hitting home runs and winning games, so they really don't need the manager. They need the manager when they're struggling, when they're having a tough time and that's when I try to be there for them. It's pretty simple—when you win you reflect that credit to the players and when you lose you accept that responsibility as a manager. I think that's the way it has to be and the way it should be.

When you lose games and get into a kind of funk, whom do you turn to for support?

That's a great question. A manager can be a very lonely man. Usually, you have one coach you can spend some time with or talk to and get it off your chest. You need a sounding board for yourself a little bit, but it can be a very lonely life. You have a coach you can depend on, you have dinner with and throw things off him. The coach is listening; maybe he sees something that needs to be changed. Normally you find one person from your staff that you can share concerns with.

Who were some of the coaches that provided support?

Well, Gene Lamont, Rich Donnelly and Tommy Sandt. Those guys were with me for a long time. It's kind of strange because I work as a scout for the Cardinals now, but I used to make a call at three or four o'clock in the morning to Tony LaRussa [when] he was managing in the American League (and I was in the National League). It was nothing for one of us to hear our phone ring three or four in the morning, in our hotel room. Because of the time change, he was out west a lot and I was back east a lot. Every once in awhile we would call each other after a tough loss and talk about it. I would talk about a game I blew that night and say, "What in the hell, I blew that game; I mugged one that night (that was our favorite expression); I let one get away that night." Even though he was another manager, he was a sounding board who listened and offered advice.

Anybody offer advice and motivation for you to become a manager early in your career?
Actually, I think Hoot Evers was probably the number-one motivational guy for me. He was a farm director for the Detroit Tigers. Hoot Evers, Bill Lejoy and Ed Catalinas advised me to begin a career in the minor league system. The Tigers organization was really instrumental in giving me a chance to have a career in baseball. Roland Hemond (Chicago White Sox general manager) believed in me enough—I was a minor league guy and he let Tony [LaRussa] hire me as a third base coach for the Chicago White Sox. If I had to look back and pick one person that really motivated me and really let me know what it's about, it would be Hoot Evers.

President Bush addressed the nation in his State of the Union speech stating, "Baseball players are setting a poor example by using steroids." What did you make of his comments?
First of all, I haven't seen obvious proof that somebody is using steroids. I don't go on hearsay. I know there's a lot of speculation; I really have no clue what goes on with that. I've been out of the big leagues for several years now and I'm not going to pass judgment on anybody [until] somebody shows proof that somebody did something wrong. I'm just not going to buy it.

From your perspective, what were some of your accomplishments?
Well, I think my biggest accomplishment was getting to the big leagues. I mean, because I was such a bad player, I was released out of Double-A (was a back-up catcher) early in my career. I think some of my most memorable experiences: being named manager of the Pittsburgh Pirates, being named coach of the Chicago White Sox, managing the Florida Marlins and Colorado Rockies. For a guy that was a lousy player, I've ended up having a pretty good career. I've been able to do wonder-

ful things that the average person probably won't do. I had the opportunity to golf with Arnold Palmer and President Clinton. That's pretty good for a back-up catcher in Double-A [laughs].

What advice would you provide future big league players?

I would just advise players to chase their dream. It certainly is a wonderful dream to have. Everybody thinks I fulfilled my dream, but I didn't. My dream was to become a big league player, not a big league manager. My hero was Yogi Berra. I wanted to be like Yogi Berra. Like I've said, my dream was to be a player, not a manager. I never really fulfilled my dream, but did the best I could with what I had. I would advise young players by telling them to enjoy the game and enjoy the camaraderie with others. Baseball is a learning experience; it's a team game, and it prepares you for life a little bit. A team is like a company where you learn how to make decisions. The main thing is to enjoy what you're doing and chase the dream [until] you see it cannot be fulfilled.

How do you want to be remembered by the fans and your players?

I don't know. I'm sure, over the years, some players liked me and some players didn't like me. I think I'd like to be remembered as somebody that was respectful to the game of baseball and had a great appreciation for it. I admired watching people do things I couldn't do. I just want to be remembered as somebody that was honest to the players—fair to the players, was straight up-front with them and told it like it was. I'm convinced—maybe some players don't agree—that I've helped my players and I'll sleep very easy in that area. I won't look back.

A humorous story while you were managing.

Well, I can remember [one time] a steal sign from the bench—if I put my arm on the back of the dugout, the guy on first base was supposed to steal second. One day, in a close game against San Diego while managing Pittsburgh, I was studying my lineup (we were down a few runs), it was late and I had a catcher on first base. I was looking down at my lineup figuring to pinch hit and I accidentally, not thinking, put my arm on the back of the dugout—sure as hell, I look up, the catcher is trying to steal second. The funny part about the whole scenario was he's halfway down to second and I pulled my arm down like I could do something about it, like it's not too late to stop him. I thought, what am I doing pulling my arm down? He got thrown out, of course, and we lose the game. There are many funny things that happened over the years when you're managing a major league or minor league team and I was fortunate to experience it.

Mike Lowell
MARLINS HOMETOWN HERO
3-Time NL All-Star

"We proved last year that if you get in as a wild card, your odds are just as good. I really don't believe that winning the division is a recipe for success because it's a short series. The team that's playing hot at that time is going to win." — Mike Lowell

Michael Averett Lowell was selected by the New York Yankees in the 20th round of the June free-agent draft. He split the 1996 season between Greensboro and Tampa (Single-A), hitting a combined .282 with eight home runs and 75 runs batted in. He led all Yankee minor leaguers with 38 doubles; second in hits (144); third in games played (137). He led all Florida State League third basemen with 421 total chances and 301 assists.

Lowell started 1997 in Double-A Norwich and ended in Triple-A Columbus. He was named the Yankees' Minor League Player of the Year and set career highs in batting (.315), runs (96), hits (156), homers (30) and runs batted in (92). He was voted the best Double-A batting prospect in *Baseball America's Managers Survey*.

He started the 1998 season at Triple-A Columbus before moving up to the Yankees in September. He had an outstanding season at Columbus, hitting .304 with 155 hits, 26 home runs and 99 runs batted in while playing 126 games. Lowell made his major league debut on September 13th against Toronto and got his first major league hit in his first at-bat. After joining the Yankees he played eight games with four hits and a .267 batting average in his brief stint.

In 1999 Lowell was acquired by the Marlins, playing in 97 games, batting .254 with 12 homers and 47 runs batted in. The following seasons he improved his batting average, home-run production and runs batted in, and was selected to the National League All-Star Team in 2002, 2003 and 2004.

In 2003, Lowell experienced a breakout year setting career highs and team-leading totals with 32 home runs and 105 runs batted in despite a broken left hand that forced him to miss the last month of the season. He led all National League third basemen with a .973 fielding percentage, mishandling only nine balls in 336 total chances and making five errors in his last 99 games. In the 2003 postseason, he became the sixth player in postseason history to hit a pinch-hit home run in extra innings when he hit a solo shot in the top of the 11th inning off the Cubs' Mark Guthrie, giving the Marlins a 9–8 win in Game 1 of the National League Championship Series.

I met up with Lowell in the Marlins clubhouse at Roger Dean Stadium in Jupiter, Florida, at the end of spring training. He was enthusiastic about the new season and the opportunity to make another championship run. He provided his recollections on the unexpected 2003 world championship team.

Conversation with Mike Lowell

Your thoughts about the championship season.

I think it begins in spring training a little bit. You hope what you see in the clubhouse is good enough to bring the team together to win a championship. If you haven't won a championship they're certainly dreams that you hope you can accomplish. Last year we saw it come together—our team chemistry was our biggest asset. I think that made us enjoy it more.

How did the unexpected championship season happen?

I think there were a few turning points, but when we finally had Mark Redman, Josh Beckett, and when Dontrelle Willis was called up, it started to happen. Early in the season Redman and Beckett went on the disabled list. We were trying to piece our rotation together, and once Dontrelle was called up he really energized South Florida [laughs]. He put us on a national stage—a young rookie from Double-A just dominating. Then Beckett and Redman came off the disabled list and our pitchers just started clicking. So I think we had many consistent pitching performances. There were days when our offense did well and our pitching didn't (we were losing those games). When we were putting runs together, once our pitchers were consistently giving us strong outings, we just went on a roll.

Did Jack McKeon make a difference?

[Sure.] I don't want to bash Jeff Torborg because with the injuries we had, he had his hands tied behind his back. I think guys appreciated him, but Jack [McKeon] has a different style. He's more in your face; he's more "I want to win right now" and we responded well to that. You know, it's a different style and I guess for our team personality it fit very well with the way Jack went about things. The victories don't lie and we had a big turnaround, a great record and got hot at the right time.

Was McKeon big on discipline or more like a teacher?

I just see him as a good manager that knows you can't treat everyone the same. What I mean by that ... different people have different personalities. Some guys—you have to get in their face and let them know what you think, otherwise they will slack off. Other guys—you don't have to talk to them for months. I think Jack understood that right off the bat, and he picked up on who you have to treat a certain way. That's why we responded well to him. I don't believe a manager is a guy who has a set way of treating guys, and it's generic for everyone. I don't think that works. I think that's one of Jack's strong points.

Talk about the 2003 season and the rumor of going to the Cubs or the Dodgers before the trade deadline.

I wouldn't say the 2003 season was a roller coaster of emotions, but a lot of different emotions. The first three months were very weird to me because I was hitting so many home runs. I really don't look to hit home runs; I've always viewed myself as a good gap hitter, a doubles hitter, but for some reason in those first three months of the season, I think I set my career high in home runs each month. I'm usually the type of guy who might hit four or five home runs a month, and I was hitting eight or nine [laughs] those first three months. It was, actually, a weird feeling to me because I was just making such good contact so many times. When you're struggling and you're not getting that many hits—you're in a rut going maybe two for 10—those two hits were home runs and that helps you mentally, that helps your numbers, and it helps you keep that strong mental approach.

I was flattered by the trade talk because I respected the fact that teams like the Cubs and the Dodgers—I think—were the big ones that the rumors were about. Franchises with such great tradition thought I was a piece that could maybe take them over the top—to get them over that hump, to really get hot. I took it as a tremendous compliment. On the other hand, I liked our team; I really didn't want to go anywhere because I thought we had

Mike Lowell taking batting practice at spring training.

a good team here in Miami. It really wasn't that much of a distraction. It got a little annoying because I had to answer the same questions every day—how do you feel going to the Cubs? How do you feel about going to the Dodgers? I kept saying, "Until I go there I'm not going to comment on it."

Then when I broke my hand, that was a little bit of a low because I missed the whole month of September. It was tough not being in the lineup, and it was an important stretch for the team. I was just hoping that my injury wasn't the reason why our team doesn't make the playoffs. It just showed you that our team stepped up—we acquired Jeff Conine and we got hot. I was just starting to feel better the last game of the San Francisco series, where I felt I had that grip strength back in my hands. That pinch-hit home run in Game 1 of the playoff against the Cubs was a big league highlight for me. I went from a feeling like I was letting the team down (when I broke my hand) to feeling like I really did something good in Game 1 of the postseason. Overall, I think it was a total focus during the season to get to the playoffs, and I think our team did a real good job of going round by round—taking the Giants in the first round, not looking ahead to who we might play and trying to beat the Cubs, not looking ahead whether it's going to be the Red Sox or the Yankees. When we got to the World Series we were like, hey, there's no further place we can go, so we might as well take care of business. We were very focused as a team.

Was it true that you were hurt while playing in the World Series?

It was true I was hurt, but I think you would have to cut both my legs off if I wasn't going to play in the World Series. I feel there were times the pain was so much less than the possible rewards, but I know I didn't warm up the last three games of the World Series because my arm was really hurting. I don't know, I just figured, at most, I would make four or five throws, hopefully; I would hit the first baseman in the chest, and we'd be all right. I got my share of ground balls and I made my throws, but I think the adrenaline is a great thing in those games. If maybe it was a Tuesday night in front of 4,000 fans during the season, it might have been a little bit different [laughs]. It was just something you have to play through.

What were your emotions playing the World Series at Yankee Stadium?

I really didn't know what to expect; I was anxious to see how loud the stadium would get, but after Game 6 and 7 in Chicago (the fans were so close to you), I thought that was the loudest I ever heard in a stadium. It was a relief to me that Yankee Stadium didn't get as loud as Wrigley

Field during Games 1 and 2 in the World Series. I think we looked at it as we're playing the Yankees as a team. We're not going into a stadium, [unless] Babe Ruth picked up a bat; I don't believe in ghosts or curses, or any of that stuff. We had our hands full with David Wells on the mound, so we wanted to get off to a good start and we did.

Talk about Game 5 and facing Wells again.

I recall the Yankees had a first-inning run, but we had a clutch two-out rally in the second inning. I remember Wells left the game with back pain after just one inning. After two straight walks, Gonzalez doubled home a run and Penny followed by knocking in two runs with a single for a two-run lead. In the fifth inning I drove in two runs with a single that gave us a 6–1 lead, and we held on to win 6–4.

Did you have an opportunity to face Mariano Rivera?

I faced him twice in the series and had one hit in two at-bats. In Game 6, I hit a double past the third baseman in the eighth inning. He throws a cut fastball with a break that is tough for right-handed hitters.

Did the Bartman incident in Chicago change the outcome of the series?

It was definitely a break, but I think what gets lost in the whole thing was, we had to get a string of hits to tie the game up. It's not like because of that dropped ball three runs came in. I think afterwards there was a big error by their shortstop when he let a possible double play get away. Then we had big hits—Derek Lee came up with a huge hit, Jeff Conine had a sacrifice fly, and then we broke the game open. I don't think the Steve Bartman incident was the reason they lost. I think it was definitely a break that we got because Moises Alou had a bead on the ball, and you can't say he wouldn't have caught it, but good teams take advantage of some of the breaks they get; we definitely did.

Talk about a winning attitude.

I think that's the mental part of baseball; I think it's easy when things are going well to have a winning attitude because you're getting hits, or if you're a pitcher you're doing your job whether it's in a relief appearance or in a starting role. I think a winning attitude develops when you're struggling. The fact that you have to keep grinding and you have to realize it's a six-month season, it's not a two-week stint. I think, in my eyes, guys earn my respect when they come out to play, and keep grinding away, even when things aren't going their way. I think that's what breeds a winning attitude.

When you're struggling, what do you do to overcome it?
    I try to work harder. You know, usually it's something not mechanical in your swing; sometimes it's bad luck, but sometimes you're being a little bit too aggressive, or you're just not focused. I think sometimes you have to work on your mental approach; sometimes you have to get in the cage, but it's something—usually it's something very subtle and it's a great feeling once you start clicking again. For me personally, I feel like I'm letting the team down when I'm not doing well. You want to get the pieces back together so you can start contributing and help the team win again.

Do you think players struggle because they peak too soon?
    I don't believe in not peaking too soon; I don't mind guys getting hot in April because when you get extremely hot—whether you're a position player or a pitcher, you can feed off that in a positive way. When things get a little bit tough, maybe in June or July, you can look back and realize that you did dominate, or you did get hot as a hitter and use that to your advantage. I really don't believe in not peaking too soon—if you want to start hot, by all means do so.

If I told you back in March of 2003 that you would hit 32 home runs, play in the postseason—defeating the Giants and the Cubs, and the Yankees in six games, what would you say to me?
    Ah, I would say, "I appreciate you being a true fan of us, but the odds were definitely stacked against us." When you're a low-revenue team and a young team, a lot of things have to go well. Your margin for error is very small. When you're a big-money team like the Yankees—if you get a superstar to go down like Derek Jeter did, when he separated his shoulder on opening day—that team is still talented enough, and has enough firepower to keep the train rolling. If we have two or three players hurt during the year, it would be an uphill climb for us. I think it would be possible; I think this team has the talent, but we couldn't afford to have two or three guys get hurt or have subpar years.

Who are the take-charge players on this team?
    Well, I've never been a big fan of guys that are rah-rah guys. I don't believe if you call a team meeting you're a team leader. I think guys who come to play every day are the leaders. Derek Lee was definitely a leader—here was a guy who partially separated his shoulder and he just kept playing. You earn respect by playing every day and when things aren't going well, like facing a tough pitcher on the mound, you don't ask for that day

off. Juan Pierre showed you what a work ethic is all about, and I think guys fed off that. I think a lot of guys in their own way were leaders, but I think it's more leaders by example. I know when we acquired Ugueth Urbina, his total disregard for any fear of any situation really helped the other guys in our bullpen. I think it's a combined effort; I think it takes more than just one guy. You know, if you want to call a team meeting, that's what we have Jack [McKeon] for.

How would you characterize yourself?

I would like to be characterized as someone who takes his profession very seriously, but I enjoy baseball more than anything else. I'd like to be characterized as a player who comes to play; I respect a lot of my peers, but I didn't fear them, and I came to play every day. I don't think slumps or nagging injuries are reasons to ask for days off. I guess I learned that from my dad—that if you can play, you play.

Why do you think this team has a chance to repeat?

We're very talented and I know we lost a couple of pieces to our puzzle, but we replaced them with very talented guys. We're kind of in the same situation—no one is giving us credit. We still have good talent, we have great starting pitching and if guys have the years they're capable of, we can be in the playoffs again. I don't think we have to win the division; we just want to make the playoffs. We proved last year that if you get in as a wild card, your odds are just as good. I really don't believe that winning the division is a recipe for success because it's a short series. The team that's playing hot at that time is going to win.

How do you prepare for the season?

Well, I kind of do the same thing every year. I'm big on the conditioning and usually take two weeks off once the season ends. I go straight into weight lifting; I like to take a break from baseball—physically and mentally—so I really don't do any baseball stuff until about January. Then about a month before spring training starts, I start throwing and hitting in the cage. I feel like you shouldn't come to spring training to get into shape, you should use spring training to fine tune yourself for opening day.

What do you hope to accomplish as far as goals for another championship season?

I don't set any goals as far as numbers, but I want to be a good run producer; I set runs batted in as a goal. I don't set exact numbers because sometimes you don't have as many opportunities as other years. If I have the opportunities I had last year, and if I don't drive in 100 runs, I'd be disappointed. If I have less opportunities and I drive in 85 runs that might be a good year. It all depends on the opportunities I have.

When you were traded to the Marlins, who were some of the players that took you under their wings?
    Ah, Alex Fernandez showed me what a veteran is. He really took care of the young guys. We were such a young team that it was tough because no one was really a seasoned veteran. My first spring training experience with the Yankees, Chili Davis, Louie Sojo and Tim Raines went out of their way to help me and give me advice about different pitchers. The Marlins didn't have guys like that on the team when I came here. Raines welcomed me not as a threat, but as someone who could help them win, and that was a nice feeling.

What advice did Tim Raines provide you?
    It's not like he had these secrets to the game, but what he has is an understanding of the game. When you see a guy whose been in the big leagues for 20 years go out and take early batting practice, you know he's doing that to get himself ready; it shows you what it takes to be a professional. He gives you advice [about other pitchers] from his experience, not what you do or should do—he didn't point out things I wasn't doing, but rather tipping me off about other pitchers.

What goes on in a winning clubhouse?
    [Laughs.] It is so different to anything I can explain to an everyday life. We spend so much time together that what's so unique about our team. Usually some people rub you the wrong way and it's tough for everyone on a team to get together, but we just have this unbelievable chemistry; we're rooting for each other nonstop. I can't explain it, but it was an intangible we had and used to our advantage.

Can you recall a humorous clubhouse incident that kept the players loose during the stretch leading up to the postseason?
    Well, one that really sticks out involves [our catcher] Mike Redmond. We had lost six in a row and we were going to Cincinnati. And they have a batting cage next to the clubhouse, so you don't have to walk through the general public area. He is wearing spikes and batting gloves, and nothing else—no clothes on at all. Redmond asked coach Bill Robinson if he could have batting practice [laughs]. And Robinson obliged and he took batting practice naked with shoes on to rally the troops. Well, we ended

up winning six in a row after that, so we made him take batting practice naked in the cage for the next four days and it kept working. Mike might not be too proud of that moment, but we sure are.

Since Redmond's naked approach worked, it appears that some players are superstitious.

I think some guys [definitely] are. The players like to go into a routine that they feel comfortable with. I know before I hit, I take the same number of practice swings. I kind of have the same approach, but I don't think if I take one swing more, or one swing less, that my at-bats will be ruined. I just feel I like the rhythm I'm in; it's worked in the past, so I just stick with it.

Is a salary cap necessary to level the playing field?

The day you can prove to me that a salary cap is good for the game, I'll agree with it. Our union is very strong and many guys sacrificed a lot to not get a salary cap because the players were kind of held hostage before free agency. I think it's an uphill climb for Major League Baseball, but I don't think players are opposed. I think you've seen salaries drop the past few years; I think the days of making $20 million a year—that was kind of a fluke because players themselves realize that's an unbelievable amount of money to be made playing baseball. You have actors that do 24 shows in a sitcom and make a million dollars an episode. So, it depends which way you look at it. I guess we're in the entertainment business and it's big business. When you're entertaining you get compensated in that sense.

Finally, does baseball have a drug problem?

I'm disappointed in a sense; I think the public opinion is everyone is on steroids. And our tests show that a maximum of 7 percent are [using drugs]. That means 93 percent of the people are playing fairly. I'm just disappointed that the emphasis is put on those 7 percent and they're using it to characterize all the players. I don't think that's fair; however, I think 7 percent is too high. I don't think seven guys out of basically four teams you're talking about are using those drugs. It's illegal first of all; you're trying to take unfair advantage, but I view it as illegal things have been around forever—from a sports standpoint or recreationally—and as an adult you're going to have to make decisions; you have to suffer the consequences. I'm not here to police or judge anyone. I'm disappointed that all players are characterized by a few, but I do think drugs should be eliminated from the game.

Josh Beckett
WORLD SERIES
MOST VALUABLE PLAYER

"Winning the World Series was exhilarating and dreams do come true. I think every kid that's ever picked up a baseball in Little League has dreamed about being in that situation, being in a World Series, being in Game 6 or 7, whatever it may be. I took a moment in the ninth inning to realize what was going on; it was a good time." — Josh Beckett

Joshua Patrick Beckett was named the *USA Today* High School Pitcher of the Year in 1999 after posting a 10–1 record with a 0.46 ERA in his senior season at Spring High School. That season he accumulated 155 strikeouts and 22 walks in 75.1 innings. He was selected by Florida in the first round (second overall pick) of the First-Year Player Draft in 1999. He became the first high school pitcher in Marlins history to be selected in the first round when Florida drafted him on June 2, 1999.

He went 2–3 with a 2.12 ERA in 13 games (12 starts) for Single-A Kane County in 2000. He was named the Marlins' top prospect by *Baseball America* and *Future Stars* following the 2000 season. Beckett was named the 2001 Minor League Player of the Year as he went 14–1 with a 1.54 ERA in 26 games for Double-A Portland (Eastern League) and Single-A Brevard County (Florida State League). He joined the Marlins on September 1, 2001, from Double-A Portland.

Beckett made his major league debut on September 4, 2001, against the Cubs, allowing one hit and striking out five over six innings and earning his first major league win. He was named the 2001 Marlins Rookie of the Year by the South Florida chapter of the Baseball Writers Association of America after posting a 2–2 record and a 1.50 ERA in four starts. In

2002, he went 6–7 in 23 games (21 starts) in his first full major league season. Unfortunately, a right middle finger blister put him on the 15-day disabled list three times during the season.

Beckett put together career highs with nine wins, 24 games pitched as he posted a 3.04 ERA in 2003. In the 2003 postseason, he made six appearances (five starts) with a 2–2 record, a 2.11 ERA and two complete-game shutouts. Josh Beckett was named the Most Valuable Player of the 2003 World Series as he pitched a series-ending complete-game shutout against the Yankees in Game 6, a 2–0 win for the Marlins on October 25th. Beckett pitched the 19th complete game shutout in a World Series–deciding game in major league history.

I sat with Josh Beckett in the Marlins clubhouse at Roger Dean Stadium on a breezy March afternoon, almost five months after his triumphant World Series performance at Yankee Stadium.

CONVERSATION WITH JOSH BECKETT

Talk about a team no one expected to get to the postseason in 2003.

Oh man, [laughs] a lot of things went right for us and we stuck together. Everybody believed in one another; we were pulling for one another. That's how dreams do come true because we all dreamed about that during the beginning of the season. Last spring we came in with such high hopes and expectations, and started off [losing] the way we did. We stuck together and came back; it just shows what kind of heart my teammates have.

What did Jack McKeon tell the team when he came aboard in 2003?

He said, "I don't need this job." That's what he told us [laughs]. That's exactly what he said: "I don't need this job." He said it like it meant, "I came here to turn you guys into winners," and he made us believe in ourselves. As soon as we started believing in ourselves, we started winning and we took off.

The new pitching coach, Wayne Rosenthal, was hired along with McKeon. How did Rosenthal help you?

Rosey is a real mechanical guy and he watches all your work in the bullpen. He makes sure that your work in the bullpen is good and your mechanics stay the same. It makes it a lot easier to get the ball over the plate consistently when you have sound mechanics and throw-to spots.

Josh Beckett completing a spring training workout.

Describe what it was like winning the 2003 World Series and earning the Most Valuable Player Award.

Winning the World Series was exhilarating and dreams do come true. I think every kid that's ever picked up a baseball in Little League has dreamed about being in that situation, being in a World Series, being in Game 6 or 7, whatever it may be. They think about pitching or hitting or whatever your position might be. I took a moment in the ninth inning to realize what was going on; it was a good time.

You appeared to show little emotion in the postseason and World Series, especially during interviews.

I expect a lot of myself and I'm not one of those guys who need a lot of encouragement. I'm very confident; I know how good I can be and it was very exciting, but I don't need that reassurance, like a pat on the back.

Do you ever pinch yourself and say, "Did this really happen?"

Oh yeah. It was exciting and a relief at the same time. We didn't have to play another game the next day. It was great winning the World Series, but kind of weird that we wouldn't have another game to play.

What was the turning point during the postseason?
  Game 5 against the Cubs was the turning point for our team. Pitching a shutout that day gave us a boost from being down three games to one. That game gave us confidence because we knew it was going to be tough. We were going back to Chicago to face Prior and Wood [tough pitchers]. We knew it was going to be tough and we ended up pulling it off. I definitely think that game was one of the turning points in our season.

What can you say about Game 6 of the World Series—pitching a shutout at Yankee Stadium and becoming the world champions?
  If I can never pitch again, nobody can ever take Game 6 of the 2003 World Series away from me. I think that's such a great thing about it; it was a great game and nobody can ever take that away from me. I think that's pretty special. What I will remember the most—we won the World Series, we won Game 6 with a shutout; that's what I will remember the most. We have a great team this year and hopefully we can win again.

Did you make any adjustments in your pitching in Game 6?
  You treat every team the same and just go out there and execute your pitches; that's all I was trying to do. You want to keep the ball down with the lineup the Yankees had. The mistakes I made that game didn't get hit; I was pretty fortunate.

How was it determined that you would start Game 6 on three days' rest?
  Jack [McKeon] told me he wanted me to pitch in Game 6 and I said, "Well, let me see how I feel today." I went out and played long toss before the start of Game 5 and I told him I felt fine. It was apparent then [that] I would start Game 6 and he didn't announce it for two more days.

What would you say was your best performance in the postseason—Game 5 against the Cubs in the league championship series or Game 6 in the World Series?
  I feel it was [definitely] Game 5 against the Cubs that I had my best stuff and allowed two hits and pitched a complete game. I know I had good stuff in Game 6 against the Yankees and pitched a shutout, but I think I made less mistakes pitching against the Cubs.

McKeon has said, "You can't rest on your laurels; last season is history." What do you feel you need to improve to get to the postseason again?

You always need to improve your game. I think it's different from one game to the next. Some days my curve ball may be good, some days my curve ball may be bad. I may need to work on that for my next start, for my next bullpen session. That's what I'm saying; I don't think that I can really pick one thing out that I need to work on for the full year besides maybe staying healthy, but I think it's different for each game.

McKeon encourages the pitchers to sit on the bench and observe what's going on. Do you agree with his approach and are you learning?

Oh, definitely. We sit on the bench and [talk shop] discuss hitters. That's where a lot of our learning goes on—just sitting on the bench and talking to one another about, "Hey, look at that guy, he's diving, or look at this guy, he's kind of pulling off a little bit. I threw him a sinker away or something." That's what we talk about.

With most players back, can this team repeat a championship season?

[Without a question], we can play in the postseason again. We're a very good team; we're going to be competitive this year, and a lot of us— me included—learned how to win in the big leagues last year. Hopefully that spills over into the new season.

What can you say about winning and leadership—the qualities of a championship team?

No doubt about it, these are important qualities. I think leadership is a little bit overrated because everybody kind of leads when they come to the major leagues. I think leadership is good when one guy speaks for the team, and that's important, but sometimes leadership is taken out of perspective or whatever you want to say; it's overrated a little bit because we didn't have any one leader last year. We all picked each other up—if Dontrelle Willis was pitching good, I wanted to pitch good; if I was pitching good, Duke [Penny] wanted to pitch good; if Duke was pitching good, Pavano wanted to pitch good, and we kind of pushed each other. It was the same way with our offense.

What can you say about Pudge [Rodriguez], what he meant to the club, and did he make your pitch selection?

Pudge is a great catcher and a great game-caller, and helped this team throughout the season. He was outstanding in the postseason, but no catcher makes my pitch selection—it's my ERA and that's why I figure I got to call the pitches; I can't let anybody call my game. When it comes to stuff like [that], I think I need to take care of that myself. Pudge would give me advice from time to time and tell me how good he thought my stuff was, [that] I need to stick with it and keep pounding away, and [work hard] things will work out.

Talk about your game preparation during the season.

I don't try to do anything different; I go about my life and try to be normal. I'm not a nervous guy; I get a lot of anxiety though, and if I start changing stuff up a lot, it just ends up being a pain in the ass.

Do you set goals for yourself as far as wins, or what you hope to accomplish this season?

My goal is to always stay healthy, to get through spring training healthy, and to try to get through the first half of the season and through the second half of the season healthy. You can't think about the result, it corrupts the process. So, I don't try to think too far ahead; I think about my next start and stop thinking about what's at the end of the road, what's at the end of the season, what's at the All-Star break—just go next start. I think about what I need to do three days from now. Tomorrow I will do bullpen work and I'm thinking about tomorrow; then I look two days ahead and then I think about my pitch day. Every year I have aspirations to win 20 games, but I don't think that's a goal I would make public. You keep that goal to yourself and go out and try to achieve it. I think about making 34 to 36 starts as an accomplishment.

When you look back at the championship season, is it still amazing?

Oh, yeah. Like I've said, McKeon kind of motivated us and we started pushing each other. We all knew we should be better than that and we started playing better.

How did the team keep loose during the season?

Mike Redmond would take batting practice naked outside the clubhouse and that was pretty funny and kept the guys loose.

Which pitcher provided the help and encouragement during your rookie season?

Ryan Dempster helped me out a lot. He was pretty much it. Back then it was kind of tough because everyone was doing their own things; we didn't know how to win at the time. So, we were kind of feeling things out. Ryan Dempster really helped me and showed me [the ropes], what it's like to be a big-league pitcher.

What do you really love about this game?

[Everything.] I'm so blessed; I'm the most-watched guy [laughs]. I come to a baseball field and work every day. I just want to improve and get better with each performance. I respect the game, but I never expect to fail. I like the challenge and look forward to another championship season.

Wayne Rosenthal
PITCHING COACH AND GURU

> *"Dontrelle Willis is a young, inspiring pitcher who came up and got in the spotlight real quick. I think he's going to be a good one; he's a hard worker and loves the game. I'll tell you right now, that boy loves the game. He lives and breathes baseball."*—Wayne Rosenthal

Wayne Scott Rosenthal was selected by the Texas Rangers in the 24th round of the June 1986 draft. He spent eight seasons in the minor leagues (seven with the Rangers) and posted a 21–32 record with a 3.07 ERA in 333 games. He was the Rangers' Minor League Player of the Year in 1987 with 30 saves and a 1.70 ERA in 56 games with Gastonia in the South Atlantic League. He made his major-league debut with the Rangers in 1991 and pitched in 36 games, posting a 1–4 record with a 5.25 ERA over 70.1 innings.

Rosenthal began his coaching career in 1994 and spent three seasons as a pitching coach in the independent Frontier League. He joined the Expos organization in 1997, where he coached at Cape Fear, was the pitching coach at Single-A Jupiter in 1998 and Double-A Harrisburg in 1999. He was named the Expos' minor-league pitching coordinator in 2000, working three seasons as a minor-league coach in the Montreal System. He started the 2003 season as the Marlins' minor-league pitching coordinator, his fourth year overall in that position. Rosenthal made his major-league debut as Florida's pitching coach on May 11, 2003, under manager Jack McKeon. He led the Marlins' pitching staff to a 3.96 ERA in 2003 and made his first major-league postseason coaching appearance in 2003 after five playoff runs as a minor-league coach. I met up with Rosenthal at a picnic table on the backfields at Roger Dean Stadium during spring training.

Conversation with Wayne Rosenthal

If I told you back in spring training in 2003 that you would become the new pitching coach in May and appear in the postseason, defeating the Giants, the Cubs and the Yankees in the World Series, what would you say?

I would've thought you're crazy. [I mean], you got to go one step at a time. I never thought I would be the major-league pitching coach in May. I was coming to spring training and performing my job as the coordinator. I wasn't even thinking about being a pitching coach. I would say if you were a betting man ... I would bet against it.

As a pitching coordinator for the big league players, what are some of your responsibilities?

My job was to help the pitchers in their pitchers' fielding practice (PFP). The major-league pitching coach would handle the games and I would handle everything else on the side. I would work out of the bullpen and get guys ready for the games, and do that until I had to report to the minor-league camps. Once minor-league camp started, the pitching coach was on his own. I would help him out as much as I can, and shadow the guys who stay behind during spring training. That's pretty much what it's like in a big-league camp. As a minor-league pitching coordinator you do whatever the major-league pitching coach wants you to do. Whenever something comes up, you discuss it with the pitching coach. In a way, you're like a puppet because you're helping out the pitching coach. Anybody who wasn't pitching in a spring training game stayed behind, and I helped out with pitchers' fielding practice (PFP).

What were you doing at the beginning of the 2003 season?

I started the 2003 season in Zebulon, North Carolina, with the Double-A team and watched them play five games. I was sent to Greensboro to observe the Single-A club and returned to Zebulon to assist the Double-A team for 12 days because the pitching coach was sick. Then, I was sent to Albuquerque, New Mexico, to watch our Triple-A affiliate team play. After that trip I went home and the major-league team called me up and asked me to help out in the bullpen for five days. Then I returned to Albuquerque for five days, was called to see the Greensboro team again, and while I was there [Greensboro], Dontrelle Willis was getting called up, and they wanted me to go up with him. He got in on Thursday; I arrived on Thursday morning to throw with him. Dontrelle was going to

Wayne Rosenthal working with the Marlins' young staff.

pitch on Friday and they told me watch the game, and stay for the rest of the weekend because there were only two games left in the home stand. On Monday morning I had a flight scheduled to Greensboro, but got a call late Saturday evening around twelve thirty, informing me [that] I would be the new pitching coach.

How did you feel when you received the news about becoming a major-league pitching coach?
    I was in the hotel room in Fort Lauderdale; I was checking out the

minor-league game reports on my computer, and my cell phone was ringing. I recognized a Miami phone number; it was Larry Beinfest [general manager] who spoke to me. He told me he was making a change—he was replacing Jeff Torborg and Brad Arnsberg. Jack McKeon was going to become the new manager and he said, "We want to offer you the major-league pitching coach job." I was kind of silent at first when he said it; I didn't know what to say. I said, "Okay." Beinfest said, "Do you accept?" I said, "Hell yes, I do, all right." He told me the time I should report to the stadium the following day, and we finished the telephone conversation.

I told my girlfriend [at the time] and immediately called my parents to tell them about my good news. The next day was Mother's Day and I was supposed to have dinner with my mom, my dad and my brother (first time in 15 years). It was one o'clock in the morning and I told my parents what was going on. About 15 minutes later, Jeffrey Loria [owner] called and he said, "Congratulations, you're going to do a good job and just be yourself." He made me feel a lot better when he called me. I didn't get any sleep that night; I slept about four hours and woke up at eight o'clock in the morning—had breakfast, headed over to the ballpark, was very nervous, and had only five days' worth of dirty clothes. I didn't have clean clothes to take on the upcoming road trip, and my dad and brother came down, and brought me slacks, shoes and extra clothes to take with me. The clubhouse manager washed my dirty clothes during my first game with the club, which was on Mother's Day. Then I met Jack McKeon for the first time.

It would be an understatement to say that you were excited.

I was excited, but I guess, I didn't show it on the outside as much as people would expect. I was more nervous—a lot of people were close to Brad Arnsberg and I knew Brad for a long time, and I didn't want anybody to have ill feelings to me because I was taking the job. I never really used politics to become the new pitching coach; I did my job and what happened, happened. I was happy being the minor-league coordinator; I had no aspirations to become the pitching coach last year; it just happened to work out.

What did Jack [McKeon] say to you when he met on his debut, as well as yours?

Marc Delpiano, the director of player development (my boss in the minor leagues), asked me if I wanted to meet the manager, and I said, "Sure, why not" [laughs]. So, he introduced me to Jack and said, "Here's your pitching coach." Jack said, "Hey, how you doing, we will talk a little bit later, I have a lot of stuff going on right now; we will get together later." The first meeting we had with the whole team—he's a fiery little guy walking around and the way he talks and says things gets you to listen. He's one of those guys you listen to when he talks to you. Nobody really knew him, but as I got to know him, he's a very, very intelligent man as far as the game of baseball, and during the year I learned a lot from him while listening to him talk.

What did McKeon tell the players?
We're good enough to win; we have a good team. We have to put it together, have some fun and try not to be too tense out there. We have about 20 weeks left in the season and if we can pick up one game a week, we'll be in the playoffs. And that made everybody feel pretty good about themselves. He told the guys he's here to have fun; he could be home, but he believes this team has the potential to win, and he made the players believe in winning—we did.

Did McKeon have to discipline some of the players?
Some needed discipline and he's the type of guy to do it. When he met with the pitchers one of the first things he did was to change the attitude about their work and pitching habits. During a meeting Jack told the pitchers, "If you don't want to pitch, we're going to get players up here who do." He told Josh Beckett, Brad Penny and Dontrelle Willis, as far as the pitchers are concerned, to work harder, take care of the running, stay in shape and don't slack off. Guys got away with a lot of stuff; you're not getting away with it now. The players are going to sit in the dugout—it's not a country club here. We're here to win. It's a business, and if you do your work, your running, your throwing and all the stuff you need to win, then we'll win. That's what he did.

Talk about the rookie sensation Dontrelle Willis and his contribution as far as helping his team get to the postseason.
Dontrelle Willis is a young, inspiring pitcher who came up and got in the spotlight real quick. I think he's going to be a good one; he's a hard worker and loves the game. He lives and breathes baseball. He has a personality about him that just shines, and brings the good out of everybody. He brings other people up when he talks, when he plays, and I think he was the catalyst for our team getting to the postseason. Watching what he did, he picked up Josh Beckett, Brad Penny, Carl Pavano—everybody on the staff—even the position players loved to play behind him because he

was quick with an uplifting personality; everybody loved to watch him, and it was fun for him to be out there. He made everybody relax and play better.

What can you say about Josh Beckett?

When I first met him he was very stubborn—a stubborn young prospect with a good arm. I think Josh and I got off, not on a wrong foot, but I told him some things I wanted him to do, and after awhile he agreed to it. I adjusted his delivery during the season, encouraged him to use his legs more and slowed his windup. He went out and worked on it, and he loved it; he picked it up real quick. Seeing what that guy did last year was amazing. He had the potential to do that. He had great stuff and you saw how he did it consistently in the playoffs and the World Series. Right now, he's in great shape; he worked his butt off during the off-season. He's taking everything seriously, he's routine oriented and he's a pleasure to work with.

Talk about Brad Penny.

Penny and I butt heads ... I don't know if you talked to him yet, but he and I butt heads. He's a guy you have to stay on all the time. I had a little trouble last year, and Jack took over, and he had to push him a little bit. I think this year is different, where he's changed a little bit; we're more comfortable, but he's stubborn. He's a stubborn country boy, I'll tell you that. But the guy has a great arm; he's a great competitor. He wants the ball, he gets that rebel attitude that's good on the mound, and that's why we butt heads because I want him to succeed as much as he does.

Talk about Carl Pavano and his magnificent postseason pitching in 2003.

What he did last year in the playoffs—the guy was very consistent. He had a 1.40 ERA with two wins in pitching 19 innings in the postseason—amazing. He had 32 starts last year, pitched over 200 innings, and the guy is a bulldog. He's a horse who wants the ball late in the game; he's an analytical guy a little bit, but mechanically oriented. We have a good relationship as far as talking to each other during the game, during side works, during off days, and he's a very solid pitcher. He may not shine you with his stuff like Josh Beckett, Brad Penny or Dontrelle Willis, but he goes out there and competes with the best of them.

What is your assessment of A.J. Burnett?

Well, I never really had a chance to work with him until this year, but A.J. has an unbelievable arm, and I'm looking forward to work with him. He has a great personality, he's a hard worker, competitor, and I can't say anything bad about him. The guy is laid back, happy-go-lucky, just wants to go out and pitch, and I can't wait to see him on game day. I've only seen him in bullpen sessions and stuff like that. I told my pitching staff to go out there and have fun, don't worry about failing.

What can you say about your bullpen, and did they help get you to the playoffs and World Series?

[Definitely.] Chad Fox came on halfway through the season and he was a pleasure to work with. He just wanted to have fun. We told him the first day when he walked in that everything was under the spotlight in Boston (his previous team), but with this team here, just go out and have fun. Go out and pitch and do the best you can on the field and have fun. Fox performed well and his success took us into the playoffs. Ugueth Urbina came here in midseason as a set-up pitcher and took over the closing role at the end of the season and into the postseason. He's a great competitor, you can't say anything bad about him, and he just came in and gave everybody a lift knowing that we had the lead in the eighth and ninth inning—the feeling was the game is over when he came in. Braden Looper had 27 saves; he threw every day. He complained a little bit like everybody else does about overuse and underuse, but the guy would take the ball and get the job done. He was a little bit stubborn at times as far as pitches, but the guy has an unbelievable sinker and came in some big games in the playoffs, and helped us out after struggling the last couple of weeks of the season.

Was it a tough decision to have Beckett pitch Game 6 of the World Series on three days rest, when you could've saved him for Game 7?

Several hours before Game 5, Josh had played long toss at Pro Player Stadium and told me his arm felt fine. Jack [McKeon] believed that as long as Beckett felt fine after his workout, he would start Game 6 on three days' rest. Jack knew that there were no guarantees to win either Game 6 or 7 and Beckett was the best choice to possibly end the World Series in Game 6. I said, "We don't do things here in a conventional way. Our pitchers work hard and have the attitude to make it work." McKeon wasn't concerned with pitch counts or innings pitched during Game 6 and decided that he would encourage Beckett to pitch for nine innings as long as he felt fine.

Do the pitchers sometimes disagree with your assessment?

Yes, and I accept disagreement. I tell them, "I'll give you my opinion, you let me know what you think. And we'll come up with a solution." I think this, they think that, let's come to a common ground. That's what I do; I give suggestions—sometimes they take it and sometimes they don't.

What did you see as the reason the 2003 team was successful and experienced a championship season?

I think the togetherness, [I mean] I've been on teams before (playing and coaching the same teams), and this team last year was brought together. They picked each other up. The bench guys that weren't playing every day were the best bench guys I've seen in my life. Guys like Banks, Andy Fox, Redman, Hollandsworth (at the end of the year), Harris and Castro—these guys were ready to play and cheering in the dugout; they were happy-go-lucky, no matter what the score was or the situation was, these guys were very loose as a team, as a family, and I think everybody played together, picked each other up and helped each other as best as they can.

Who did you see as a leader on that championship team?

We had a lot of leaders by example, but Pudge [Rodgriguez] was a leader and he held that pitching staff together. He did a great job with the defense. You have two guys up the middle that lead by example—Rodriguez and Juan Pierre lead by example. This was a team where the guys were playing together and working together, and leading on the field.

You had a lot of opportunities to work with Pudge. What can you say about him?

Pudge to me, as a rookie coach, was a veteran player behind the plate that helped me out a lot and took the pressure off me. I let him do a lot of things like going out to the mound and talking to the pitchers, stuff like that, and it took the pressure off me to do it. He will be missed, but we have to move on with what we have right now. He led that pitching staff to where we were. He worked those guys and he got on their ass when he needed to; he patted them on the back when he needed to, he pumped them up, he kept them going, and I think he was very valuable to this team.

With the loss of Pudge, who is going to work with the pitching staff?

I think Ramon Castro is going to play more than Mike Redmond. I love Mike Redmond to death. Can he catch everyday is the question. If he can catch every day, I would love it. He's intelligent, he knows how to handle pitchers, and he does a great job. When you talk to him during the meetings about hitters, he knows every hitter. He helps me out a lot with the meetings and knowing how to pitch guys and stuff like that. Castro is learning because he was in the meetings, but didn't get a chance to catch when Pudge was here. Now he's getting a chance to catch, and he really has to pay attention to what the hitters need, and what the pitchers can throw. He's learning how to handle the pitchers, he's catching the main guys he needs to know every day, and he's becoming more comfortable behind the plate.

Do you have meetings with the pitchers and the catchers, and what do you discuss?

Every new series we have a meeting with the catchers and the pitchers, where we go over their hitters, how to pitch them, some tendencies, mostly a game plan of how we want to pitch the opposing lineup—hitters and pinch-hitters, everybody. It's more of a solid base—it's not pitch by pitch, but more about hitter's tendencies—we're going to pitch this guy hard-in and stay all day long, just throw him hard stuff; if we throw him something soft, it's going to be off the plate. For a dead pull hitter—if you throw him anything soft that goes away from him, he'll pull it and pull it on the ground, stuff like that. We talk about the little tendencies, so they'll have it in their mind of how to pitch other players. We have a 10-minute meeting at the start of a new series; if we play the same team next week, we don't have another meeting.

How do you handle poor outings by the pitchers and problems with their mechanics?

I get together with the starters during their side work. When Beckett pitches a game and I see something, we'll look at the film and I'll show him what he's doing; we'll go from there. I work with the relievers when they go out to the outfield to throw. If I see something, I will address it then; sometimes I will do shadow work or something off the mound to show them what we need to do. Sometimes during a game, I'll go out to Chad Fox and tell him to keep that front leg back; you're drifting a little bit. He understands what I mean and he fixes it. Sometimes they fix it themselves; sometimes you have to give them key words quickly—"Hey, get it down, just stay back and ride it to the plate, and let it go." I work hard with the starters and the relievers with shadow work and bullpen sessions.

How would you characterize this team?

I think this team loves to have fun. This is a business, but it's a game. You go on the field and play a game. These guys have fun with each other.

They have handshakes before the game, they're joking around in the clubhouse, the togetherness, and it's great to see. I don't see any big egos in that clubhouse. Guys on this team don't act weird because they're making a lot of money. Overall, this team has a lot of chemistry. You have a leader like Juan Pierre who's a great competitor; he leads by example, plus in the dugout he leads with his voice.

You talk about how the players joke around in the clubhouse and the handshakes. Are these important qualities for a championship team?
  [Definitely.] Watch our dugout before a game and watch Dontrelle Willis and Juan Pierre before every game [except] when Willis pitches. They do a little rap together out in the outfield. They put their fists together and they jump up in the air, and they stamp it down. Everybody has different handshakes and it's fun to watch. Luis Castillo has about six different handshakes. He does this thing with A.J. Burnett before every game. Little things like that loosen everybody up—here we go, we're ready to play a game now. We have a good chance to repeat, but let's worry about winning games first and the playoffs later.

Do you think this team can repeat and why?
  I think we have a different bunch of guys, but it's the same attitude. I think we have a very good team. I think it's different from last year, but with the starting pitching we have and the leaders on the field, as far as the infield and Pierre in the outfield, we have our whole outfield back, and three-quarters of our infield back.

Do you set goals for yourself?
  I do, but my goals are for the players. First of all, I want all my pitchers to be healthy all season. My job is to keep them healthy all year long. I want each of my starters to have close to 200 [pitched] innings; I want each of them to have double-figure wins. I want Fox to get a couple of saves (maybe), but mostly to get us to the ninth inning to get to Armando Benitez. Armando will blow some saves, no doubt about it; Gagne is the only guy who hasn't blown a save in over a year. I want to give Benitez a chance to get in the game, win a ballgame and save the game. I want little things for the pitchers to accomplish like developing another pitch, work on a slide step and work on holding runners; work on this and that, that's my goals as far as a pitching coach. This year is my first full year as a major-league pitching coach and I'm excited about the new season.

Dontrelle Willis
THE JOURNEY OF THE D TRAIN
2003 NL Rookie of the Year

> "The whole year, the way everybody played and everybody came together ... you can't dream that. We won the World Series as a unit and we had 25 guys contributing. What we accomplished that season was something very special and awesome."—Dontrelle Willis

Dontrelle Wayne Willis graduated from Encinal High School in Alameda, California, in 2000 and was named the California High School Player of the Year in 2000 after going 10–1 with a 0.70 ERA and 111 strikeouts in 70.0 innings. In 2000, he joined the Cubs in the Rookie-level Arizona League and went 3–1 with a 3.86 ERA in nine games. He pitched for Single-A Boise in the Northwest League in 2001 and won eight of his 10 decisions with a 2.98 ERA in 15 starts. He was chosen by *Baseball America* as the sixth-best prospect in the Northwest League.

In his first season in the Marlins system in 2002, Willis posted a combined 12–2 record with a 1.83 ERA in 24 games (all starts). He went 10–2 with a 1.83 earned run average in 19 games with Kane County and 2–0 with a 1.80 ERA in five starts at Jupiter. He was named the fourth-best prospect in Florida's minor-league system.

Willis began the 2003 season with the Double-A Carolina Mudcats and went 4–0 with a 1.49 earned run average in six starts, pitching 36.1 innings for the Mudcats. He joined the Marlins on May 9, 2003, and made his major league debut that night, facing the Rockies and collecting no decision. He collected his first major-league win in his second start on May 14 at San Diego, allowing three runs on five hits in five innings with nine strikeouts.

Willis began his big-league career with a 1–1 record over his first three starts before posting an 8–0 record with a 1.05 ERA over his next 10 starts, including wins in seven consecutive starts. He was selected to the National League All-Star Team, replacing injured Dodgers pitcher Kevin Brown. He went 9–1 with a 2.08 earned run average in his 13 outings prior to the All-Star Game.

Willis led the Marlins to the postseason and World Series crown, and pitched out of the bullpen in the World Series. He set the Marlins' single-season record for wins by a rookie and finished tied for the team lead with 14 wins (14–6, 3.30 ERA in 27 starts). He was named the National League Rookie of the Year. Willis and I had our conversation at Pro Player Stadium, in the Marlins clubhouse at the beginning of the 2004 season, a day after he earned his first win.

Conversation with Dontrelle Willis

You started the 2003 season at Double-A and joined the Marlins early in May. Did you expect to pitch in the major leagues that soon?

No, no. I didn't think about coming up then or in September. I just wanted to play good baseball wherever I was pitching—at Double-A, Triple-A and try to accomplish things there. I just figured that if I play well at each level, then hopefully I would get an opportunity to play in the big leagues. I just wanted the opportunity to compete and pitch every fifth day. That was my plan.

When you made your major-league debut, what was that like?

Well, it was exciting and I was nervous—all rolled into one. I was facing a good Rockies team with Helton (a batting champion almost every year), Larry Walker (another great player), Preston Wilson—all those great hitters that make a living off guys making mistakes, and to go out there and compete with those guys on the same level—not thinking about their great numbers, but getting myself out there to compete on a level like that.

Talk about your rookie season.

It was good coming up early in the season; we won the World Series. I enjoyed both aspects of it—me doing well and me struggling, all of it; it was a learning experience. I'm a firm believer of taking a negative and turning it into a positive.

Dontrelle Willis in the dugout at Pro Player Stadium.

How did you turn your experience into a positive?

I'm a guy that likes to put everything in perspective, and I try to be positive, even when I do well or struggle. I realize now you have to grow up, be a man, and take responsibility. When you do well or struggle, that can be a learning experience and you try to improve. You have to learn how to keep your composure, you learn how to fail and fail with class. You keep your head up, and you're learning and taking something from it. Through that, I think it made me relax [coming] into the World Series ... it made me more confident.

When you joined the team, you quickly piled up nine wins (eight consecutive wins). What was that like?

It was exciting because we were playing well. It was an exciting time, but at the same time, it was nothing more than trying to help my team win. I really didn't notice the winning I had—how big it was until after we won the World Series.

Which players helped you when you joined the team?

The whole team, [I mean] everybody took part in helping me. Even players from different teams helped me. Juan Pierre and Pudge Rodriguez provided knowledge that I was able to take in, and encouraged me to be a good player. Burnett and Penny have been phenomenal. They're teaching me to play the game the right way ... the professional way.

How did the pitching coach help you?

Well, he worked on my mechanics [a little bit] between starts. He encouraged me to pitch, throw the ball the way I had been throwing. Rosenthal didn't change my delivery. Like McKeon, he encouraged me to have fun when I was pitching. He said, "Go out and play the way you know how to play."

What was it like having Rodriguez, a great veteran catcher, to work with you?

Early on he helped me with a lot of hitters because I didn't know the hitters, but after I faced the hitters a couple of times, I figured out what I wanted to do. He's a Hall of Fame catcher and one of the best in the game. He helped me focus on the physical part of pitching, as well as the mental part of it.

When did you see the team start to click and believe you would play in the postseason?

There were so many different points where everyone was just picking up each other throughout the season. When I struggled, someone would pick me up, and I picked up other guys when they were struggling. There were so many different points, but Jack came in and motivated us; he played a big part. He encouraged us to work hard, work on our mechanics and have fun at the same time. Once we started winning, [Jack] had us believe in ourselves, and we knew we had the potential to get to the playoffs.

Many players [even Hall of Famers] never had the opportunity to play in the postseason. What was it like to play in your first postseason?

It was really a blessing to be able to play against the best in the world. I went out there and competed physically and mentally every day against players that I grew up watching and admiring. In the postseason, Jack had me come out of the bullpen and it was exciting. He wasn't afraid to use me, Beckett and other guys to help get us a win.

How did you approach pitching in the postseason, and did McKeon talk to you?
I just went out there and threw hard; I didn't have a significant approach. I'm not thinking about winning or losing, but I'm concerned about staying healthy. McKeon gave me a lot of insight on things I needed to work on. He just wanted me to throw strikes and he wanted me to do well. He would rather see me give up 10 hits than walk 10 guys, so he wants me to be aggressive and throw strikes.

Players have dreams of playing in the World Series. What can you say about defeating the Yankees in the World Series?
You can't dream anything like that. I can't say that was a dream come true, that was unreal. The whole year, the way everybody played and everybody came together ... you can't dream that. We won the World Series as a unit and we had 25 guys contributing. You can't field the balls by yourself and you can't hit the balls by yourself, you need to do that as a team. What we accomplished that season was something very special and awesome. What made this huge—we beat the best team in the world. We did it against the Yankees, at Yankee Stadium, against their best pitchers in the postseason. Winning awards and [stuff like that] doesn't compare to winning a World Series.

My dream would be to start Game 7 of the World Series. Being able to start and take the ball in Game 7, [win or lose] with everything on the line, that's my biggest dream. I want to be the guy they call in that pivotal game.

What was it like pitching in Yankee Stadium in the World Series?
It was exciting to face the best players on that team and there's a lot of history there; it doesn't get any better than that.

Which Yankees pitcher was the most impressive during the World Series?
I would have to say Andy Pettitte because he's pitched in the big stage [Yankee Stadium] and he's had great success, not only during the season, but also in the postseason. He's the person I would like to talk to, and hopefully I will get a chance when we play in Houston.

What is it about Pettitte that is impressive?
He never got out of what he wanted to do. He always went out there

and pitched his game. He has that tenacity on the mound—that confidence that he's going to get it done, regardless what the score was.

To be successful and pitch in the postseason, do you need to develop a certain type of attitude?

I think there's a balance; I think you want to be confident, but at the same time, you can't be arrogant—you can't sell your opponent short. You want to be confident at what you're doing, and you have to respect the people you're going up against. I think that's the biggest thing you have to balance out.

What was the clubhouse like during the postseason?

For us it was relaxed, [no one expected us to win] and everyone was having fun, everyone was working hard and we did a great job of balancing that. The guys were loose and they were pulling for each other.

When you look back on what you and your team accomplished in the 2003 championship season, do you feel like it really happened?

You can't dream anything like that, you can't. The way every game was won, how we came back from a deficit, the ninth-inning magic we had so many times, how we recovered from the deficit against the Cubs, [I mean], you can't dream things like that. We won the World Series as a unit—guys like Juan Pierre, who doesn't say a lot, but he does it with his play. Mordecai does it with his knowledge and being around the game a long time. Beckett and Penny became emotional at the right moment. They were fired up in the postseason. Cabrera doesn't talk a lot, but he goes out there and shows examples of leadership by the way he plays. That season was just awesome.

Where were you when Beckett got the final out in Game 6 of the World Series?

I was throwing in the bullpen, and when he tagged Posada out to end the game, I just started running down the stairs past the monuments in the outfield. I started screaming and it was awesome beating the Yankees in the World Series.

Tony Perez
THE HEART AND SOUL OF THE BIG RED MACHINE
7-Time National League All-Star
2000 Hall of Fame Inductee

"In 1975-76 we had the best team. We had eight guys who would go out there every day and they knew how to play the game, and they knew how to win. We had players like Bench, Morgan, Rose, Concepcion, Griffey Sr., Geronimo, Foster and myself— these were players that played hard and knew how to win."—
Tony Perez

Atanasio Perez, better known as Tony Perez, has been involved in major-league baseball for the past 40 seasons as a player, coach, manager and special assistant to the president. During a 23-year playing career, mostly with the Reds, Tony Perez was an extremely productive hitter, batting .317 in 1970, with 186 hits, 40 home runs and 129 runs batted in, and in 1973 he hit .314, with 177 hits, 27 home runs and 101 runs batted in.

Perez was one of the most consistent first basemen in baseball for over two decades. He produced 90 or more runs batted in for 11 consecutive seasons (1967–1977) and over 100 runs batted in seven times. He played in seven National League All-Star Games and was the most valuable player in the 1967 All-Star Game when he hit a game-winning home run in the 15th inning.

Perez played in five World Series, including four with the Reds, and won the championship in 1975 and 1976. Known as the glue that held together the Big Red Machine, he hit a sixth-inning two-run home run in Game 7 of the 1975 World Series to propel the Reds to a 4–3 win.

His career total 1,652 runs batted in are the second-most by a Latin

American player (behind Rafael Palmeiro) and he is tied with Orlando Cepeda for sixth in home runs by a Latin player with 379. Perez was inducted into the Hall of Fame on July 23, 2000. He assists the players during spring training and during the season, both as an instructor and advisor to the president.

I met up with Perez on the infield at Roger Dean Stadium in Jupiter, Florida, at the beginning of spring training. He is very congenial and a popular instructor in the Marlins organization and has the opportunity to work with both the up-and-coming ballplayers from the minor-league system and the veterans in camp. His overall recollections shed some light on postseason play past and present with the Reds and the Marlins 2003 championship season.

CONVERSATION WITH TONY PEREZ

When did you come up with the Reds, and what was it like back then?

I came up in 1965 and these guys didn't tell me much. I observed Frank Robinson and learned a lot from him because he was the type of player I always wanted to be. He played hard, he was a power hitter who knocked in runs and he just wanted to win. I think he helped me more than anybody in baseball because I always looked up to him.

When I came up, Frank Robinson and Vada Pinson were there to help the young players. Other guys I looked up to were Leo Cardenas and Deron Johnson when I first came up to the big leagues.

What can you say about Frank Robinson?

One of the best players I've seen play. He was a hard-nosed player with the desire to win and to play the game right. I remember when I came to the Reds Frank was a starter. I had seen him play for a year or so in spring training, and I knew the type of player he was. I watched him [all the time], the way he played, and what he tried to do with men in scoring position. That helped me in my career because Frank played the game hard and tried to win all the time, and I think he passed that down to me. Playing against him in the 1970s was something special.

You played 23 years in the big leagues, most with the Reds (16 seasons). What do you recall about playing with the Big Red Machine?

Well, there are a lot of memories, [I mean,]—from the 1970s on we

Tony Perez working as an instructor at spring training.

had the best team in baseball. I think we dominated and had a lot of good players. We had eight guys who would go out there every day and they knew how to play the game and win ballgames. That lineup helped the pitching and was probably the most dominant at that time.

Let's talk about the Reds championship team you played on in 1975 and 1976.

At that time we had the best team. In 1975-76, we had the best team.

We had eight guys who would go out there every day and they knew how to play the game and they knew how to win. We had players like Bench, Morgan, Rose, Concepcion, Griffey Sr., Geronimo, Foster and myself—these were players that played hard and knew how to win. We had Driessen, a guy who came off the bench to help us get to the postseason. Then the pitching we had wasn't the best in the world, but the guys knew how pitch, and the pitchers knew how to do their job.

Which pitchers got the Reds to the 1975 and 1976 World Series?
You're talking about Jack Billingham, Gary Nolan, Don Gullett and Fred Norman. We had other players like Pedro Borbon and Clay Carroll—these were guys who knew how to play the game and pitch.

You played in five World Series, including four with the Reds. What was your most memorable World Series?
Well, the 1975 World Series against the Red Sox, when they came back in Game 6 and beat us, and tied the series. I think that was the best World Series because we came back in Game 7; we won the game 4–3 and beat the Red Sox. That was a great series, and everybody still talks about it.

Was Game 7 of the 1975 World Series the most memorable one?
For me, yes, because I hit a two-run home run to come back, when we were down 3–0, to make it 3–2. Then we tied the game at 3–3, and won the game on Joe Morgan's base hit. That was the best game I played.

What was it like to hit two home runs and drive in four runs in Game 5 of the 1975 World Series, and break out of a 0 for 15 slump?
That was great [smile] because I was down, 0 for 15 and struggling a little bit, but the series was tied (2–2) and I never looked back. I said, "The next game is going to be mine," and I hit two home runs, and we won the game. Then I hit another home run in Game 7 and we won the World Series.

Talk about Game 7 of the 1975 World Series.
I remember Game 7 being a great game, and our pitching staff performed well. Considering we were down 3–0 in that game, the pitching staff came through and gave us a chance to come back and win the World Series. That series was exciting and my favorite one.

In 1976, the Reds played the Yankees in the World Series. What was that like?
The Yankees are rich in tradition, but we knew we had a better team.

We proved it by going out and beating the Yankees four in a row. We took two games at home, and then we go to New York. The fans there tried to intimidate us, but we weren't intimidated. We just came there, won the next two games and the World Series. It was special to beat the Yankees in four games because not many teams did that before, but I think the 1975 World Series was the one we really enjoyed. It was a tough series and we had to play hard to the end (seven games).

Did you believe that you would sweep the Yankees in four games?
No. We didn't think we'd beat them in four games because they had a great ball club. We had great pitching and clutch hitting, and we beat them because we had a better team.

What was special about that team?
It was everything—we had speed, we had power, we had great players and great defense. The pitching held up and that team would beat anybody. I still believe the 1975 championship team was stronger than the 1976 team.

In the 1972 World Series you had 10 hits and a .435 batting average. The Athletics defeated the Reds in that exciting seven-game series. What do you recall about your performance?
I hit well in that series, although, the other guys weren't hitting well early in the series. We had a good team and found a way to make it an exciting seven-game World Series. We didn't have good offense, but it took the Athletics seven games to beat us. I recall we almost won the World Series when one of the Athletics players made a great catch in left field late in the game and we lost that game.

Do you remember the 1970 World Series against the Orioles?
I think we got beat badly because we didn't play well and we didn't have the pitching to compete with the Orioles. They had the best pitching in baseball that year and they proved it; they beat us.

Seems like the Reds got to the postseason about every year in the 1970s. Why do you think the Big Red Machine was successful?
We had the best eight players going out there every day. We knew how to play, we knew how to win, and we played together. Besides having talent, that team had a lot of confidence. We knew if a player didn't perform well one day, another guy would do well the next day. This was a veteran club that thrived on winning.

Did you feel the Big Red Machine would repeat year after year?

Oh, yeah [smile]. With those eight players—Rose, Morgan, Bench, Griffey, Concepcion, Foster, Geronimo and myself—we would win in 1975 and repeat in 1976. We could've won again in 1977, but I was traded, and we never had the chance to repeat again.

Were you disappointed when you were traded from a championship team?

Yes. I was disappointed, but what could I do? You don't want to be in some place they don't want you, and they have somebody else to play for you.

You have been referred to as the glue that held together the Big Red Machine.

Well, I was a guy who wanted to play every day and win every day. I played this game to win ... I never played for myself. Everybody knows that and my teammates respected me for that. I knocked in a lot of runs and contributed to my team.

Along with the great players you've talked about, what can you say about your manager, Sparky Anderson?

Sparky Anderson was a great manager. He knew how to handle the players and how to get the most out of them. He knew he had a good team, a veteran team, and he knew the guys just wanted to go out and play. He focused on the pitching staff, and the smartest thing Sparky did was to let us play, and he took care of the pitching.

Let's talk about your present role with the Florida Marlins.

I'm a special assistant to the president of the team. I help the players on the field during spring training and throughout the season, and I help out in the front office when they need me. I work with Bill Robinson, the hitting coach, and we exchange ideas about hitting. In the championship season I worked with Derek Lee, Alex Gonzalez and Luis Castillo. With Lee, I told him not to pull the ball, but to drive the ball in the gaps, and stay behind the ball—use your legs and hands, and I told him to relax.

As the special assistant and instructor with the Marlins in 2003, did you think the team would play in the postseason?

When we left spring training nobody thought we could win a wild card or anything like that. We knew we had a young team, but we didn't expect to put it together that season. When we started the season, we didn't play good baseball, and changes were made with a new manager and a new pitching coach. Then we picked up Willis and Cabrera, and some of the other players who helped us win the World Series. The guys played with a lot of heart. We started rolling and rolling, and it continued in the World Series as we beat the Yankees.

What was it like defeating the Yankees in the World Series?
It was unbelievable. Nobody expected that; nobody even expected the Marlins to beat the Giants or the Cubs. The team was playing great baseball at the right time, and it carried over in the playoffs, and we ended beating the Yankees in the World Series. To beat the Yankees any time—I remember when we beat the Yankees in 1976, it was special; any time you beat the Yankees it's the best you ever do in baseball because they're one of the greatest teams ever. They have always been the team you have to beat. When you say "New York Yankees," you're talking about a tradition, about baseball, about a World Series and all that.

Who was the spark plug on the 2003 World Championship team?
Well, I will tell you what—[I think] Rodriguez, the catcher, gave the club a spark the way he put everything together when Jack [McKeon] became the manager. You have to give Jack a lot of credit because he put this team together, and he told the guys what to do, and they did it. I think Pudge Rodriguez, a veteran player, was the guy that kept the pitching together, who led this team, and then when we got Cabrera, and guys like Castillo and Gonzalez [the Latin players], who followed each other in the batting order—each guy encouraged each other—at that point the team became successful.

What did McKeon do to get the team to the postseason?
He always told the guys to play hard, he didn't accept excuses, and he wanted his team to play good baseball. Being an older guy who's been around with lots of experience, the players respected more of that than anything, and responded to him. Young guys looked at a 73-year-old guy like McKeon and believed they have to play for this guy because he shows you respect, and you have to respect him. The players looked at him as a leader.

What's the difference between the 2003 championship team and the 1997 team?
Well, the 1997 team was supposed to win. I think everybody expected that team to get to the postseason. That team had veterans [experienced

players] like Sheffield, White, Renteria, Conine, Kevin Brown, Leiter—all the players who've been around and played the game for a long time.

The 2003 team was young and no one expected that team to win when the season began. Guys like Rodriguez, Lee and Conine showed the young guys how to win.

Do you see the Marlins repeating and getting to the postseason again?
I think we have a good team; we have good pitching, a young pitching staff, and it all depends on what they do. I think we'll score enough runs to win, but we're going to have to wait and see.

Another accomplishment in your career, along with winning two World Series championships, was your induction into the Hall of Fame in 2000. How special was that?
Well, one of the greatest things that happened to me or any player with a great career is to be in the Hall of Fame with all the immortals of the game. The best players in the game—to be selected and to be honored with a plaque for the rest of my life [his voice cracks, tears fill his eyes], even when I pass away, that plaque will remain in the Hall of Fame in Cooperstown.

When you were inducted into the Hall of Fame in 2000, which players were there honoring you that day?
Frank Robinson was there, Willie Mays, Bob Gibson, Orlando Cepeda, a lot of guys—Al Kaline, Ernie Banks, Reggie Jackson, Gaylord Perry—they were all there to honor me. They congratulated me and they told me that I deserved to be inducted, and that I waited too long. I was just happy to be there. I've experienced two World Series championships and was inducted into the Hall of Fame; it doesn't get better than that.

Robin Yount
THE BREW CREW'S MOST VALUABLE PLAYER
*1982, 1989 AL Most Valuable Player,
3-Time American League All-Star,
1999 Hall of Fame Inductee*

> *"So we had basically a do-or-die game, the last game of the season, in Baltimore. The winner was going to the playoffs and the loser was going home. So we're fortunate enough to win that game. I hit a home run in the first inning and had another home run and triple in that game. The other players came through and we won 10–2."* —Robin Yount

Robin Yount played his entire 20-year career with the Milwaukee Brewers. He was a consistent player with a .285 lifetime batting average and a member of the 3,000 Hit Club, amassing 3,142 hits. Yount was the American League Most Valuable Player at two different positions: in 1982 as a shortstop and in 1989 as a center fielder.

Yount's baseball career began with a one-year stint with Newark in 1973, and then he joined the Brewers at the age of 18 in 1974, where he played through the 1993 season. He had a batting average that eclipsed the .300 mark six times in his career and had a breakout year in 1982 with a .331 average, league leading—210 hits and 46 doubles—had a career-high 29 home runs and drove in 114 runs (earning his first MVP). Yount played in the 1982 World Series batting .414 with 12 hits in 29 at-bats in the seven-game series, and hit a home run in Milwaukee.

In 1989, Yount had his second MVP season with a .318 batting average in 160 games, 195 hits, 21 home runs, and knocked in 103 runs. He was selected by *USA Today* as the Player of the Decade for the 1980s. He was a three-time American League All-Star (1980, '82 and '83) and was inducted into the Hall of Fame in 1999. He was the bench coach for Arizona in 2004 and resigned when manager Bob Brenly was fired early in the season.

Yount and I met up in the Diamondbacks' dugout early in May 2004 and talked about postseason play in 1981 and 1982, and the Diamondbacks' championship season while defeating the Yankees in the 2001 World Series.

CONVERSATION WITH ROBIN YOUNT

Early in your career, you had a one-year stint in the minor leagues, and were called up to the Brewers at the tender age of 18 in 1974. Talk about the beginning of your career, and what was it like back then.

Oh, I think as far as baseball goes, my dreams were no different than any other kids [growing up], and that was to play in a World Series somewhere along the line ... maybe hit a home run in the World Series, be a world champion—those types of dreams. I think any kid who's played baseball probably has those, or [had those], and I was no different.

Early on in my career, I was an 18-year-old kid that didn't know a whole lot about playing at the major-league level. I had a lot to learn, and I was in a position where I was given the opportunity to gain major-league experience at an early age because there really wasn't any pressure on the organization to win in those days. The Brewers were a new organization and at that time they were five years old, and had never played .500 ball throughout the history of the franchise. I was able to play in the big leagues and learn, and be able to make a number of mistakes without the concern that I may get sent back to the minors, or anything like that. It was an opportunity that a lot of young kids wouldn't have had with a different organization.

Who were some of the people that helped you when you came up in 1974?

In my first year, Harvey Kuenn was probably the biggest influence, from a coaching standpoint, that I had at that time, early in my career, and he was around for most of my career. The first real player that I became close with was a pitcher, Ed Sprague, whose son later played in the big leagues too. It's funny because we had so much in common. Sprague was

10 years older than I am, and he's the first guy that took me under his wings from early spring training days before I made the team. He talked to me a lot, asked me to play golf with him, and I didn't know anybody. During spring training you play a lot of golf before the season begins, and he was the first guy to ask me to golf with him. I got to know him real well, and it turned out we had a real a lot in common—the fact that he was 10 years older than I was to the day—our birthdays are September 16th—we both loved to fish and play golf, and both our wives' names are Michele. And to this day we're still close friends; it's kind of a neat coincidence.

You mentioned Harvey Kuenn helping you when you came up with the Brewers.

He helped me in more ways than just baseball. He was our hitting coach when I came to the big leagues. The best thing about his style of being a hitting coach was that he didn't really try to change much, but he was there, and recognized what you were doing when you were going well. When you got into a slump, he was able to see the difference, where you were headed, and he would try to get you back on track before you got too far out of whack. He knew everybody goes through slumps; that's just part of the game. He was real good at recognizing when you were starting to get away from whatever it was you did when you were going good, and catch that early enough to not let you get so far in a tailspin that it took a long time to get back on track. More than that, he was a great influence on me, as far as teaching me how the game was supposed to be played, how to conduct yourself both on and off the field as a major-league player. I have a great dad,

Robin Yount in the dugout at Pro Player Stadium.

and learned a lot from him growing up, but as far as being away from home, Kuenn was a father figure to me.

You had a great 20-year career with the Brewers, piling up 3,142 hits, two Most Valuable Player Awards and inducted into the Hall of Fame in 1999. Were you disappointed that you played in the postseason only in 1981 and 1982?

Yes. Obviously that was what I played for. As a player, that was always the goal I set, to win a World Series. It was disappointing after 20 years to not have accomplished that, but on the other hand, I will feel fortunate that I got to play in the World Series, and a very exciting one at that. An extremely exciting last couple of weeks of the season that we had to go through to win our division. Then the playoffs with the Angels was a great accomplishment, and then the seven-game World Series. I wouldn't trade the experience for anything other than winning it. We were about three innings short of accomplishing everything that I wanted to, and it's disappointing, but like I said, I feel fortunate that I was able to at least experience that feeling that a lot of players never get to.

Talk about your postseason in 1981 against the Yankees.

I think we felt that we were as good as the Yankees that year. That was the strike season. The reason we played the Yankees was because they broke the season in two halves as a result of the strike [during the season]. I think, obviously, the Yankees won one of those halves and we won the other. We felt we had a chance to beat them because we had been playing really well up to the playoffs. I think in that series, if I'm not mistaken, it was the best three out of five. We played the first two games in Milwaukee, and then had to go to New York for the remaining three games. I'm pretty sure we lost the first two in Milwaukee, and then went to New York, and won two. We thought we would win Game 5 at Yankee Stadium, and I was disappointed that we were beaten.

Most of us had never been in a playoff situation before. It was a great experience, and it gave us some postseason experience that became really big the following year [1982] when we did go all the way. We were climbing that ladder in those years. The year before we got in the playoffs, I think we had something like 86 wins in 1980, and finished third in our division. That was our first real good team; we had a successful year and we started knocking on the door of a championship. Then the following year, we won those halves, got some postseason experience, and then in 1982, we played in the World Series.

Were you disappointed in 1981 when the Brewers were eliminated in the division series?

No, no. Of course you're disappointed when it ends, but it was just part of that steppingstone of getting to the World Series, and it was a great experience for us.

What was the make-up of that team?

It was pretty much the same make-up in 1981-82. We had a bunch of characters on that club. It was a great mix of personalities, and in those days it was really a close-knit group of people because there was not nearly as much movement of players in those days, as there is now. Families became close, not just the players—the wives and the kids—and players spent a lot of time doing things both on and off the field. It was special because many times you don't get that opportunity to get as close with your teammates as that group did.

In 1982, you had a breakout season, and get to the postseason with a .331 batting average, a career-high 210 hits, scoring 129 runs and 114 runs batted in. What did you do that season that got you the MVP and your team into the World Series?

The reason you put numbers like that up has to do with the people around you. We had the best offensive team in the game for a couple of years there, in my opinion. We had hitters [1–9] that were all bona-fide offensive players. You put a group together like that, and that makes everybody a better player. And we had that for a number of years there, where we were a pretty good offensive team, and that certainly plays a major role in putting numbers like that together.

You're saying that when everybody is playing well, you feed off that, and it improves your game?

Oh, yeah. There's no question about the confidence factor and the snowball effect that takes place when things are going well. We went to the ballpark for a couple of years there, just expecting and knowing that we're going to win that day. And when you really and truly believe that, and feel that, it's amazing how often that happens.

Talk about the 1982 postseason.

Well, the whole season came down to the last day where we're playing Baltimore, and we ended up being tied with them with one game to go. We had basically a do-or-die game, the last game of the season, in Baltimore. The winner was going to the playoffs, and the loser was going home. So we're fortunate enough to win that game. I hit a home run in the first inning and had another home run and triple in that game. The other players came through and we won 10-2.

Then we started the playoffs against the Angels; we had to fly out of Baltimore to the West Coast and open up the league championship series in Los Angeles. It was one of those best out of five series, where you played the first two games in Anaheim and then went back to Milwaukee for the last three games. And we lost the first two games in Anaheim, then head back to Milwaukee for three do-or-die games. We had to win all three if we were going to continue and we did.

Then we played in the World Series and took that to a seventh game. In probably a three-week period, from the end of the season to the end of the World Series, we found ourselves playing in five games that were do-or-die situations, and we won four of those games. That was great; it couldn't have gotten any better. After winning four of those, and going to the seventh game of the World Series, we were all convinced we were going to win that game before it started because that was just the way the season was going, and we came in with a bunch of confidence that we would win Game 7. We had won four do-or-die games already. We had the lead, 3–2 going into the sixth inning, and then the Cardinals scored four runs to win it 6–3. It was a great experience, and we didn't pull off the last game; it sure felt like we won Game 7.

Did the players expect to win the World Series in 1982?

I think we did; I know we did. I think by the time we made it to the World Series, we believed we were a better team than St. Louis, but they beat us in a short series. I'm sure they wouldn't agree with that, but that's okay.

In 1982, you had an outstanding World Series with a .414 batting average, 12 hits, drove in six runs and scored six runs. Were you satisfied with your postseason play?

Every athlete wonders how they will do when they get to the ultimate competition and big-time game. It was fun to do well in that forum, and that side of it was satisfying. The only down side was the outcome of Game 7; everything else was wonderful.

Sounds like you were disappointed losing the 1982 World Series to the Cardinals. If I recall, the Brewers were ahead 3–2 in games.

I was absolutely disappointed when we didn't win. This is what you've worked your whole life to accomplish, and you're this close, hell yes, I was disappointed, but I wouldn't trade that experience for not being there. I would rather have gotten there and lost Game 7 than never been there at all. I had no problem dealing with the disappointment, but sure it hurts, and I'm over it [laughs].

Did you expect to play in the postseason the following season?

Oh, yeah. We certainly expected to be back the following year, but you find out real fast that it's not that easy, and things didn't go nearly as well the next year for us, as it did in 1982. We were in first place with, maybe, a month or so to go. We had fallen way behind earlier in the season, made a good run at catching back up, and getting into first place, but we kind of shot our wad with a month to go, and didn't finish strong enough to pull it off.

As a player, what was your greatest accomplishment in baseball? Why?

Playing in the 1982 World Series was my greatest accomplishment. That was the goal that was set from day one, and being able to live out that dream was by far the highlight of my career. It would've been sweeter if we had won.

In 2001, when the Diamondbacks defeated the Yankees in the World Series, you weren't coaching that season, but it must have been exciting to see the Diamondbacks come back from a 3–2 deficit.

I wasn't here in 2001; I was involved in motor sports as a co-owner of a Formula Atlantic racing team, and traveling around the country with the racing team. I remember being at two of the World Series games in Phoenix (Phoenix is home to me). I was at Game 6 and 7. I recall Game 6 was a blowout win for the Diamondbacks, who tied the series at 3–3. In Game 7, I remember Gonzo's [Luis Gonzalez] hit over the shortstop's head to win the World Series. Mariano Rivera came in the ninth inning, and Grace began the inning with a base hit. Then there was a bunt that Rivera threw past second base into centerfield, which was a huge play and Womack followed with a double to tie the game at 2–2. If I recall, Counsell got hit by a pitch to load the bases, and Gonzo followed with a bloop single to win it. That was a great World Series and a huge comeback for this veteran team.

Was the 2001 Diamondbacks similar to the 1982 Brewers?

That Diamondback team had a lot of experience and was more similar to our team than the Marlins in 2003. They were given respect with veteran players, a couple of horses on the mound [Johnson and Schilling], they had power—they hit a lot of home runs that year, and with Womack they had speed at the top of the lineup. And like I've said, they had a lot of experience and won a championship.

In 2002, you became the first-base coach with the Diamondbacks. Did you see the team having the chance to repeat and win another title?

Anytime you have Randy Johnson and Curt Schilling on your team together, you have a chance to do a lot of damage. We had a good year, we really did. Down the stretch, we were banged up, and in September we didn't hit as much as we did early in the year. We were pretty banged up at the time when the playoffs came around. We kind of lost the momentum at the wrong time—for the first five months, we were really on a roll, and then in September we kind of lost that momentum going into the playoffs and never got it back. St. Louis was on a roll when we matched up against them, and they took care of us pretty easy. We certainly had a good team, and anytime you have Johnson and Schilling on the hill for you [consistently], you have a good chance to get to the postseason.

Were the injuries in 2002 a factor in the division series?

Oh, yeah, no question. Gonzo got hurt diving for a ball in St. Louis and collided with Tony Womack a week before the season ended. Gonzalez had a shoulder separation and didn't play in the postseason. We played St. Louis at the end of the season [prior to the playoffs], and when he got hurt, he was certainly a key factor in the offense of that club.

In 2004, you're working as a bench coach with the Diamondbacks. What does this team need to do to get to the postseason again?

Well, getting back to the postseason: we're real young now, we have an infield of kids, a young catcher, a pretty young pitching staff too, for that matter. The outfield is veteran guys, but you really need pitching; without pitching you're not going to win [consistently]. When the young pitching staff gets some experience, and learns to compete at this level, we'll be competitive again, and have a chance to win. Young players [all] go through growing pains early in their career. As a coach, you can tell them everything that you've learned and know about the game, and try to help that process. In the meantime, they still have to experience it for themselves to really understand what you're trying to teach them—what we're going through right now. We're trying to teach these young guys what it takes to win. It takes a little while, and so, that's where we're at. There's no substitute for experience and we're just a little bit short on that right now, but we'll keep teaching, and hopefully they will get the hang of this, so we can get there quick because we have a lot of talent here. It's young.

What is your role as the bench coach?
My job is to keep the manager aware of as many of the options that we have and he decides which way he wants to go. While the game is being played, my role is to give him as much information as I can as to what's happening in the game itself, and he decides which way he wants to go with that. My job goes back to teaching and helping the young players with learning to play the game, and like I said earlier, what it takes to win. And teaching that—whether it be before the game in batting practice, or while the game is going on—after something happens, you come back and discuss what happened, and there's different ways to do those things. I look at it more as an opportunity to help the young players learn the game.

What can you say about a player like Luis Gonzalez, who's been to the postseason and the young players look up to?
He's played the game a long time, and he's experienced just about everything you can as a player. He won the World Series with his clutch base hit, and he certainly is a positive influence on these young players too.

Which players inspired you during your career?
I was always a George Brett fan; I loved the way George played the game. He always played like it was a Little League game; he was always having fun, yet serious about the competitiveness, and winning the game as anybody that ever played, but did it in a way that made you feel like I said, you were watching him play on a sandlot or in the Little League. What I admired most about him was that he was able to keep that boyish attitude about the game of baseball—even at the big-league level, but with the intensity of winning was certainly the priority in his mind. It's a funny combination, but he was able to do that. There's lots of intense guys that want to win real bad, but few can play like you're still in the Little Leagues, if that makes any sense.

Since you're talking about Brett, it's interesting to note that you and Brett were inducted together in the Hall of Fame in 1999.
Yes. That couldn't have been planned any better. It's just like, if I could've planned it, that's the way I would've.

If I spoke to Brett and asked him who inspired him, he would say Robin Yount.

We became good friends through all of this. We respected each other as players, for our playing abilities—the abilities didn't matter as much as the way he played the game, like the way I did. When we played against each other, it was that same fierce competitiveness, but we could laugh at each other, and joke with each other as the game was going on, yet we still wanted to beat each other's brains in; it was the best way to play the game.

What do you see as all the ingredients needed to get to the postseason?

Like I've said earlier, you've got to have those guys on the mound out there. You start with pitching, as far as I'm concerned. Even as much as I was a hitter, and loved the offensive side of it, but you still win consistently with the pitchers. If I was trying to put together a championship team, and starting from scratch, that's where I would begin—pitching, defense, and then you figure out a way to score runs later [laughs]. If you can hold the other team down, you're going to win more games than you lose.

Sounds like you want to manage your own team one day.

I don't have any ambition to do that right now. I'm not crazy about all the other stuff that goes along with it, away from the field, and all the side stuff that goes with the job. I'm really enjoying my job as a bench coach, and I don't know how long I'm going to last. I'm enjoying what I'm doing right now.

How do the good teams that get to play in the postseason keep loose during the season?

Every team has a different cast of characters, so it can be done in many, many different ways. Sometimes you don't even try; it's something that's not contrived or anything. It's sometimes personalities that keep you loose. I think every team needs a guy or two like that to have that way about them. If it's contrived, it doesn't do the job. Every team needs the class clown. On the 1982 team, half the team were class clowns, and that's what made it great. It was fun and I loved playing on that team.

Complete this thought: Here's a player that played 20 years in the big leagues, came up as a raw 18 year old, played for the same team his entire career, experienced a World Series and was inducted into the Hall of Fame.

I don't want to say that I enjoyed every minute of it, but I enjoyed most of it. I loved to compete, and was most proud of coming to the ballpark every day, ready to play and help my team win. Every kid dreams of hitting a home run in the World Series, and I hit a home run in Milwaukee in the 1982 World Series. I was an introverted kid when I came to the big leagues, and played my entire career in Milwaukee, which was ideal for my personality.

Luis Gonzalez
Gonzo's Championship Season
4-Time National League All-Star

> *"I dreamed about hitting a home run because of the kind of season I had. In reality, I was happy about that bloop single. Every kid or adult that enjoys sports dreams about being in a situation like that, and I was no different."* —Luis Gonzalez

Luis Emilio Gonzalez was signed in 1988 as Houston's fourth pick in the June draft and split his first professional season between Asheville and Auburn, playing 70 games. In 1989 he hit .286 while playing in only 86 games due to an injured right shoulder. In 1990 he was playing for Double-A Columbus and was tied for the league lead in home runs with 24 and played on the Southern League All-Star Team.

In 1991, Gonzalez, now a big-league rookie, appeared in 137 games with the Houston Astros, collecting 120 hits, and leading the team with 50 extra-base hits (a club record for rookies). In 1993, his batting statistics improved with a .300 batting average, 162 hits, 82 runs scored and 72 runs batted in. In 1995 he started the season with Houston and was traded to the Cubs in June, and hit .290 in 77 games.

From 1996 through 1998, Gonzalez played with three different clubs each year—Cubs in 1996, Astros in 1997 and Detroit Tigers in 1998. From 1999 through 2001, his batting statistics improved significantly, and in 1999 he had his first breakout season, as he established career highs with a .336 batting average, 206 hits (leading the league), 26 home runs, 111 runs batted in, 112 runs scored and made his first All-Star Game appearance. In 2000, Gonzalez became the first Diamondback in franchise history to play in 162 games, batting .311, 192 hits, 31 home runs and 114 runs batted in.

But it was in 2001 that Luis Gonzalez had his second breakout season, as he established career highs with an eye-popping 57 home runs, 142 runs batted in, 128 runs scored with a .325 batting average, made his second All-Star Game appearance and played 162 games. He will be remembered for his heroics in Game 7 of the 2001 World Series, when he hit a single that traveled a little over a 100 feet to win the World Series. His regular season performance was recorded as one of the top power displays in big-league history.

Gonzalez had a productive 2002 season with a .288 batting average and put up improved statistics in 2003 with a .304 batting average, 176 hits, 26 home runs, 104 runs batted in and his fourth All-Star selection. We sat alone in the Diamondback dugout discussing how his career improved over the years, leading up to postseason play and Gonzo's 2001 championship season.

Conversation with Luis Gonzalez

You came to the big leagues with Houston (1990–'95), the Cubs ('95–'96), a brief stint with Houston in 1997, Detroit in 1998 and Arizona (1999–2004). When did your career take off?

I think my career took off towards the tail end of Detroit, and then coming into Arizona because I changed my batting stance. I became more involved with working out, trying to get bigger and stronger. I was always a consistent .270 hitter, and then I became more of a power hitter, pulled more balls, opened up my stance, and it helped elevate my playing abilities to the next level.

Late in your career you became more of a power hitter.

I changed my batting stance in batting practice and found a hitting approach that I was comfortable with. I kept it simple and wasn't stressing out about hitting, and brought this hitting approach to spring training in 1999. I started off the new season with a 30-game hitting streak and became a better player.

What did you focus on early in your career?

I think earlier in my career I was just more worried about [the first couple of years] staying here. Once you play for a long time, you worry about staying healthy and being consistent. I think that's my biggest goal every year out there—is being a rock on your team and going out there, and being able to play every day. I think your teammates appreciate what you do when you're able to go out there, and try to put up consistent numbers year-in and year-out. It's not a lot about batting averages, although you try to hit .300, things like that. Where I hit in the batting order, my main goal is to try to knock in 100 runs and score 100 runs.

As you became more mature, did you change your approach to the game?

I did. I think what helped me a lot was before I came to Arizona in 1999, my wife and I had triplets. I think that opened up my eyes a little bit more, and made me more of a relaxed ballplayer. I realized that there are more valuable things than stressing out so much on the field, and it made me enjoy the game much more. I realize there are more valuable and precious things than playing baseball all the time. I didn't take the game home with me because when I come home I want to be just dad. It didn't matter if I was 4 for 4 or 0 for 4, or got booed or a standing ovation at the ballpark—my kids didn't know any different.

Luis Gonzalez being interviewed at Pro Player Stadium.

You've been to the postseason four times. What would you say was your best postseason?

I would say by far the 2001 World Series because us being able to win the whole thing the first time we played in a World Series, and winning the whole thing; that was like reaching the top of the mountain for me.

What was your worst postseason?

My most disappointing postseason was my first year with the Astros.

We had a lot of high expectations and we had great ballplayers. We believed we could go all the way with Bagwell, Biggio and all those guys with Houston. We had Caminiti and Finley, and we lost early—we got swept by Atlanta. I think another one that really sticks out in my mind was in 1999, when the Mets knocked us out of the playoffs early, on a home run by Todd Pratt. Finley jumped up in center field and it just nicked off his glove, and it went over the center field wall to beat us, knocked us out of the postseason.

In 2001 you had a breakout season with a .325 batting average, 57 home runs and 142 runs batted in. What do you believe contributed to that monster season?

I think you have to have good surroundings and good teammates around you. You still have to go out and do it between the lines, but you need to have good people around you. I think that whole year everything was going my way. Being selected as a starter for the All-Star Game, winning the home run derby, it was just a storybook season for me from start to finish, and to cap it off, I was the guy that came up in Game 7 of the World Series and had the game-winning hit. There's no better way to close my storybook season than getting the game-winning hit in the World Series.

You talk about having good teammates. What did your teammates do in 2001?

You look at our team, our ballclub in 2001 was very much a veteran club, and I think what we did, we quietly pushed each other. There were guys on that team that if they didn't have a good game, we knew somebody else on the club would have a good game at the plate. I think we just went out there and played hard every day. We considered ourselves a blue-collar team. We didn't have any flashy guys. We had a lot of guys that hit home runs that year. We ran around the bases hard, we didn't try to show anybody up, and we believed that we could win. We played hard together and we just had a great chemistry, mix of guys.

Did you know the 2001 Diamondbacks won the World Series in just four years as an expansion team?

We knew we were the fastest team to win a World Series as an expansion team. That was a great accomplishment for not only us as players, but for our organization to be able to do something like that. I will tell you, it was a lot of fun and hopefully we'll get the opportunity to do that again sometime. We've had a big change of guys here; we still have three or four guys that were from that team, but for the most part in this game today, so many guys move to different teams and it makes it very difficult to repeat, and do things like the Yankees have done for so many years.

Being down 3–2 against the Yankees in the 2001 World Series, what happened in Game 6?
    We were down 3 games to 2, but we felt like we outplayed the Yankees the whole time. We were up two games to none, then lost three in a row in New York, and we felt like we played well. They just beat us on some big home runs late in the game, on three consecutive nights. We came back in Game 6, and we felt pretty confident with Pettitte going up against us, that we were going to be able to go out and beat the Yankees. I think our biggest asset was when we walked out onto our home field we knew we would win that series because every game was decided on the home team's field. And when we walked onto the field and saw our fans giving us support, we felt pretty good before the game. We jumped on Pettitte early, scored a lot of runs, so we felt we had a great chance of winning the World Series after that game.

What about your heroics in Game 7, with a single to win the World Series?
    Well, that was a dream situation—in my dream, I dreamed about hitting a home run because of the kind of season I had. In reality, I was happy about that bloop single. Every kid or adult that enjoys sports dreams about being in situations like that, and I was no different. I was on the on-deck circle thinking (after Counsell was hit by a pitch thrown by Rivera), I've played this scenario out a million times in my mind, and now I'm actually living that dream, so the first thing that went through my mind was don't screw it up, and the second thing was, what happens if I don't get that game-winning hit? What are my parents, my wife and kids, family and friends going to think? That went through my mind. And if you get that game-winning hit everybody loves you. Millions of things go through your mind in those short seconds that you have before you get in the batter's box.

What were you actually thinking while you were on-deck?
    When I was on-deck and Counsell was at the plate, I was actually thinking that he was going to get the big hit to win the game. And I was thinking—where do I want to be when that winning run scores (because there were runners on second and third base)? Do I want to run to home plate and jump on the guy there? Do I want to go to first base with Counsell? I want to be where all the TV cameras and the photographers will

be, so I can end up being in all those publications and things like that. It ended up me being the center of attention after Counsell was hit.

What went through your mind when you faced Mariano Rivera with the game on the line?

Well, he had struck me out in my previous at-bat, so when the Yankees decided to bring the infield in, I thought I had to make contact and try to put the ball in play. I had to try to get it somewhere in the outfield. Fortunately for me, the infield was playing in, and I hit it just far enough out of the infield to short left center field to get the game-winning hit. As soon as it left my bat, I knew where the infield was playing, and the ball was going to fall in for a hit. It was one of those situations where I was jumping up and down, telling myself, I can't believe this is happening to me because I'm a sports fan, and I'm used to seeing situations like this on television.

When the game ended, what were you thinking?

You want to enjoy the moment; you don't know how many times you will get to do it again. The fans, my family, my teammates all mauling me at first base—it was an incredible feeling. My only regret (after I got the game-winning hit) was there were so many media outlets on the field, and they took me off the field to an interview room, so I wasn't able to celebrate with my teammates and fans on the field. That was my only regret. If I had to do it all over again, I would like to be part [more] of that celebration and make the media wait a little bit because they will always be there. I realize the media wants to get the live shot and cover the situation, see what's going on and things like that. After I was interviewed, I ran into the clubhouse and the champagne was almost gone—I felt like I missed a huge part of that celebration.

You've experienced the dream of a championship season with a veteran club. With many players gone, what do you hope to accomplish this season?

My dreams are just like every other player's and that's to get to play in the postseason again. I think the most important thing is staying healthy and being the hot team at the right time. You look at a team like the Marlins who won the World Series in 2003. We did it in 2001, and Anaheim won it in 2002. You don't necessarily have to be the best team, you just have to be the team that is hottest at the right time. You need to get that good karma and confidence going, and once your team gets that confidence going, you feel like you have a good chance of winning it. The mental part of this game plays a huge role. Once you get that mental aspect going and believe in yourself, and your teammates, then you have a very good chance of winning again.

Are you saying the 2003 Marlins could possibly have not been the best team?
  Well, no. I think in 2001—I didn't feel like we were the best team out there at the time [during the season]. When the postseason came, the Marlins were the best team out there. I covered the first round of the playoffs and remembered when the Diamondbacks played their best baseball [during the playoffs], and that's what the Marlins did last year, and Anaheim did in the postseason. They found ways to get wins. When you can do stuff like that, you start believing in that karma, and the baseball gods are looking down on you and things like that. Everything kind of steamrolls from there.

Talk about the make-up of the 2001 Diamondbacks. Who were some of the leaders on that team, and can you give me an example of some of the things they did that makes them leaders?
  I think Matt Williams was probably one of our silent leaders. We called him Sergeant because he was a player that was always game faced. We had other players that led by example. You look at Randy Johnson and Curt Schilling—those guys took the ball every day when they were asked and went out there, and pitched with everything they had. We had players like Finley, myself and other guys, and I'm a little bit more vocal in the clubhouse. I want to play hard on the field; I enjoy that aspect of the game, and having fun in the clubhouse, but when we're out on the field, everybody was on the same page. Jay Bell was another big inspiration on our team, and like I said earlier, we had a great mix of guys, it was all older players. We had one or two young guys, but the older guys kind of led by example, and everybody kind of followed in that direction.

During the championship season, how did the players keep loose during the season?
  I think we gave each other a hard time if someone made a bad play or something like that, but we kept each other in line. We pushed each other, we demanded a lot out of each other, we always felt if somebody was in a slump or bad streak, somebody else had to try to pick that player up or pick up his slack to cover for him, and that's what we did. We had a great bunch of guys on the bench. When a guy needed a day off those guys were there to step in for each other.

Every good team goes through losing streaks. How did the Diamondbacks deal with that in their championship season?

We would try different approaches like no batting practice, and Bob Brenly used a million lineups that year. I think I was probably the only consistent guy hitting third in the order, but for the most part, we mixed in a lot of guys in and out, and it seemed like every button he pushed was working that year—every move that Brenly made, every pitching change or whatever, seemed to be working for us.

When you look at a team like the Yankees, why do you think they get to play in the postseason every year?

I think consistency plays a big part in their success. The guys they run out there have been together for so long, and I think Steinbrenner, Joe Torre and Cashman—they bring in one or two players, and they don't do an overhaul, they retorque a little bit, and tinker with one or two guys. They try to get the guys they feel that are going to fit in right with the main guys on the ballclub.

What is it going to take for the Diamondbacks to play in the postseason again?

It's going to take for us to be a little bit more consistent. We've been so up and down all year, our offense has to be a big part of that. We don't have Curt Schilling anymore. We have a lot of guys that are very capable pitching up here, but we're going to have to score some runs, and I think that's what we have to do. We have to have big years from a lot of different guys.

You see the game on a different level than most fans do. Talk about the characteristics, the qualities that good teams need to play in the postseason.

I think they have to be able to take advantage of mistakes on the other side of the field. They have to push the envelope a little bit. You have to be aggressive, you can't play afraid or scared out there to make a mistake, and you need a good lead-off hitter and guys that know how to get on base—good teams play fundamental baseball. When you do things like that, you find ways to win. You do the little things, you bump guys over, you get the sacrifice fly and things like that. If you make a mistake on the field, you got to be able turn a double play; you need a lot of different intangibles going your way to make a successful team.

How do you make up for the loss of Curt Schilling?

Well, he's a huge loss, and there's no getting around that. Every time he took the mound he played hard and he pitched with everything he had. He was one of the most studious pitchers in the game. You have to find a way and have other guys on your team that are able to go out there, and find ways to win games, even when they don't have their best stuff. You find ways to win with your offense picking you up. Our pitchers have to go out there and be that much better than the other guys you're facing.

Were you surprised by the Marlins winning the World Series?

No. At the end of the season they were playing well, and I came in here for the playoffs, to cover the games for ESPN on radio. I saw the Giants all year, playing against them in our division. I saw the way Beckett was pitching and he was phenomenal. Their whole pitching staff was tough, and Pierre and Castillo were doing all the little things. I saw the way they were playing, and you had a good sense that these guys were right on target to win the World Series.

How did a team with a small payroll and without great players defeat the Yankees in the World Series?

I don't think it has anything to do with salaries. I think it's all about heart and these guys had big hearts out there, and they believed in themselves. That Marlins team got hot at the right time; they had great pitching from their young pitchers, played fundamentally sound baseball, and defeated a very good Yankees team.

Mark Grace
PROFESSIONAL HITTER AND GOLD GLOVE WINNER
3-Time NL All-Star and 4 Gold Gloves

> *"You finally get to the World Series after 15 years in the big leagues [against the Yankees], and after the tragic events of September 11. The Yankees were in New York, and were near and dear to everybody's heart. So we were kind of wearing the black hats that year. I think the nation grew to like us. We were heavy underdogs, but we weren't intimidated by the Yankees."* —Mark Grace

Mark Eugene Grace was signed by the Chicago Cubs as their 24th round selection in the June free-agent draft. His 1986 pro debut was at Single-A Peoria; he won the Midwest League batting title with a .342 average, 159 hits and 95 runs batted in. In 1987, he played 123 games at Double-A Pittsfield, batting .333 with 151 hits, 17 home runs and 101 runs batted in.

In 1988 Grace, now a big-league rookie, appeared in 134 games with the Chicago Cubs, collecting 144 hits, 34 extra-base hits and batting .296. The following seasons he improved his batting average, and in 1990, he hit .309 with 182 hits and 82 runs batted in. In 1993, he established career bests in hits (193), runs batted in (98), made his first All-Star Game appearance, and finished fifth in the league with a .325 batting average.

From 1994 through 1999, his batting statistics improved significantly, and in 1995, he led the league in doubles with 52, had a .326 batting average with 180 hits, 92 runs batted in and made his second All-Star Game appearance. In 1996, Grace had a .331 batting average with 181 hits, and in 1997 he was selected to the All-Star Team (third time) with a .319 batting average and 177 hits.

Grace joined the Diamondbacks in 2001, after 13 seasons with the Cubs, and was instrumental in the Diamondbacks' world championship that year. In the ninth inning of Game 7 of the World Series, he will be remembered for the single off of Mariano Rivera to begin the inning. His base hit ignited a two-run rally that gave the Diamondbacks a 3–2 win and their first championship.

Grace retired at the end of the 2003 season after an outstanding career with 2,445 hits, a .303 batting average, 511 doubles and 1,146 runs batted in. He was a four-time Gold Glove winner with a .995 career fielding percentage. In 2004 he became a television analyst on the Diamondbacks Television Network and Fox Sports Network.

I met up with the outgoing Grace in the Diamondbacks' dugout during the 2004 season. Grace reflected on his postseason play with the Cubs and talked about his 2001 championship season, his first year with the Diamondbacks, and his contribution to winning the championship.

CONVERSATION WITH MARK GRACE

Let's talk about the beginning of your career coming up with the Cubs.

I was signed by the Cubs as their 24th round draft pick, and I wasn't supposed to do anything. My early dreams, once I was drafted, was to eventually make it to the big leagues if I could. I wasn't supposed to make it to that level, and once I realized I was good enough to play at the big-league level, then it was, all right, now let's make a good career out of it. I kind of went year to year as far as that was concerned.

Talk about your rookie season.

I was called up early in the season [from the minor league] in 1988, had a good season, earned the *Sporting News* Rookie of the Year Award, and Chris Sabo was the *Associated Press* Rookie of the Year. I hit .296 that season, did some good things; I didn't set the world on fire by any means, but it was good enough to buy myself a starting position day-in and day-out.

Once you realized you made it to the big leagues, did you set goals like getting to the postseason every year?

Well, when you play for the Cubs, the postseason usually wasn't in sight. I'd say my goal was always to hit .300. If I hit .300, then I knew I'd be driving in runs and I knew I'd be out to be driven in. So that was always my thing, just hit .300, and I didn't set goals as far as the amount of home runs, or amount of runs batted in. I would drive them in when they're out there, and be on base to be driven in. That's what I always thought was the biggest parts of offense.

What year was the closest the Cubs got to the postseason?

We got there twice—once in 1989 and once in 1998 with the Cubs. We lost to the Giants in the earthquake year, and they went on to lose to the Athletics. In 1998, we were the wild-card team, and we lost to the Braves in the first round (division series).

Let's talk about your first postseason with the 1989 Cubs.

We were Don Zimmer's team. We called ourselves "The Boys of Zimmer." We were a good team, and the two main cogs in our offense were Andre Dawson and Ryne Sandberg. I was in between those two guys; I was hitting third, they were hitting second and fourth. Our pitching staff was a good pitching staff. We were anchored by Rick Sutcliffe, Greg Maddux, Mitch Williams was our closer, Jerome Walton was the Rookie of the Year that year and had the leadoff spot in center field. We had a pretty good, talented team.

With that talent, did you see the Cubs playing in the World Series that season?

No. [Serious.] No. We didn't think so, and we didn't. We were hoping to finish .500 that year. We overachieved and we felt we were better than the Giants, once we got to the postseason, but they ended up beating us in a great series. We didn't think we were going to the postseason until about the last month.

When I spoke to Jack McKeon and Mike Lowell, they said the same thing—they didn't think they [the 2003 Marlins] were going to the postseason until the last month.

They just got so hot, they were on a roll when they got to the postseason, and it continued through the Cubs series. You had a

Mark Grace interviewed at Pro Player Stadium (courtesy of Oscar Huete).

feeling it was their year, and they could beat anybody and they did. They had a great pitching staff, they had Pierre at the top of the lineup, Derek Lee was clutch and played good defense too. They had some bombers in the middle of the lineup—Cabrera blossomed, Lowell had a great year—and they were a fun team to watch.

Getting back to the '89 Cubs, who were some of the take-charge players?
Andre [Dawson] and Ryno [Sandberg] weren't really take-charge guys; they did the proverbial lead by example—play every day, play hard every day, and play well every day. That was kind of what we did. Zimmer was our take-charge manager; Sutcliffe was our take-charge pitcher. We all fell in line, and you watch Andre and Ryno, they never missed a day of batting practice, never missed a day of infield practice—they were just grinders, hard workers and that's why they were great.

How did the players on the 1989 team stay focused day-in and day-out?
Oh, I don't know ... psychedelic drugs are always good. It's not so much that you get tight, you get nervous, and I'm sure everybody gets nervous. If players tell you that they're not nervous, they are lying. It's about channeling nervousness into excitement or fear. If you can channel it into excitement, that's what the great players do, but if you channel it into fear, those guys aren't around very often, and there are a lot of people that do that.

How did you deal with the pressure of playing in the postseason?
You have to focus on being confident; you want to be up there in the big situations, and when you're on defense [in big situations], you want the ball hit to you. You're nervous, but excited, and hoping, you say, "Come on, Ryno, get on base so I can drive you in." I think that's the way you have to be in this game. If you don't believe in yourself, nobody is going to believe in you; so you have to be that way.

Do you agree that you need to establish long-term goals and high expectations?
You can't be satisfied and you have to work hard. I never set long-term goals; I just set game goals. Let's try to get something every day—get a hit or two every day, and I realize it's not always going to happen, but that's what you have to try to do.

Talk about playing in the 1998 postseason against the Braves.
That was another Cub team that wasn't supposed to do much. We

had picked up Rod Beck—he was our closer, and he saved over 50 games that season. He did a great job, but our offense just centered on Sammy Sosa. That was the year he hit 66 home runs and that was the big story. He was the main cog; I contributed as well, and I can't think of anybody else at the moment.

How did you feel about leaving the Cubs (after a 13-year career) and coming over to the Diamondbacks in 2001?

The Cubs got rid of me—they showed me the door. So, I had to find a job somewhere else, and the Diamondbacks called about five minutes after the Cubs nontendered me. I was living in Arizona at the time, and it was a no-brainer for me. I accepted the Diamondbacks' offer; it became a great decision, and we won the World Series that year.

Talk about the 2001 championship season.

It was a magical season and we were so talented. We came into spring training expecting to win the World Series that year. We were anchored by Randy [Johnson] and Curt [Schilling] in the rotation. Gonzo hit 57 home runs; we had Tony Womack, Matt Williams, Jay Bell, myself, Finley—a bunch of guys that had a great year. Byung-Hyun Kim was our closer; we had a great season and we just steamrolled everybody that year. We had a great pitching staff, we had a lot of power, we had some speed and great pitching, and were a pretty well-oiled machine that year. We had more veterans on that team than any other team.

Talk about the postseason, beginning with the division series against St. Louis.

We played St. Louis in the first round, and beat them in five games. Tony Womack had the game-winning base hit to score Danny Bautista for the go-ahead run in Game 5. That was awesome.

What about playing Atlanta in the league championship series?

After that nerve-racking series against St. Louis, we made quick work with Atlanta, taking four of the five games in the championship series. Johnson and Schilling were outstanding, and Counsell, Finley, Williams and myself—we had clutch hitting throughout the series.

The World Series—was that magical?

Of course. You finally get to the World Series after 15 years in the big leagues [against the Yankees], and after the tragic events of September 11. The Yankees were in New York, near and dear to everybody's heart.

So we were kind of wearing the black hats that year. I think the nation grew to like us. We were the heavy underdogs, but we weren't intimidated by the Yankees. We knew we could beat them; we knew if we could get through the Dodgers or Giants in our division, and then get through St. Louis and the Braves in the postseason, we knew the Yankees couldn't be much better than those teams; we felt confident we could beat them.

Talk about Game 4 of the World Series.

I hit a big home run in Game 4; we lost that game in the 10th inning. I hit a bomb off El Duque [Hernandez] in New York. I had an opportunity to hit a home run in Yankee Stadium, hitting an upper deck shot in Game 4 of the World Series. Unfortunately, they came back and beat us a few times in that series. That was a pretty good moment for me.

Game 7, in the ninth inning—you're down a run, and you're leading off, facing the best closer in the game (Mariano Rivera). What happened?

I started the ninth inning with a base hit off Rivera, and then Bob Brenly made a brilliant move when he sent in a pinch-runner for me. So, I was out of the game, and Rivera threw the ball into center field on a force-out. Womack doubled to tie the game, and about five minutes later, it all happened quickly. About 10 or 11 pitches later, we were jumping for joy when Gonzo got the game-winning hit. I will never forget all the emotion that was going through me—of happiness, of joy, of relief, of accomplishment. There were so many things—just a bunch of grown men crying our eyes out on the field.

What was it like facing Rivera in Game 7, in the ninth inning, and down a run?

He sucks. [Laughs.] He's tough, I mean, you have to battle against him. He's a big bully with his fastball. You have to go up there and say a few "Hail Marys" and hope he gives you something to hit. Fortunately, that was the first postseason blown save of his career—couldn't happen at a better time for us.

When you got to the dugout in the bottom half of the ninth inning, what were you thinking?

By hook or by crook, I got to get on base. Somehow, some way, if I have to stick my head in front of one, hit by a pitch, I would do it because you could get over a concussion after a month or two, and that was my attitude. I had to find a way to get on base, and two pitches later, I got a base hit up the middle.

Was winning the World Series the pinnacle highlight of your career?

Yes, without a doubt—not even close. That's what we play for every season, to get to the postseason, to have a chance to play in the World Series, and we believed in spring training that we could win that World Series that year. We knew how to play, we knew how to play the right way, and we knew how to win.

You see the game today from a different perspective, as a broadcaster than a player.

The game looks a lot easier sitting up in the booth. The pitches don't look as fast, the players don't look as big or strong, the balls don't look like they're hit very hard; the game looks very easy up there. You have to remind yourself constantly that the game is not easy.

As a broadcaster and playing with these guys, is it difficult to critique their performance in a different role?

I'm not there to critique these players; I'm a positive guy—I don't get on guys because I popped up with the bases loaded a lot; I made errors, I made lots of mistakes, so, I'm not going to get on guys if they make mistakes. The only time I will be critical is if I see lack of hustle or I see mental mistakes, and I will criticize that. Striking out with the bases loaded or making bad pitches in big situations, I'm not going to criticize that.

Any humorous stories during the 2001 championship season?

During our playoff run in 2001, I was always the leader in the shower chorus. We would always sing in the showers after every win, and I was always the head honcho leading with Jimmy Buffett tunes or whatever it would be in the showers. They liked seeing me naked, which was the biggest thing.

Tommy Hutton
THE PHILLIES' STEADY PINCH-HITTER AND COMMENTATOR

"What I remember is a great group of players—we had a good bench and a good bunch of guys there. The fact that I could look back and say that I played with Mike Schmidt, I played with Steve Carlton—two Hall of Famers—Bob Boone was a tremendous guy, and we all wanted to kill Larry Bowa, but we loved him because we were glad he was on our side."—Tommy Hutton

Thomas George Hutton had a 12-year major-league playing career with the Dodgers (1966, '69), Phillies (1972–77), Toronto (1978), and Montreal (1978–81), and compiled a .269 career pinch-hitting average with 79 career pinch-hits. In 1977 he guided the Phillies to the league championship series as a productive pinch hitter and had a .309 batting average that season. He was named to the 1972 Topps All-Rookie Team.

After retiring from baseball, Hutton became a radio broadcaster with the Montreal Expos from 1982–86, and joined the New York Yankees' radio broadcasting team from 1987–89. Hutton spent seven seasons (1990–96) as a color commentator with the Toronto Blue Jays as well as conducting weekly assignments for ESPN.

Hutton joined the Marlins in 1997 as a television analyst and begins his ninth season with the team. A veteran sportscaster, he worked as the color analyst for the 2000 National League Championship Series and World Series for Major League Baseball International. He earned two World Series rings as a broadcaster in 1997 and in 2003, and he found it ironic that he never accomplished a championship season as a player, but experienced the World Series crown in a broadcasting role.

Conversation with Tommy Hutton

Talk about your 12-year career, playing with the Dodgers, Phillies, Blue Jays and Expos. You delivered 79 pinch-hits during your career. Any memorable game-winning hit that you contributed?

When I look back on my career, I think about perseverance, and someone who had average talent, but I was able to make the most of it. I learned how to be a part-time player, and that's probably one of the reasons I became a decent pinch hitter. A lot of guys who don't accept that role, they're not good pinch hitters. I remember a big game-winning hit in Chicago, a pinch-hit home run that won the game. And Tug McGraw was our winning pitcher, so he took me out for a great steak dinner afterwards [laughs].

Your recollection of that exciting National League Championship Series against the Dodgers in 1977.

The things I recall are negative things because we lost [laughs]. I remember pinch-hitting in the game we lost, which was Game 4, and pinch-hitting early in the game. That was kind of unusual for Danny Ozark to send me out there like that in the fourth inning to pinch-hit. Normally I would pinch-hit toward the end of the game, so that was unusual. The well-known play in left field when Ozark didn't make the other defensive move that he usually made. He usually put Jerry Martin in left field for Greg Luzinski with a lead; he didn't do that, and a fly ball just got off the top of Bull's [Luzinski's] glove, and that was a key hit for the Dodgers. I remember the last game that Carlton pitched against Tommy John—it was a rainy day, and it really hampered Carlton more than John because he was a power pitcher.

What do you remember about the 1977 Phillies team, and which players made significant contributions to get to the postseason?

What I remember is a great group of players. We had a good bench and a good bunch of guys there. The fact that I could look back and say that I played with Mike Schmidt, I played with Steve Carlton—two Hall of Famers—Bob Boone was a tremendous guy, and we all wanted to kill

Larry Bowa, but we loved him because we were glad he was on our side [laughs]. Bowa was a feisty type of player, but you wouldn't want anybody else other than him on your side in certain situations, and if you played against him, you didn't like him. Garry Maddox in center field was unbelievable with the great catches he made. We had a good group and a good bunch of guys.

Your contribution was mostly in a pinch-hitting role?

Yeah. I had an interesting situation in 1977. That year I only had 80 or 90 at-bats, but we had some competition on the bench with the bench guys. McCarver was there, and the last day of the season—of course, we made the playoffs by then—I was hitting close to .300. I was one for two at the time, and came up for the last time in that game. If I had walked I would've ended the season hitting over .300, something like .302, and if I made out I would've ended the season under .300, and I singled. So I ended up at .309 and the bench guys loved it.

As a player, is the postseason like a new season with a different kind of mind-set, and a different level of play and motivation, separate from the regular season?

Well, more so then because the championship series was the best of five games and that was tough. I think we felt, and probably still do, that we had a better team that year, but the best of five is really tough. We split in Los Angeles, and we thought that was good for the Phillies because it meant that the series would be settled at home, and we rarely lost at home. After winning one game and losing one game, we lost the next two games, but I remember Game 3 was exciting and a disappointing loss.

What do you recall about Game 3 of the 1977 League Championship Series?

I remember we had a 5–3 lead with two outs and the Dodgers batting in the ninth inning. I just remember we had the lead, the Dodgers had Vic Davalillo pinch-hit, and he bunted his way on base. Next it was Manny Mota pinch-hitting and he doubled—it might have been the one that hit off of Luzinski's glove. It seemed like the Dodgers were sending up pinch hitters who were like 50 years old [laughing]. In that inning there was an error, and Lopes hit a ball that caromed off of Schmidt's glove, and Bowa made a smooth pick-up and threw to first ... a bang-bang play, but the speedy Lopes just beat the throw (Bowa thought he had the out at first), and Mota scored the tying run. Then Lopes stole second base, and Russell got the base hit up the middle that drove in the go-ahead run for a 6–5 win. I guess my memory isn't that bad.

You're saying the regular and postseason are two different seasons?

Oh, yeah. What you've done during the regular season just got you to the postseason. I think that was displayed by what Jack McKeon did last year, by bringing in some of his starters out of the bullpen. His attitude was—hey, it doesn't matter, you just have to win this game right here, and he had Beckett and Willis pitch in relief. It's a totally different season because it's a short series, and you use all your players in different situations.

In Game 6 of the 2003 World Series, McKeon was questioned about using Beckett, considering he had only three days' rest from his previous start.

McKeon felt good about it; he had a great approach and said, "I don't want to have to play Game 7 in Yankee Stadium; I want to win Game 6. There's no sense saving Beckett, we've got to win Game 6." It turned out great for McKeon.

After retiring from playing you started a new career in radio broadcasting with the Expos (1982–86). You joined the Yankees' broadcasting team (1987–89). In your new role in broadcasting, was your perspective of the game different from when you played?

When I first started I worked with the Expos, then it was a little difficult because most of the guys on the field were my former teammates, so that made it a little difficult to be as objective as I wanted to be. When I began broadcasting I knew I wasn't a superstar player, so I knew I wasn't going to get a big job because of my name and my career, so I approached it wanting to learn how to broadcast, and wanting to

Tommy Hutton in the broadcast booth.

become a broadcaster, as opposed to an ex-player who does color. I worked on doing play by play, which I did with the Expos and the Yankees, and radio and television. I think it helped, starting in radio (worked on radio for three or four years). That's the way I approached it—I wanted to become a complete broadcaster as opposed to just a player who's up there in the booth.

You're becoming the Vin Scully with the Marlins.

[Laughs.] No. I've been with too many teams; he's been with one team [laughing].

From 1990 to 1996 you became a color commentator with Toronto, as well as doing weekly telecasts for ESPN. During that span, did you get to work the postseason, and experience the Toronto Blue Jays' postseason and world championship?

You know, I didn't. I was at home ... of course the postseason comes and national TV takes over. I was doing TV with Toronto—the only broadcast that Toronto did was their radio. The only thing I did was a newspaper article for the *Toronto Sun*. I was home in Florida, and I watched every game, and then one of the writers would call me to put together a story for the Blue Jays during the postseason (1992-93).

What do you recall as some of the factors that contributed to the Blue Jays' success in the postseason?

One of the big things was they played like a six-inning game because they had Duane Ward and Tom Henke. Ward would pitch a couple of innings, and Henke would close it out. If they had a lead after six innings, it was difficult to beat them. These guys were dominant in 1992-93 postseason and World Series, and that was one of the keys.

Alomar was great, Molitor and Joe Carter were talented players, the pitching was good, but when they had the lead their bullpen would close the game.

You had the dream of many in broadcasting, by working as the color analyst for the 2000 National League Championship Series and World Series for Major League Baseball International. What do you remember about that World Series?

Well, that was fun because it was in New York. I worked with Gary Thorne, who I had worked with before with ESPN, and we had done some games together—he's a terrific broadcaster—and we didn't have to travel. We got to stay in one hotel, so that made it nice. It was just exciting because it was the Subway Series, and there was a lot of excitement in New York. You could feel it as you walked down the street, with Yankees and Mets souvenirs, and that was the fun part of it because you knew the rivalry with those clubs, with the city and the boroughs. We also had a broadcast every night on the international telecast a hit with some talk show host in England because we were heard all over the world [laughs]. So some guy in England would ask us a couple of questions about the World Series, and we would talk to him every night.

What was your observation of the 2000 World Series with the Yankees and the Mets?

The Yankees dominated and it wasn't as exciting as the Marlins and Yankees in the 2003 World Series. I think if you talk to the New York people they will tell you it was an exciting World Series; it wasn't exciting for me.

In 1997 the Marlins play in the postseason as a wild-card team. What do you recall about that team, and did you believe they would win the World Series?

Everybody had a stronger belief in spring training that the team would win the World Series in 1997, and nobody thought about it in 2003 because they had a solid group of terrific players in '97 like Sheffield and Alou. They had a good team, they had good pitching, and at that time, they were probably the top five or six in payroll too. So Wayne Huizenga at that time had gone out and put together a pretty good team. It wasn't until some moves were made later in the year when they got Craig Counsell, which was amazing. He was hard-nosed, he was solid, he wasn't going to make the fancy play, but he would make the routine play. That's the type of manager Jim Leyland was, and that was what he wanted. In Game 7 of the 1997 World Series, Counsell had the big at-bat with his sacrifice fly that tied the game in the ninth inning, and he scored the game-winning run in the 11th inning.

Luis Castillo was here, but Jim Leyland still thought he was a little too raw, a little too much of a rookie, and Counsell was the perfect fit for this team. Then the Marlins got Darren Daulton. The first or second game after Daulton joined the club, there was a collision at the plate—he ran over some catcher, and that sent a pretty good message of an example to the club that this guy was a leader. He was a big acquisition. I remember Mark Kotsay had come up and he was young, and I will always remember a funny incident that took place in St. Louis. Daulton had just been with the club a short time, so he didn't know anybody, and he was trying to get to know the guys and he asked Kotsay, "Where did you play last year?" And Kotsay said, "College" [laughs]. I thought that was a great line.

In 2003, Torborg was replaced, and McKeon inherited a team with a 15–22 record in May. Did you ever dream that team would make a run at the postseason?

No. [Absolutely not.] That team had no clue. We wondered where they found Jack McKeon. Actually, [laughs] we didn't know where he was, was my first thought. Where did they find Jack? I remember when he was with Cincinnati, and he was telling me at the time he made different moves, and he would say, "What are they going to do, fire me?" And so, he was in retirement. We all tried to figure out how they found Jack McKeon, and he put it all together—everything came together when he took control of that team.

What about playing and defeating the Giants and Cubs in the postseason, and defeating the Yankees in the World Series?

I think the fun part about that was nobody expected the Marlins to beat the Giants; nobody wanted them to beat the Cubs because everybody in the nation was rooting for a Cubs–Red Sox World Series. The Cubs are seen all over the United States, so nobody knew about the Marlins, and nobody wanted them to beat the Cubs. Baseball fans and the media didn't think the Marlins would come close to beating the Yankees because they're the Yankees. The unexpectedness of defeating the Yankees—that's what made it so sweet.

Did you think they had a chance to beat the Yankees?

Oh, yeah, sure. I think anybody that followed our club knew they had a chance to beat all three of those teams because we knew the type of pitching the Marlins had; we knew the type of defense they played, the way they were able to score runs, but we were a team nobody ever followed [wasn't on TV very often], so, nobody thought they had a chance, except for the people that saw them. And I'm sure the Braves, the Phillies, those teams said, "The Marlins are going to be pretty good in the postseason." We could see from the booth that the guys on the field were having fun and that made it more special than in 1997.

From your perspective, compare the 1997 team with the 2003 team. How were those two teams different and were they similar in any way?

They were similar because they had a lot of ballplayers like we were just talking about. They had players like the Counsells and the Daultons, and they had guys last year that just went out and grinded, and played hard. Mike Lowell is like that, and when Jeff Conine came over he was that kind of player. Juan Pierre is the most fun player to watch, and just watch him prepare and work. In that respect, both teams were the same, but the 2003 team wasn't as experienced as the 1997 team. The key last year was picking up Urbina and that certainly helped, and it was similar to 1997 with Robbie Nen. You want to have a closer at the end of a game because that was a big shot in the arm for the club too, when the organization went out and got Urbina. All of a sudden it meant, we're trying here, so I think that psychologically helped.

Did Conine make a difference in 2003?
He's a leader, and he's the first to tell you that he doesn't have a lot of great talent, but has just made himself a quality major-league player, and an example for young players to watch him. His great defense against the Phillies in the September drive, helped to get the team to the postseason, and his great defense in the division series, when he threw out J.T. Snow to eliminate the Giants.

With the Diamondbacks, Angels and Marlins winning the World Series, is it realistic to believe that teams with a smaller payroll and without great players have a chance to play in the postseason again?
Sure. It happens every year. Minnesota gets in the postseason every year, and they don't have a big payroll. If you have the quality minor-league players that are developed in the organization, with it all starting with pitching, you can do it. Oakland has done it, Minnesota has done it, so there's no question that it can be done. And I think there's probably more parity in the game than people seem to think.

Can the Marlins repeat?
Yeah. Not if they continue to play at the current rate they're playing, but they have a chance because they have the pitching. If A. J. Burnett comes back and is healthy, they can go out there four days in a row with four number-one starters. They don't need to score a lot of runs.

Which teams do you see as making a run to the postseason and what are some of the characteristics of those teams?
Actually, you're asking that question at a time when we're playing what I think is the best team—Houston. The characteristics: They got power; they have some grinders like Berkman, Biggio and Bagwell. They

have tremendous pitching, a great bullpen, they can beat you with singles, with doubles, with home runs, so I really like Houston the way they play. I think the Cubs are going to be good because of the pitching, but they have some injuries now too. We've seen all of the west teams; San Diego is probably the most impressive West Coast team that we've seen, in my mind. I'm more impressed with San Diego than the Dodgers. I think the Braves are in trouble; the Cardinals' starting rotation isn't really strong, so that may hurt them, but I really like Houston.

With the addition of Clemens and Pettitte in the Houston rotation, would it be a major disappointment if Houston doesn't get to the postseason in 2004?

I think they're expecting it. I don't know about a major disappointment because those guys all know what can happen in this game, but I think it certainly feasible that they will be there. It's tough in the postseason, and Houston hasn't gotten by the division series because the Braves always beat them. When you think of what the Marlins have done in the last seven years by winning a world championship twice, that's amazing.

Any final thoughts about postseason play?

I think it's ironic that I played all those years, but my two World Series rings are as a broadcaster [laughs].

Juan Pierre
TEAM LEADER AND MASTER OF THE SMALL GAME

"I try to keep everything team oriented. I don't like to put up numbers like I want to steal 60 bases. I want to steal enough bases to help the team in a way that we win. I'm not going out there to just steal bases to have big numbers, but my goal is to get the team to play in the postseason again, and play in the World Series." — Juan Pierre

Juan D'Vaughn Pierre was selected in 1998 by the Colorado Rockies in the 13th round of the June First-Year Player Draft. He began his career in 1998, playing in the Northwest League Single-A with Portland, and led the league in hitting with a .352 batting average, as well as the stolen base leader with 38 steals. He spent the entire 1999 season at Asheville in the Single-A South Atlantic League and led the league in games (140) and hits (187), and compiled a .320 batting average, also finished second in steals with 66. Pierre played a combined 111 games in 2000, for Double-A Carolina with a .326 batting average, and with the Triple-A Colorado Springs club (hitting .471).

In 2000, his rookie season in the major leagues, Pierre appeared in 51 games for the Rockies and batted .310 with 62 hits and scored 26 runs. In 2001, he experienced a breakout season; he appeared in 156 games, compiled a .327 batting average, was second in the league with 202 hits, scored 108 runs and piled up 46 stolen bases. He completed the 2002 season with a .287 batting average, 170 hits, scoring 90 runs and collecting 47 stolen bases. That season he appeared in 152 games with only two errors (.995 fielding percentage).

In 2003, Pierre established single-season records for the Marlins, as he played in all 162 games, hitting .305 with 204 hits, scored 100 runs and compiled a career-high 65 stolen bases (leading the major leagues). That season he had 29 bunt hits and 45 infield singles, which was reminiscent of the dead-ball days. He was chosen the team's Most Valuable Player by the South Florida Chapter of the Baseball Writers Association of America.

In the postseason, Pierre had a .301 batting average with 22 hits and scored 12 runs. He established a Marlins' playoff record with four hits in Game 2 of the National League Division Series. His outstanding performance in the small ball game and exceptional defense guided the Florida Marlins to their second world championship.

Pierre had an outstanding 2004 season, with a .326 batting average, and a National League–leading 221 hits. He scored 100 runs and was tied for the league lead in triples with 12 and played in all 162 games (two consecutive seasons). In 687 at-bats, he had only 35 strikeouts and has been a valuable team leader.

I met up with Pierre at Roger Dean Stadium toward the end of spring training and listened to him talk about his first championship season (in his first year) with the Florida Marlins.

CONVERSATION WITH JUAN PIERRE

Many big-league players that I've interviewed have told me that Juan Pierre was the main reason the Marlins won the World Series in 2003. They feel you're a student of the game.
 I try to learn the game by watching what's going on because I'm not a big guy, so I need to find a way to help myself out, as well as help the team out, by learning about my opponent or about the field, about the whole game in general. I would say I'm a student of the game, just trying to get better and finding a way to win. The goal is to get better personally and as a team. The personal stuff you do is to help the team—the bunting, the base running, that's to help the guy behind me—where I can steal third, he doesn't have to get a hit to get a run batted in, and that helps the team. I try to keep everything team oriented. I don't like to put up numbers like I want to steal 60 bases. I want to steal enough bases to help the team in a way that we win. I'm not going out there to just steal bases to have big numbers, but my goal is to get the team to play in the postseason again, and play in the World Series. If the team is having a good season, the individual accomplishments will be there as well.

Jack McKeon talks about your outstanding work ethic with the media and anybody that's listening.

I believe you have to be focused, always work hard, and never let anybody tell you you can't do it. I was a guy they always told was too small to do this, and too little to do that, and I just persevered and didn't let it get to me ... get me down. I knew inside what I can do and in my heart, with hard work, I knew I could be successful and became successful by dedicating myself to working hard every day.

McKeon said you have a tremendous amount of pride and want to be perfect in your game. Do you agree with that?

I definitely agree with Jack, and appreciate what he said, but I just go out there and play hard. If guys follow me by what I do on the field then fine. I'm not too much of a vocal guy, I kind of just go out there and play hard, and give it all I've got for nine innings, every night out. I don't like coming out of the game, I always like being in the game. So, in that aspect I'm a leader, and that's how I do it, but I'm not the vocal one in the dugout, I just go out there and play the game hard.

Talk about a winning attitude, and how do you endure over 162 games?

I think we evolved into a winning attitude after a while. We started the 2003 season shaky, but we started playing better baseball, and before you know it, we were expecting to win instead of going out there and trying not to lose. I think it carried over, and everyone just pulled together as we continued to win; it became a lot of fun towards the end of the season.

You indicated the team was shaky at the beginning of the season. How did you turn it around?

I think, collectively, everybody looked at themselves in the mirror and realized that they could do more for the team, and help the team win. We started playing together as a team, and I remember something happened during the season. It was during the Boston Red Sox series, that we started sticking together after the 25–8 loss we had, and the next night we came back from being down 9–3 to win in the last inning. I think that pulled us together as a team.

When you came over to the Marlins, who were some of the players that took you under their wings?

I latched on with Derek Lee, who had been around the Marlins for a while. He talked to me about baseball-related issues and family things,

Juan Pierre laying down a bunt (courtesy of Oscar Huete).

and I was closer to Lee than anyone else. When Dontrelle Willis was called up, he was new to the team, and we latched on together.

What was the 2003 championship season like?

That was pretty much like a storybook right there. We started out slow, then we came together as a team, and nobody picked us to do anything. We kind of went up against giants every time we played bigger and better teams, but we came out on top, and it was a good feeling because I've been pretty much an underdog all of my career. People told me I couldn't do this or I wasn't going to play in the big leagues, so it was a dream season—the fact that we silenced all the doubters, everybody thought we would fizzle away against the Phillies, and we had no chance against the Giants and the Cubs, and definitely didn't have a chance against the Yankees. We played our game, we started to shine and it was a great run.

On September 25, 2003, the Marlins defeated the Phillies 8–4, and clinching no less than a tie for a wild-card playoff spot. Do you remember what happened that evening?

Oh, yeah. It was a big game, a real big series for us. We were one game up on the Phillies, and winning that game would put us in a good position to clinch a spot in the playoff the next game. I remember I wanted to get out and get going like I always do, but I wanted to put extra emphasis on these two games. I wanted to play hard because they had just beat us pretty good in Philadelphia. That evening, I had two hits, scored two runs, and did what I'm paid to do in that sense. I remember I got my 200th hit that night on a bunt off Jose Mesa. I beat it out, and he threw the ball into right field. I received a standing ovation when I got to second base, with my 200-hit total displayed on the scoreboard. That was the first time ever I had a standing ovation, and it was nice being appreciated for the dirty work because my game isn't pretty, and that was special.

The following night the Marlins win the wild card with a 4–3 win against the Mets. That game you go 3 for 3 and score a run.
   It was a special night and we knew what was at stake. We knew what we wanted to do, and I actually caught the last out in that game. I will always remember raising my arms in that win. The whole buzz of working hard all year long, and having a chance to clinch in front of the home crowd, and it was a big crowd. It was just a good feeling all around as we came together, and accomplished our goals; that was great. It seems like everybody wrote us off, and we got the job done [smiles].

You began the postseason against the favored Giants.
   It was great to play the Giants, but we were excited to be there, and we felt we could beat those guys. We were the underdogs and probably nobody expected us to win a game. We play Game 1 in San Francisco and Schmidt threw a great game against us. In Game 2, Castillo and me got on base, and I scored three runs, had four hits and drove in three runs, and I think it helped us by winning that game because we were going home and knew we could beat these guys. It was just a good feeling playing the Giants, playing against Barry Bonds, the best ever to play the game, and it was a great feeling. Game 2 was one of the biggest games of my career, and when we tied the series, we just knew we could beat the Giants in the next two games at home.

The Giants are defeated in Game 4 as Pudge Rodriguez holds onto the ball for the final out in the series. The Marlins advance to the league championship series as the nation is rooting for the Cubs.
   Nobody in the world wanted us to win. Cub fans felt so bad about their team not winning for so many years, and they had the better team on paper. I had the opportunity to play against another great player, Sammy Sosa, and watched him make his quest to try to win a world championship.

Again, it was an exciting series, and all the stakes were against us. We're down 3–2, and we're going to face Mark Prior and Kerry Wood, and have to beat them on the road. Nobody in a million years thought we had a chance to win. We pulled together as a team and got it done. That was probably the most exciting and intense series, even more than the World Series because the Cub fans wanted it so much, and the country wanted the Cubs to win.

Next up, the New York Yankees in the World Series.
    Enough said. Coming into Yankee Stadium with all the history, the team they had was a great team, and again we were the underdogs, not expected to be there, but it was an awesome feeling—my first time at Yankee Stadium, and taking in the monuments with all of their greatest players was exciting. Again, we felt like we had a good team, and we could play with these guys. We didn't think they were that much better than us.

What was it like playing the Yankees in the World Series?
    That was the icing on the cake, I should say. You dream about winning the World Series, and to win it against the Yankees, in Yankee Stadium, was the icing on the cake. The World Series always seems to go through New York, and to win it there was a great feeling.

What was it like facing Rivera and being down a run in Game 3 of the World Series?
    He was pretty tough, I mean, his fastball moves like a slider, and he's pretty tough. I faced him one time and struck out, and it was a good thing we left him in the bullpen a lot; we didn't have to face him because we had the lead a lot in that series, but he's the best closer in the game.

Any memorable games in that World Series?
    Of course, when Alex [Gonzalez] hit the home run in Game 4, that was a great game at home, and provided the momentum for us to get back into the series—we were down 2–1—and if the Yankees win that game it would've been really tough to come back and win. Also, Game 6, the replay of me running in from the outfield was shown a lot, and my whole career from Little League on up just flashed in front of my eyes, and just felt like it was worth it—all the work, the sprints, all the times hitting in the cage was well worth it because you practice so hard, and my whole career from T-ball on just flashed in front of my eyes. The goal is to get to the postseason and win a championship, and that was the first one I ever won; it was a great feeling.

You recall Game 5 when you knocked in Derek Lee in the fourth inning?

Oh, yeah. I doubled off Contreras and knocked Derek Lee in, and got a good count to hit in—I think it was a 3-1 or 3-2 that I worked the count, a fastball count, and I put good wood on it. Any time I drive in runs is a great feeling. I forgot to mention Game 1, when I had two hits and drove in a couple of runs, stole a base, and just set to tone. I think it set the tone of the series when Castillo and I got on base, and realizing from there what we can do. We realized what we wanted to do throughout the series was to put pressure on their defense, and we started right off the bat, and it continued the whole series. When we got on base the threat of stealing was a distraction for their defense. Any time you get on base you're going to be a distraction, and maybe the pitcher doesn't concentrate on the batter as much, so the batter gets a better pitch to hit.

When Game 6 ended, what was it like winning your first World Series?

It was the greatest feeling beating the Yankees, at Yankee Stadium, but I felt like I missed something. While you're playing, you're so in tune trying to win the game that you miss the fun part of it. The games are fun, but the highlights and all that stuff—you just don't get the opportunity to enjoy it. I didn't even watch TV during the World Series—not even Sports Center. I felt like I missed something, but that feeling was, man, we just won the World Series, and I can't believe we won the World Series.

With most players back, the goal is to repeat. Do you ever look back and say, "I can't believe we're the champs?"

No, no. Now it's just remembering it a little bit, but now it's time to move on. You're trying to do it again. You remember those good times last year, but you're trying to look forward to this year. And definitely, there isn't a day that goes by that I don't think about the World Series.

Nobody in the media and in sports publications picks the Marlins to go to the postseason.

[That's good.] We have a lot of you guys, so we don't need the young guys thinking they're better than what they are. I'm glad the media isn't taking too much notice about us, and thinking it was magic last year. We have a good ball club, but it's going to be tough; it's all about consistency. If we get good pitching like we had last year, and coming up with those timely hits, then we'll be all right. I'm glad the media isn't picking us to do anything, but I'm quite sure our opponents know about us when they come out of the dugout.

Juan Pierre

Do you see another championship season?

[Without a doubt.] We basically have the same make-up and kept our pitching intact. I think we're actually a better team where everybody pulls for each other here. It's going to be tough—we've seen the Angels win it, and the kind of year they had last year with everybody gunning for them, so it's going to be tough, but I think we can pull it off.

What are some of the qualities of this team?

This team has a winning desire. We had a taste of it last year, and we know what that winning feeling is all about; we want to keep it. The guys don't like losing anymore. Once you get comfortable with losing, it's hard to start winning, and I think we have that winning attitude. It's a long season, 162 games, and hopefully we can carry it out.

Which players did you want to model when you came to the big leagues?

When I was younger, I was watching guys like Rickey Henderson and Vince Coleman, and I wanted to be like them. As I got older, Kenny Lofton was the type of player that I tried to pattern myself after because he would hit home runs, but he still played the short game, and was an All-Star and made a lot of money doing it. When I was in high school, Lofton was the guy I wanted to be like. All the older guys—Vince Coleman, Willie Wilson and Rickey Henderson—I had watched them play, and I admired those guys that stole bases and made the game fun. Last season Rickey Henderson talked to me about running, and certain situations to run in, and how to be aggressive. I'm just in awe when they come up to me and want to speak to me.

How would you characterize yourself?

A guy who brings energy to the park every day, by getting on base, and creating a little havoc and a winning attitude. I play hard the whole game, the way it should be played, and that's the best compliment anyone can ever give me. That's what I take from the game; to give myself the best chance preparing every day, and go out there and just play hard.

Chipper Jones
BASEBALL'S BEST RUN PRODUCER AND SWITCH-HITTER
1999 NL Most Valuable Player,
5-Time NL All-Star

> "I'll never forget my first postseason game, maybe one of the greatest games I've ever played in my life. We opened up in Colorado on the road, and I hit a home run in the sixth inning to get the game tied. We were down a run in the bottom of the eighth, and I made an outstanding defensive play to save us two runs. I led off the top of the ninth inning with a home run to put us up 5–4, and we ended up winning by that margin."—Chipper Jones

Larry Wayne Jones, Jr., graduated from the Bolles High School in Jacksonville, Florida, in 1990. Leading his team to the state championship in his senior season, Jones batted .448 and was recognized as the Florida High School Player of the Year in 1990. He was promptly selected by the Braves, who made him the first pick of the first round of the 1990 June Amateur Free-Agent Draft.

Jones began his professional career in 1990 at Bradenton, Florida, in the Rookie-level Gulf Coast League, hitting .229 in 44 games. He spent the 1991 season at Macon (Single-A) and was selected the most outstanding major league prospect for the South Atlantic League. The starting shortstop in the All-Star Game, Jones completed the 1991 season with a .326 average and tied for first in the South Atlantic League with 104 runs; second in triples (11), runs batted in (98), and hits (154); third in total bases (245).

In 1992 he played 70 games at Single-A Durham prior to being promoted to Double-A Greenville. He began his Double-A season with an eight-game hitting streak and in one stretch hit safely in 27 or 28 games. Chipper completed the season with 33 multihit games and established a Greenville franchise record with 11 triples. In 67 games he had outstanding statistics—a .346 batting average with 92 hits, 17 doubles and 11 triples—and was named the Southern League's top prospect by a poll of the league managers in *Baseball America.*

In 1993 Chipper was promoted to the Triple-A affiliate Richmond Braves and had a breakout season. He was named the Minor League Player of the Year and was chosen the number two prospect in the International League by *Baseball America.* He led the International League in hits (174), runs (97), total bases (268) and triples (12). Jones joined the Braves on September 10, 1993, and collected his first major league hit in his first at-bat, against the Reds, on September 14.

During 1994 spring training, Jones had a terrible injury that would place him on the disabled list the entire season with a complete tear of the anterior cruciate ligament in his left knee. The injury occurred in a game against the Yankees at Fort Lauderdale Stadium on March 18. Jones underwent successful surgery and looked forward to spring training in 1995. The 1995 campaign would be his first in the big leagues.

In 1995 Jones had an excellent rookie season, and many believed he would be chosen Rookie of the Year, but he finished second to the Dodgers Hideo Nomo in the Baseball Writers' Association of America Rookie of the Year balloting. He did, however manage to pick up the *Sporting News'* Rookie Player of the Year, voted on by the players. Jones led all major league rookies in runs batted in with 86; he had 23 home runs, 139 hits and scored 87 runs.

In the 1995 postseason, in Game 1 of the division series against Colorado, Jones connected for two home runs, with the game-winner, a solo homer in the ninth inning. He had an outstanding postseason that year batting over .410 with 14 hits, three home runs and seven runs batted in, and guided the Braves to the 1995 World Series. Chipper had a .286 batting average with six hits and scored three runs in his first World Series win.

From 1996 through 2003 he continued to post MVP-type statistics, and in 1999 was named Most Valuable Player by the Baseball Writers. That season he had a .319 batting average, 181 hits, 41 doubles (career high), 45 home runs (career high), 110 runs batted in and 116 runs scored. Jones has driven in 100 or more runs in eight consecutive seasons, has scored 100 or more runs in seven of eight seasons and has hit more than .310 in five consecutive seasons. In 2001, he had another breakout season with a

.330 batting average, 189 hits (career high), 38 home runs and 102 runs batted in. He was selected to the National League All-Star Team in 1996, 1997, 1998, 2000, and 2001.

Chipper and I had our conversation in the Braves dugout on June 23, 2004, at Pro Player Stadium, in Miami, Florida. We talked about playing in the postseason his entire career, and the possibility that the postseason run could end in 2004.

CONVERSATION WITH CHIPPER JONES

In 1995 you were chosen Sporting News *Rookie of the Year by the players, and you led all major league rookies with 86 runs batted in. How would you describe your rookie season?*

Chipper Jones in the dugout at Pro Player Stadium.

It was a very exciting time.... I had spent the year before on the disabled list [all year], so I was really chomping at the bits to get out there, and soak up as much knowledge from some of the veterans that we had on our ballclub that year. I had a few real good ballplayers take me under their wings early on in spring training. Fred McGriff, David Justice and Marquis Grissom all helped me out tremendously. I just wanted to go out there and be one-ninth of the equation, and help us win ballgames. Bobby [Cox] threw me in the three-hole opening day. We had a good, solid regular season and started the postseason with a bang, and ultimately brought home a championship. So, it doesn't get any more exciting then that.

What was it like playing in your first postseason in 1995?
Well, I got my feet wet real early. I'll never forget my first postseason game, maybe one of the greatest games I've ever played in my life. We opened up in Colorado on the road, and I hit a home run in the sixth inning to get the game tied. We were down a run in the bottom of the eighth, and I made an outstanding defensive play to save us two runs. I led off the top of the ninth inning with a home run to put us up 5–4, and we ended up winning by that margin. So it was certainly one that I will always remember.

It seems like certain highlights (hits and defensive plays) you always remember.
You have a handful of highlights, a handful of big hits or big defensive plays in the course of your career that stick out, and make an impression on people as being momentum-shifting hits, game-winning plays, and that was certainly one of them.

In Game 2, you collected three hits and sparked a rally from a 4–3 deficit into a 7–4 lead. What happened in Game 2?
Again, that was a situation where we were down and when I came up in the ninth inning, I wanted to set the table for some of the big boppers that we had—McGriff hit behind me, Justice hit behind me and Ryan Klesko hit behind me. Being able to run a little bit, and putting some pressure on the defense would allow me to give those guys opportunities to drive in runs. That was a situation where I was fortunate enough to get on base and give Fred McGriff opportunities to drive me in, which sparked a rally. Colorado [laughs] is notorious for giving up big innings, and luckily we had a big inning in us right there. Marquis Grissom hit two home runs in that win.

In the 1995 league championship series against the Reds, you had another outstanding series, with a .438 batting average, and immediately contributed in Game 1.
That was a situation where we were dominated by the starting pitcher [Pete Schourek], and my job is to go out there and get on base. I'm leading off the ninth inning with a hit, and I knew that Fred McGriff had a lot of success against that particular pitcher. I scored the tying run in the ninth inning, and Mike Devereaux got the game-winner in the 11th inning,

driving home Fred McGriff with a single to center field for a 2–1 win. Again, opening up on the road, and coming back from a deficit, was a huge momentum-builder. And if you can steal a game on the road, early in the playoffs, you know you got the advantage.

You recall your two-run homer in the seventh inning of Game 3, leading the Braves to a 5-2 win?

That home run, I believe, was off Xavier Hernandez, to the opposite field. It was a situation where I was trying to drive the ball to the gap, and really get myself in scoring position; with one big hit we could take the lead. I got a fastball out over the plate, and drove it into the gap, and [luckily] playing in old Fulton County Stadium, which was called the Launching Pad, and if you hit a ball good in that old ballpark, chances are it was going to carry out, and that one did.

What do you remember most about playing in your first World Series in 1995?

I think the comparison between our dominant pitching and their dominant offense. That's where I really learned early on in my career that good pitching is going to shut down good hitting 90 percent of the time. I can remember the feeling that I had every time another one of their hitters stepped to the plate, that the game could change on one swing. Our pitchers did an outstanding job of keeping them off balance. I think they hit .179 for the whole World Series, which was outstanding for our pitching, as the Indians led the league in hitting that year. I think they hit around .300 as a team that year. The World Series is all about match-ups, and it was an intriguing one that we dominated. We had a pitching staff with Maddux, Glavine, Smoltz and Avery against the likes of Albert Belle, Jim Thome, Manny Ramirez and Eddie Murray. And they had a real murderer's row. To watch our pitchers peck away at their weaknesses as hitters was fun to watch.

What can you say about your pitching staff?

It was certainly a pleasure to play behind them because, when the catcher put down a signal in a location, you could bet that ball was put in that location. It makes it very easy for you defensively to position yourself in the right spot, to make a great play behind them. I remember that they made my job so easy, and if they were coming inside on a right-handed hitter, and I shaded myself towards the line, I was in position to make a great play behind them. That was probably the reason why we were one of the top defensive teams in the league that season. Those guys put the ball in the spots they wanted, and that's another reason why two or three of them will be in the Hall of Fame when they're done.

Was the '95 team the best club you played on?
   I don't think so. Talentwise, I don't think it was; it certainly was when Maddux, Glavine, Avery and Smoltz were in their prime. From a pitching standpoint it was the best pitching staff that we had, but from a 1–25 player standpoint, I think the team we had probably last year (2003), with the amount of offense we had, was a better team. I think that was a team that probably on paper had a little more talent, but it just goes to show you that talent doesn't always win out in the postseason.

In 2003, you win your division easily, but get eliminated early in the division series against the Cubs.
   Again, we had an awesome offensive ballclub and while we had good quality pitchers, we didn't have the dominant starters, the guys that could go out there and strike out 10, 12, 14 hitters in a game, and get the big outs with strikeouts. The bottom line is, we ran into a Chicago Cubs team that shut down our offense and put some runs on the board against our pitching staff, and when that happens, you're going to lose.

What about the Marlins defeating everybody in the postseason?
   I thought they were the best team at the end of the year. For 162 games they probably weren't the best team during the regular season. It just goes to show you a team that is young, that has an opportunity to jell through success out there on the field, and gains confidence along the way can beat anybody come postseason time. They had two or three starting pitchers with dominant stuff—guys that could go out there and strike out a bunch of guys any time. And those pitchers—Brad Penny, Josh Beckett and Pavano pitched really well—those guys put it together at the right time and got it done.

You think Glavine would've made a big difference for the Braves in 2003?
   Oh, I don't know. Certainly you would like to have that feather in your cap, but the economics of baseball didn't allow it to happen. This ballclub is finding out every year that it's going to be that way. We have to push through, and hopefully we'll give ourselves an opportunity.

In 1996, you had an outstanding season with a .309 batting average, 30 home runs and 110 runs batted in. In the division series you sweep the Dodgers in three games, and defeat the Cardinals in a tough seven-game series. What do you recall about your outstanding performance?

Ah, I don't remember much individually—there were a couple of hits here and there that I remember—but I just remember that being the first time in my career our backs were against the wall. We were down three games to one; not too many teams go down three games to one, and come back to win it. Fortunately, we had an outstanding offensive performance in Game 5 to really shift the momentum. I think we won 14–0 up there in St. Louis. Then we came home, we drilled them again, and that was pretty gratifying because we were down, and being dominated up to that point in the series. Having the whole city of St. Louis being really excited about going to the World Series, everybody was kind of counting us out. Like the champs that we were, we bounced back, and really put three solid games together, and went on to the World Series.

In the 1996 World Series, the Braves win the first two games in Yankee Stadium, and it appeared Atlanta would win a second-straight world championship.

Well, David Cone threw a gem against us in Game 3, which made it 2–1. He threw an outstanding game against us. I think everybody will tell you Game 4 was the turning point. We had a 6–0 lead off Kenny Rogers, and the roof caved in on us, beginning in the sixth inning, as the Yankees scored three runs. Then in the eighth inning, Jim Leyritz hit a three-run homer off Mark Wohlers to tie the game at 6–6. The Yankees won it in the 10th inning and the series was knotted at two games each. I think every baseball fan will tell you that the series turned on Jim Leyritz's swing of the bat. The momentum shifted and the Yankees beat us 1–0 in Game 5, and we lost 3–2 in Game 6.

Do you feel you matched up with the Yankees that year?

If people ask me what happened to us in the postseason over the past few years, with the exception of 1996, I can honestly say that I think we got beat by a better ballclub. In 1996, that was the one year I thought that we really should've won the World Series and didn't. To be that close—to be up 2–0 after going into New York, and beating them up pretty good, the way we did, I really thought we should've handled them in that series. We weren't facing any slouches; those were guys that were brought there to win that World Series, and they certainly played a lot better in the last four games than they did in the first two.

In 1997–98, you play in the division and league championship series, and get eliminated in the league championship series. What do you recall about that series against the Marlins in 1997?

Um, how basically they won it the same way they did last year. I think we ended up beating them by nine games over the 162-game schedule. We really played well against them, and at the end of the season, they just got hot. They had a lot of veteran ballplayers that knew how to win, knew how to bounce back from momentum shifts and whatnot. They took it to us pretty good. I think obviously one of the highlights was probably Kevin Brown getting sick, and Livan Hernandez pitching in his place, and striking out 15 of us at Pro Player Stadium. I think Game 5 was a huge game; the series was knotted up at two games apiece, and Hernandez had a clutch performance in that game. Kevin Brown shut us down in Game 6.

What about postseason play against San Diego in 1998?

I thought San Diego had a real good ballclub, and they were better than us at that particular time in the season. After the Marlins had kind of abandoned the ship, and sold off all of their key players, Kevin Brown goes to San Diego. He was obviously their ace out there, and he shut us down again. Sterling Hitchcock, a guy we hadn't seen all year—I believe he was the series MVP and he was outstanding against us. I just remember us having a tough time scoring runs and when we did score runs, we couldn't shut them down.

In 1999, you had a breakout year with a .319 batting average, 181 hits, 45 home runs and 110 runs batted in. What would you attribute to those outstanding numbers?

I don't know. Everybody talks about being in a zone, and it just seemed like for the last two months of that season, and in the playoffs, I was in that proverbial zone. It didn't matter who was out there on the mound and if they threw it over the plate, and I could get my bat on it, I was doing some damage with it. You can't explain it; you just ride it as long as you can, and my workout regimen has never changed [even in that year]. The ball was jumping out of Turner Field, so that was probably the reason for the big numbers.

Did you finally feel the '99 team would get it done in the postseason, and defeat the Yankees in the World Series?

Well, looking at the roster, that was not one of our better teams that we've had here personnelwise. Certainly I thought we had enough talent to be able to compete better than we did in the World Series, but again, you're talking about one of the greatest teams of all times in that Yankees ballclub. They took it to us pretty good. I think we had the lead in Game 1 for about six or seven innings, and then didn't see it again the rest of the World Series. It was a tough pill to swallow, but I would say that was one team that along with the '95 team really overachieved.

Your best postseason?
It would have to be the first one [1995]; nothing beats the first one. You go out your rookie year, and not only do you perform well and help your team win ballgames, but you help them achieve the ultimate goal, which is to win the World Series. And that's something that will always stick out in my mind.

Your worst postseason?
I would say probably 2001. We got swept in the division series by the Cardinals. We had a pretty good ballclub that year; we had a good offensive team, we had a lot of high expectations, but again, we kind of came into the postseason on a down note, not playing real sound fundamental baseball, and on the flip side, St. Louis was playing really good and they took it to us.

Considering how easy you win your division each year, what can you say about your dismal play in the postseason?
Um, there is no explanation for it, really. Different players react differently to pressure situations, and in the postseason, teams on the other side are not going to let guys like me beat them in clutch situations. So it's going to take somebody else to do it. Whenever I come up in a big situation, usually they pitch around me, and somebody else had to come through. Those guys just weren't able to do it enough in the postseason, to be able to put us over the hump.

What about the Marlins winning two world championships as a wild-card team?
It just goes to show you what you do in 162 games during the regular season doesn't mean much. Whatever team comes in on a roll, comes in the hottest and playing the best baseball, normally is going to win. You run into a pitcher who is dealing or a team that has two pitchers that are really on a roll, bottom line is you're not going to beat those guys. If you don't jump on them early, they gain confidence against you, they just get stronger, and that's what happened to us many times.

Do you feel the 2004 club has a chance to make another run at the postseason?
We have to play a lot better baseball then we have been. We have to

solidify our bullpen, we need to find some semblance of a consistent offense. If those things happen and we stop throwing the ball all over the yard, we'll be able to compete. We've played terrible baseball up until this point, and we're only five games out, so we can consider ourselves pretty lucky.

Finally, what is the formula to achieve success in the postseason?
   It's all about pitching, defense and timely hits; that's the formula. If you have solid pitching, you play defense behind that solid pitching, and you get timely hits with runners in scoring position, you're going to win ballgames.

John Smoltz
BRAVES TOP GUN TURNED CLOSER
*1996 NL Cy Young Award,
5-Time NL All-Star*

> *"We had a great team, and beat a great team in Colorado and Cincinnati on the way to playing Cleveland in the World Series. We faced three of the top-hitting teams you could face, and we shut them down. It was just a dominating pitching performance. I remember Game 6 was tremendous; that was the game Glavine won 1–0, which ended up winning the World Series."* —John Smoltz

John Andrew Smoltz was acquired by the Braves in a trade with the Detroit Tigers for Doyle Alexander on August 12, 1987. He began his career in the Braves organization with Triple-A Richmond in 1987. After winning 10 games at Richmond in 1988, he was called up by the Braves on July 23 and made his major league debut the same day, beating the Mets 6–1. He earned two wins in his first season. In his first full season in 1989, Smoltz became the youngest pitcher in Braves franchise history to be chosen to the All-Star team, and he piled up 12 wins that season.

In 1990, he began dominating National League hitters while earning 14 wins and six complete games. He started out slow in 1991, with a 2–11 record in the first half of the season, and turned around the second half, with a 12–2 mark and a 2.62 earned run average. He earned 14 wins that season and added two wins in the division series against the Pirates. In 1992 he led National League pitchers with 215 strikeouts, while piling up 15 wins and a 2.85 earned run average, and he earned four wins in the postseason, as he was named the MVP of the National League Championship Series against Pittsburgh.

Smoltz underwent successful arthroscopic surgery in 1994 but won only six games that year. In 1995, he rebounded from his injury the previous year with a solid pitching performance, winning 12 games. In the 1995 postseason, he pitched in each series without a decision and earned his only World Series championship. In 1996, Smoltz had a breakout season, with 24 wins and a 2.94 earned run average. In addition, he won the National League Cy Young Award, and dominated throughout the postseason by winning four games with an amazing 0.95 earned run average.

In 1997, he became the staff workhorse by making 35 starts, and pitching a career-high and league-leading 256 innings, while winning 15 games. Off-season surgery limited Smoltz to only 26 starts in 1998, but he posted a career-high .850 winning percentage with a 17–3 record and picked up a win in the postseason [division series]. He was plagued by elbow problems throughout the 1999 season and earned 11 wins. Smoltz missed the entire 2000 season after tearing a ligament in the elbow of his throwing arm and underwent successful Tommy John surgery.

In 2001, he was converted to relief work and became one of the most dominant closers in the National League over the next two seasons. Beginning in 2002, Smoltz set a National League record and led the major leagues with 55 saves. In 2003, he accumulated 45 saves, and over a two-year period piled up 100 saves (only Smoltz and Gagne have also done this). He had 44 saves in the 2004 campaign.

Smoltz and I sat in the Braves dugout discussing the Braves' unbelievable postseason run during the past 12 seasons. While talking about his starting role over the years and his contribution in the postseason, Smoltz indicated that he would prefer to perform again in a starting role, as opposed to being a closer.

CONVERSATION WITH JOHN SMOLTZ

You initiated a 16-year career with Atlanta in 1988, but in 1989 you had your first full big-league season with 12 wins and an All-Star appearance. What was it like back then?

I was obviously new to everything, and just trying to find a way to be successful. It happened real fast in the first half of the season, and then it stalled out in the second half of the season. So I had gone to the All-

Star Game in my first year; I was numb, but I realized I had to constantly make adjustments and that's what I've been trying to do ever since.

How did the pitching coach and other pitchers help you that year?

Well, they gave me insight to the hitters and what to do, and how to upgrade my pitches. I was constantly trying to improve everything that I was doing.

Has Leo Mazzone been a positive influence in your career?

Yes. He has helped me a lot. Obviously, it is easier to learn when you've spent many years [14] with one person. We seem to know each other's mannerisms and everything.

What do you and Mazzone talk about?

Mechanics. We're always talking about mechanics; that's the biggest thing. Throwing the pitches where you want to throw them and as far as the quality of pitches, that will come when you're mechanically sound.*

In 1991, you win 14 games during the season, and win two games with a 1.76 earned run average in the league championship series against the Pirates. What do you recall about that series?

That was the most dominating pitching series ever. Steve Avery won two 1–0

John Smoltz interviewed at Pro Player Stadium.

---

*In the August 2003 *Baseball Digest*, John Kuenster spoke to Leo Mazzone about Smoltz, and indicated that he became a closer after his elbow surgery, and he encouraged Smoltz to be a pitcher, not just a thrower. Smoltz has maintained a starter's mentality as a closer.

games, and we shut them out at their home park the last two games. The Pirates shut us out one time in our park, and it was an incredible series.

You made your first World Series appearance in 1991 against the Twins, pitching 14 innings with a 1.26 earned run average. What do you recall about Game 7?

I remember I can't believe we didn't win it. I didn't give up a run in Game 7 of the World Series [usually that results in a win], but unfortunately Jack Morris didn't give up a run either. He pitched the entire 10 innings and was unbeatable that night. The Twins scored in the bottom of the 10th to beat us 1–0.

In 1992, you piled up 15 wins with a 2.85 earned run average and nine complete games. In the league championship series you win two games against the Pirates, and are named MVP of the series.

Again, it was a dream come true; just getting a chance to pitch in the postseason. We were there the year before, and you never know if you're going to get back. I remember having a three games to one lead against Pittsburgh and then having to pitch Game 7. It was unfortunate, but it ended up being the most dramatic Game 7 probably ever to get you into the World Series.

What happened in Game 7?

Well, this was a game where we had a hiccup there and we're losing 2–0, and I gave up two runs. The ninth inning was incredible; there was nothing to say about it other than it was incredible. We benefited from a lucky error that Jose Lind never makes, and just an incredible pinch-hit by Francisco Cabrera with two outs. We get the tying and winning runs as Sid Bream slides across the plate.

In the 1992 World Series you get your first win and appear in two games. What was that series like?

Well, once again we had a chance to win the World Series and it didn't work out. Toronto ended up beating us, but every time I went out to the mound, and every time I was in those situations, I felt like our team was going to win. Even when we had gone out on the field, I thought our team was going to win, but ultimately came away short.

Toughest Toronto hitters in the 1992 World Series?

Roberto Alomar was obviously in a league of his own at that time, as well as Dave Winfield, who they obtained late in the season. They had the right lineup for the type of team they had, and they were a tough team. I think [even] David Cone got a hit off me in that series because he was a pretty good hitter in the National League, and he was a good fit for that team.

In 1993, you have another good season with 15 wins and start 35 games. The Braves get eliminated in the first round, and you lost for the first time in six postseason decisions.

Well, in the game I pitched, we ended up losing 2–1 on two unearned runs. Mitch Williams, the Phillies' closer, had an outstanding series, and it seemed like every time he came in, the bases were loaded, nobody out and he got out. It was one of those series where I had the most disappointing loss I had gone through at that time, because there was no way we should've lost that series.

In 1994, you had your only losing season with a 6–10 record. Was that a disappointment for you?

Yes and no. I went through surgery; I had some arm problems and I tried to battle through it; it just didn't work out, and the next thing, I ended up having surgery, which was a big part of my struggle.

You came back in 1995 from arthroscopic surgery and pitched in the postseason. What was it like winning your first World Series?

Ultimately and obviously that was our best year, and the most memorable year because it was the only one we won. We had a great team, and beat a great team in Colorado and Cincinnati on the way to playing Cleveland in the World Series. We faced three of the top hitting teams you could face and we shut them down. It was just a dominating pitching performance. I remember Game 6 was tremendous; that was the game Glavine won 1–0, which ended up winning the World Series. He limited Cleveland to one hit and David Justice hit the winning home run, and the rest was history.

In 1996, you had a breakout season with 24 wins, six complete games and a 2.94 earned run average. What contributed to that great season?

I was healthy; I was almost two years removed from surgery, and I was healthy again. I hadn't been healthy there for three or four years, and I really felt like I could do a lot of great things while I was healthy, and ultimately it was a dream year. We just didn't finish it off in the World Series.

In the 1996 postseason, you dominated by going 4–1 with an excellent 0.95 earned run average. You won at least one game in each series and the World Series. Seems like the '96 postseason was your best pitching.

It was one of them. I pitched under adverse situations in the previous postseasons, which were better, but I was pretty healthy now, and really shouldn't have lost a game. I lost 1–0 on an unearned run against Pettitte in Game 5 of the World Series, and ultimately it should've been a dream year for the team and me personally, but we came up short because we didn't finish the job.

You've been to the postseason nine times, with only one World Series title. Is that a disappointment in your career?

It would be a disappointment depending on how we're viewed—if people just look at that. Disappointment comes from the fact that we didn't win as many as I thought we should've, but man, we had many opportunities and were very close.

You've indicated that not winning the World Series more often has been a disappointment. Despite that, what can you say about playing in the postseason?

I can honestly say that we were pretty darn good, and you have to be real lucky and good to win the World Series. We won one and should've won three, at least. There's a couple where you could say we shouldn't have won, but that's what competition in sports is about.

What are baseball historians going to say about the Braves from the 1990s to the present time?

They're going to say that most teams tried to model what we did and it won't ever happen again. The fact that we had a run like that with the amount of pitching we had, you'll never see that in baseball again. I think it will be looked at as one of the most unique opportunities, but most people are going to think about what we didn't do.

In 1997, you win 15 games and meet the Marlins in the league championship series. What do you recall about that playoff, and did you expect to win?

Expected to win—I feel like we gave them the opportunity to win. We made terrible plays, terrible breaks early, and just gave them every chance to win the series. Now they went ahead and won it, but I honestly feel like we gave them more chances than they should've had in beating us because that team was built to beat us. They won the wild card and ended up ultimately winning the World Series.

You had another outstanding season in 1998, with a 17–3 record and a 2.90 earned run average. Was that another breakout year?

That was another year coming back from arthroscopic surgery, and it was just one of those years I had quietly. I was hurt and on the disabled list twice; I was 5–2 at the All-Star break, and then went 12–1 in the second half. Again, ultimately we didn't get it done against a very good San Diego team, but we had our chances.

In 2001, you take on a new role as a closer. Is that something you wanted to do?

The club asked me to do it. It was a strange situation, but it allowed me to stay here all this time.

What is the role of a closer?

Basically, three outs can be easy to get at any time in an inning. The last three outs are the hardest thing to get. You face failure every single time, and it's a mental challenge, as well as a physical challenge because you can potentially pitch in 80–84 baseball games a year and the pressure mounts. Everything is a rally, and nobody takes the last inning for granted; they're all grinding and want to beat you, and we don't play against time. That's why it's so hard to find a closer that closes out 95–98 percent of the games. One season I saved 55 out of 59 [games] and the next 45 out of 48.

Talk about your role as a closer beginning in 2001 through 2004.

I'm a starter by nature and this was a need of the club. They asked me to become a closer, and we were able to work it out. It worked out the first two years, but ultimately we still didn't get past the first round of the postseason with me as a closer. We haven't done it yet, so I will assess my value of what's better for the team, and if they feel like it's better for the team [for me] to be a closer ... we'll see.

Which role do you enjoy more?

Starter. We're going to see what happens at the end of the season, but I would prefer being in the rotation again. I definitely feel like I can win at least 15 games and help the team.

It doesn't appear you enjoy being a closer.

I mean, I want to win a championship; I love to pitch and I like to be used, but I also like structure. I like to know when I'm pitching. My first two years as a closer, I pitched an awful lot, and I had an injury because of it. I think that's fixed, but this year has been tough, and I'm trying to ride it out—figure what's best for the team. I know I can pitch and I want to pitch again, and it's hard not to. I want to pitch a few more years and we're going to work very hard to try to work it out here.

How does a closer prepare to pitch in the ninth inning?

Every closer is different. I sit around and watch the game, relax, and then I start going through a different routine in the fifth inning: I start to loosen up, I'll get stretched, I'll get my arm worked on, every once in a while I'll get in the hot tub and then I come down, and get ready in the seventh inning for what might be my job in the eighth or ninth inning.

What is the psychology of pitching in the ninth inning?

Well, the ninth inning is about failure, and what keeps me in a position of trying to do this job is—I think I can give it up every time I go out there, which keeps me at a level of not thinking I've got it licked. So the fear of pressure motivates me and makes me better.

What is your routine during the first three innings?

I'm just sitting down in the clubhouse watching the game on TV. Depending on the score, I start getting ready around the fifth inning and rest until my body is ready. Sometimes I take a shower, but for the most part I'm getting loose.

Who is the best closer in baseball?

Gagne. He's taking it to a different level; he hasn't blown a save, and who knows if he'll ever blow another one.

Was the loss of Glavine in 2003, and especially in the postseason, a huge loss?

It was a huge loss. Our team was going in a different direction; it was going to start spiraling down with the structure of our salary and it has. We just had to plug in the pieces that we were left with. You can't replace what we lost in two years. It doesn't mean you can't win, but you certainly can't replace them. If everyone else does their job, we have a chance to get to the postseason.

In 2004, you're making a run without Glavine, Maddux, Sheffield and Lopez. A big loss?

I don't know if it's doable, but until we're eliminated we can still think we have the chance to run off this string, and that would be incredible.

Finally, since you've lost three big starters, do you see the 2004 club playing in the postseason?

It depends on what we do; it depends on what moves we make and if we get healthy; if we don't get healthy and we squander these next 12, 14 games, no.

Javier Lopez
QUIET SUPERSTAR
3-Time NL All-Star

"We beat the Indians in the World Series and in Game 2, I hit a two-run home run off Dennis Martinez, that put us ahead in the sixth inning. Later in the game I picked Manny Ramirez off first base in the eighth inning to end their rally." —Javier Lopez

Javier Lopez Torres was signed by the Braves as a nondrafted free agent on November 6, 1987. He began his professional career in 1988, playing for the Gulf Coast Braves, and hitting .191 in 31 games. Javy spent the 1989 season in the Rookie-level league at Pulaski, batting .261 in 51 games, and in 1990 he led all Midwest League catchers with 11 double plays. He was selected to the Carolina League All-Star team in 1991, and was tied for first in home runs with 11.

In 1992, Lopez played 115 games at Double-A Greenville with a .321 batting average, 142 hits, 28 doubles and 16 home runs. After an outstanding season, he was called up by the Braves and hit .375 (6–16) in 9 games. He went 3-for-4 with a double, three runs scored and a run batted in while playing in his first postseason against San Diego.

In 1993 Lopez was promoted to the Triple-A affiliate Richmond Braves and had an outstanding season with a .305 batting average (a club record for a catcher), 116 hits, 17 home runs and 74 runs batted in. He joined the Braves on August 17, 1993 and went 6-for-12 in four starts. He hit .375 (6–16) in eight games.

In his rookie season with Atlanta in 1994, Lopez played 80 games with 13 home runs and 35 runs batted in. In 1995, he increased his offensive statistics significantly in his second full season at catcher with a .315 batting average and 105 hits. From 1996 through 1998 he continued to increase his batting statistics—runs batted in (consecutive years)—69, 68, 106; home runs (consecutive years)—23, 23, 34.

In 1999, Lopez had a great beginning of the year, hitting .317, when a partial tear of the anterior cruciate ligament ended his season after just 65 games. He recovered from his injury in 1999, and had a solid performance in 2000, with a .287 batting average, 138 hits, 24 home runs and 89 runs batted in. From 2001 through 2002 his batting average, run production and home runs decreased—batting average (consecutive years)—.267, .233; home runs—17, 11; and runs batted in—66, 52. He had one of the greatest seasons for a catcher in 2003 with a .328 batting average, 150 hits, 29 doubles, 43 home runs (almost half of his hits were extra-base hits) and 109 runs batted in. He was selected to the National League All-Star Team in 1997, 1998 and 2003.

He was acquired by the Orioles on December 22, 2003, and was signed as a free agent to a three-year contract through 2006. Lopez had an outstanding 2004 season, hitting .316, and has been a clutch performer.

Lopez and I had our conversation in the Orioles clubhouse in Fort Lauderdale, Florida, toward the end of spring training. We spoke about postseasons past with Glavine, Maddux and Smoltz, and a new beginning with the Orioles in 2004.

Conversation with Javier Lopez

What was it like catching Glavine, Maddux and Smoltz?
First of all, it was a great honor to catch for the best pitching staff in baseball. These guys [definitely] make my job easy when they pitch. I have to say that each individual has a totally different approach to pitching—as far as controlling the game. Both Maddux and Smoltz are right-handed and Glavine is a lefty.

Describe Glavine.
Glavine is the type of guy who likes to throw a lot of change-ups. He doesn't throw hard, but he likes to spot the ball on the corners. He tries to make the hitters chase the ball as much as they can. And if he gets a called strike on the outside corner, he will try to spot the ball over there all day long. He is not a powerful pitcher; he knows how to use his pitches.

Describe Smoltz.
  Smoltz is a powerful pitcher who likes to challenge hitters with his fastball. He throws 95 plus, and he has a tremendous slider and split-finger pitch, and he's considered one of the best in the game right now [as a reliever]; he's a strikeout pitcher.

Describe Maddux.
  Maddux is another guy like Glavine; he is right-handed, he throws a little bit harder and his ball moves a lot more than Glavine's. And he has a lot more pitches than Glavine. He's got a curve ball and a slider, and Glavine is usually change-up and fastball.

What did you learn from these pitchers?
  I learned there's always a way to win a game; there's always a way to manipulate and to win the game. The game of baseball is not just a game; you have to be pretty smart out there when you play. You have to know the hitters, you have to know the pitchers and that's pretty much what I learned from them. Every game is a new game and what you learn from these great pitchers helps you improve your game as well, and makes you a better player. I've become more patient as a hitter over the years from being able to work with these great pitchers.

Leo Mazzone has been described as a pitching guru.
  Leo is the type of coach that likes to work hard with every pitcher. He wants every pitcher to be like Glavine, Maddux and Smoltz because he knows how to convert a pitcher into one of the best in the game, as long as the pitcher is willing to listen to him and does what he says. He's probably the best pitching coach in baseball; he's very strict and wants the best for the pitcher.

From 1995 through 2003 you played in the postseason with the Braves every year. Why is this team successful?
  I guess because of the atmosphere here. The manager and coaches provide lots of encouragement and confidence—even the owner and general-manager are very confident. We have talented players that know how to prepare for games, know how to win games and the guys respect each other.

What do you recall about playing in your first postseason in 1995?
  I remember I had a tremendous postseason and drove in three runs in each series. We beat the Indians in the World Series and in Game 2 I

hit a two-run home run off Dennis Martinez that put us ahead in the sixth inning. Later in that game I picked Manny Ramirez off first base in the eighth inning to end their rally. I had a few hits in that World Series, but in Game 4, I had a key double that drove in a run in the ninth inning to help us win. In the playoff against the Reds, I hit a three-run home run in the 10th inning of Game 1, to provide a comfortable lead and a win. Our pitching was tremendous with Glavine, Maddux and Avery. I think Glavine won two games, but in Game 6, he pitched a one-hit shutout to give us the championship and that was exciting.

Javy Lopez completing workout at Fort Lauderdale Stadium.

Did you see the Braves winning another championship in 1996?

Definitely. We had a great team, our pitching was outstanding and we were pretty confident that we would win the World Series again. We had an easy time in the playoffs against the Dodgers—we swept the Dodgers in three games; we came back from a three games to one deficit and just beat the Cardinals the next three games, and just dominated in those three games. Coming into the World Series, we were very confident as we won the first two games in Yankee Stadium. I remember Andruw Jones hit a home run in his first two at-bats and that got everybody pumped up. I didn't hit well in the World Series, but I remember the Yankees got hot and swept the next four games to win the World Series. We should've won the World Series, but for some reason we couldn't get it done.

In the 1996 league championship series, you were named

the series MVP with an amazing .542 batting average, 13 hits and five doubles, which set a playoff record.

That was a tremendous performance I had in the series, after taking the Dodgers in three games. I had a lot of confidence and was pumped up. I was making good contact at the plate and really couldn't do anything wrong in that series. [Laughs.] I had five doubles, two home runs and drove in six runs; that was probably my best postseason performance.

How can you explain the postseason letdown from 1996 through 2003?

It is something that is hard to explain since we've played in the postseason throughout my career. [Laughs.] I don't know the reason why we haven't won more championships, and it's hard for me to explain. It seems like a bad dream or a spell has been put on the team. Well, we definitely had a great team for the last 12 years. I guess the reason why we've only won one World Series is that our luck isn't there at the end. For some reason, whoever plays against us at the end has more motivation than us. The reason why, I don't know, but that's how it is. Anybody can get hot at a particular moment. A lot of teams that finally made it to the playoffs are very happy and so pumped up to get to play in the postseason because it's a short series, and the team that is really motivated and pumped up is going to win the World Series.

That would explain how the Diamondbacks, Angels and Marlins won the World Series.

In the last three years, look at the teams that won the World Series. The Diamondbacks, Angels and Marlins were wild-card teams that made it to the playoffs, and they were so pumped up that they carried that motivation throughout the postseason. On the other side, the Braves clinched like a month before the playoffs started, and weren't as pumped as the Marlins were, since they became the world champions.

Talk about your relationship with Bobby Cox.

He is a player's manager who brings confidence to his team and a winner. He's been a tremendous manager for many years. I tip my hat off to him because he's been great, not only with the team, but for baseball. He is one of the most-recognized managers out there right now with the most wins. I don't think there's anybody in baseball or anywhere out there that could say anything bad about him because he gets his team to the postseason every year. He never gets angry with the players and treats us like professionals. When we make mistakes he takes the blame. So you really try hard not to make mistakes.

Did you do anything different in 2003 to get to the postseason?

We had a potent offense in 2003, and for some reason I was very confident about having a productive season, and something inside of me calmed me down from everything. I felt good about myself—whether I had a good or bad game, I felt the same. I worked harder in the winter and lost 35 pounds; I felt stronger and more flexible than I did in other years.

Do you feel the 2003 club should've done better in the postseason?

Definitely. I think we won like 101 games that season; we led the National League in hitting and won our division very early. That club had as much talent as the previous ones, and we should've gone further in the postseason. Unfortunately, the Cubs beat us in five games; that series they got hot at the right time and Wood won two games, and in Game 5 he had a dominating performance and shut us down in a 5–1 defeat.

You had your best season in 2003 with a .328 batting average, 43 home runs and 109 runs batted in. Knowing your contract was up in 2003, was that a factor that contributed to your outstanding season?

That's not the reason because in 2002 I had the opportunity to put up good numbers [near the end of my contract year], and I didn't do anything close to that. In 2002, I had the worst year of my career. As a player and the person that I am, I wanted to bounce back from the worst year of my career, and I guess that was the reason … that's my motivation for 2003. I don't want to be in that position again because 2002 for me wasn't fun at all and it was my worst year. I worked hard during the winter to bounce back and to just forget what happened in 2002.

Now with the Orioles, what is it going to take to get to the postseason again?

It's going to take a lot of hard work, a lot of hustle and learning how to win as a team. You have to play hard baseball and it's not easy; it's harder to make it to the playoffs than to win the playoffs. The playoffs are either a five- or seven-game series that you play. To make it to the playoffs, you have to make it through 162 games, and it's a lot harder to do that.

With the mix of older veterans and younger players on the Orioles, what is your role in getting this team into the postseason?

Well, as a veteran, I have to help the pitchers as much as I can, and the younger guys playing infield. I have to show them what I learned from my experience in the big leagues, and we have other veterans that can help the younger guys. There has to be a lot of consistency, motivation and good pitching. We have veterans like Palmeiro, a tremendous player and the type of guy that could put up good numbers to lead us to the playoffs. Tejada is another veteran that leads by example and has played in the postseason. With this club it's going to take a lot of work, a lot of patience and we have to look forward to today's game [not tomorrow's].

Why have the Braves teams made it to the postseason year after year?

Everybody always seemed to be on the same page—the veterans took pride in being successful and winning. The younger players and guys coming from other teams saw what we accomplished and wanted to be a part of a successful team.

Do you miss playing with the Braves?

Yes. That was the only team I ever played with and spent 10 years with them. It became more of a family than a team, and I will definitely miss them. I miss spring training in Orlando [with the guys], but at the same time, I feel comfortable here with the Orioles now that I've changed teams. What I hope to accomplish is to put up good numbers and help the Orioles play in the postseason.

Tom Glavine
BRAVES PITCHING GREAT, FUTURE HALL OF FAMER
9-Time NL All-Star and 2-Time Cy Young Award Winner

> *"Game 6 was one of those games that I was locked in or in a zone, or whatever you want to call it. It was probably the best game I pitched—if not the best game I ever pitched, certainly one of the top two. It was a game that I had good stuff, I had real good location and I was able to make all my pitches."—* Tom Glavine

Thomas Michael Glavine was drafted by the Braves in 1984 and he led the South Atlantic League with a 2.35 earned run average with nine wins in 1985 while pitching at Single-A Sumter. In 1986 he was promoted to Double-A Greenville, winning 11 games and being selected to the Southern League All-Star Team. He began the 1987 season at Triple-A Richmond and was promoted to Atlanta on August 14th and made his major-league debut on August 17th at Houston.

In 1988, Glavine had a disappointing rookie season with a 7–17 record and a 4.56 earned run average. In 1989, he began the season with a 5–0 record prior to spraining his left ankle at Chicago on May 16th. He piled up 14 wins that season with four shutouts. He had 19 quality starts in 1990 and earned 10 wins.

Glavine had a breakout season in 1991 with 20 wins, a 2.55 earned run average, a league-leading nine complete games and he won the Cy Young Award. He made his first All-Star appearance in 1991. In 1992, he was the Cy Young runner-up to Greg Maddux, piling up 20 wins with a 2.76 earned run average, and he made his second All-Star appearance. He had an outstanding 22–6 record in 1993, was selected to the All-Star team for the third time and finished the season tied for the league lead in wins. From 1994 through 1997, he averaged 15 wins each season and he was selected to the National League All-Star Team in 1996 and 1997. Glavine collected two wins in the 1995 World Series and was named World Series MVP. In the deciding Game 6, he pitched a one-hit shutout against Cleveland with a 1–0 win.

In 1996 and 1997, Glavine averaged 15 wins with a 2.97 earned run average. He won his second Cy Young Award in 1998 with 20 wins and a career-low 2.47 earned run average. In 1999, he reached double digits in wins for the 11th consecutive season, posting 14 wins.

Glavine led the majors with 21 wins in 2000, the fifth time in his career he had won 20 games in a season and the 12th consecutive season with double digits in wins. He was named National League Pitcher of the Year by the *Sporting News*. In 2001 he collected 16 wins and in 2002 had an outstanding season with 18 wins and a 2.97 earned run average. Through the 2002 season, Glavine had reached double digits in wins for the 14th consecutive season and was selected to the National League All-Star Team for the eighth time in his career.

He was signed as a free agent by the Mets on December 9, 2002, and had a disappointing 2003 season with a 9–14 record. In 2004, Glavine earned seven wins up to the All-Star break and was selected to the National League All-Star Team for the ninth time in his career. He should reach the 300-win milestone over the next two seasons barring any injuries.

Glavine and I met up at spring training and in the Mets clubhouse at Pro Player Stadium in Miami, Florida, in early July 2004. Our conversations reflected upon his postseason experiences with the Atlanta Braves while pitching in nine postseasons.

CONVERSATION WITH TOM GLAVINE

What are the characteristics of a championship team?

You have to have unselfishness, unity, guys that are willing to sacrifice. When you're on a championship team, everybody has got to be willing to do whatever they have to do for your team to be successful. Sometimes it's not the most glamorous thing; it's not the guy who hits the home run, it's the guy who moves a runner over, whatever the case may be. You have to have guys that are willing to work hard and just be very unselfish when it comes to putting team goals first.

How did the Braves get to the postseason year after year?

We had talent, we had luck and we had commitment. I think those three things really helped, but to win that often you need to have a little bit of luck, which we had. We stayed healthy a lot, which is a tough thing to do obviously. We had talent and guys who were committed to working hard every day, and making it happen.

You've been a five-time World Series participant. Which World Series would be your most memorable?

I would say the 1995 World Series because we won. The other one that would be close would be the 1991 because it was so unexpected, but there's something that makes it a little bit better when you win.

In the 1995 World Series you notched wins in Game 2 and Game 6, and earned MVP honors. What do you recall about your performance in Game 2?

Um, I recall it being a little bit shaky. I wasn't totally on my game, but was kind of able to survive long enough for Javy Lopez to hit a big home run that gave us the lead in the game. It was really about trying to survive and keep the game close, and give our offense a chance to win the game.

In Game 6 you pitched a shutout and won the World Series.

Game 6 was one of those games that I was locked in or in a zone, or whatever you want to call it. It was probably the best game I pitched—if not the best game I ever pitched, certainly one of the top two. It was a game that I had good stuff, I had real good location and I was able to make all of my pitches. And fortunately it came on that night because we had only one run to work with and didn't have much room for error.

What were you feeling after that outstanding performance in Game 6?

I don't want to say an out-of-body experience, but just being one of those games that was special; it was a special game. Even now when I'm struggling a little bit [whether physically or mentally] that's the game that I kind of go back to and say, "Here you were in this setting against this lineup, and you were able to do this, you're capable of doing that." That was the kind of game you draw strength from it and certainly look back on as one of the best games I've ever pitched in my career. To be able to identify that is one thing, but certainly to be able to identify it in that setting, in that atmosphere and to have it come together then, was something pretty special.

Which World Series would be a disappointment?

I think the 1996 World Series against the Yankees. We went into Yankee Stadium and won the first two games of the series, and went back home and lost the next three games. Two of them were real close games and in one of the games, we had a five- or six-run lead that we blew. Looking back on all the World Series games, I think the ones that we lost, we can make an argument that the teams were better than us, but I think in 1996, that was the only one that I really felt that we kind of let get away from us.

In 1991–93, and in 1998 and 2000, you had outstanding 20 win seasons. Were you disappointed that the Braves were eliminated in the postseason?

You're always disappointed when you're eliminated. Having a good year individually is nice, but the problem with it is, you're the only one that gets to enjoy it. When you win a World Series, everybody gets to enjoy that, and everybody is in on all the hard work that went into it. Personal accomplishments are always good and they're gratifying, and obviously they're an indication of having done some good things, but in the end, those kinds of things you're left kind of celebrating by yourself versus celebrating with your teammates when you win.

Tom Glavine at Pro Player Stadium.

In the 1996 World Series you were an inning away from having a 3–1 lead. The Yankees found a way to come back to win the series. Did you see the Braves matching up evenly with the Yankees?

I thought we were two pretty well-matched-up clubs, and in the end, a late inning home run by Jim Leyritz in one game that brought them back 2–2 instead of us being ahead 3–1. I remember in Game 5 Paul O'Neill making a great play in right field that would've resulted in an extra-base hit that probably would've given us the lead and given us a win in that game. So, you look back in that series, which was close like that, and you can find one or two defining moments [that series certainly had it], but I felt like we matched up with them, and we're every bit as good as them; it's just in the end there were a couple of plays that they made that we didn't.

Seems like the Braves get to the postseason every year. What would you say is the reason for their early elimination?

It can be any number of things; it's hard to put a finger on it. I think some years we just ran up against good pitching, and the old cliché "good pitching beats good hitting" is true—particularly in the postseason. There were a couple of series where the starting pitchers didn't pitch well and got our team in a hole, and we got eliminated. So, you really can't narrow it down to one thing, but I think the one thing that makes it more difficult is when you have a team perform so well over 162 games and a certain atmosphere, and hits well and does all that stuff, I mean, you get into a short series and you hear Bobby Cox say it all the time, "You get into the postseason and it's a crapshoot." You just don't know what's going to happen—all it takes is one or two hot pitchers to beat a club. That certainly happened to us a number of times. We ran up against Schilling and Randy Johnson in 2001, when they were in Arizona. You run up against Kevin Brown and a couple of guys in San Diego that got hot in the 1998 postseason. That happens and that's why in a short series you can't afford to make mistakes because you don't have time to come back from it.

Most memorable playoffs?

I think the most memorable series would be the 1992 league championship series against Pittsburgh, when we came back in Game 7, and Sid Bream slid into home plate to win the game. Cabrera got the clutch hit and that was one of those come-from-behind wins that came out of nowhere. Still to this day, that slide is so memorable in Atlanta and Atlanta Braves history. Even though we won in 1995, we won, but we didn't have that defining moment, so to speak, that captured the essence of the series. That slide with Sid Bream in Game 7 of the 1992 playoffs defined that whole playoff year and certainly that series.

Toughest hitters you faced in the World Series?

In 1995, that whole Cleveland team was tough. I remember their seventh or eighth hitter had 30 home runs, or something like that. That lineup had Lofton, Vizquel and Alomar at the top. Then you had Thome, Albert Belle, Eddie Murray and Manny Ramirez in the middle. So, there was no let up with that lineup. Aside from maybe Atlanta's offense last year (2003), for me personally as a pitcher, that was probably the deepest and toughest offensive lineup that I faced as a pitcher. That's what makes postseason pitching [in particular] so tough. You get up against a pretty darn good offensive club that you don't have a whole lot of room to make mistakes.

What about the 1996 Yankees lineup?

They had a good lineup. I remember Cecil Fielder being in the middle of it and Wade Boggs being in there. Bernie Williams, Jeter and Paul O'Neill were tough hitters. If you looked at the Cleveland lineup in 1995 as being a powerful lineup, then you noticed the Yankees lineup in '96 as just being a very well-balanced, disciplined lineup. The kind of lineup that was going to make you work to get pitches, work to get them out; didn't get themselves out a lot and even though you may not have necessarily been worried about the long ball as much as you were with the Cleveland lineup, you knew that as a pitcher you were going to have to work, and they were going to string together good at-bats. You were really going to have to bear down on every single hitter to make pitches, and not let them string together a big inning.

Is your ultimate dream to pitch in another World Series—maybe be the starting pitcher in Game 7?

I guess so. I think ultimately I would just like to pitch in another World Series and win it. If it happens in Game 7, great. I'd rather have it happen in Game 4, probably so you don't have to go through the drama of a Game 7. We all dream about Game 7s and whatnot, but it's a very pressure-packed, gut-wrenching experience to pitch in a Game 7. I wouldn't care if it's Game 7 or Game 4. I just want to be a part of another world championship team and pitch in a World Series.

Up to the 2003 season you participated in postseason play your entire career. Was it weird not pitching in the 2003 postseason?

Yeah, it was very different—when you get used to doing something, I mean, it was different. I don't think I really noticed it so much in October, but I certainly noticed it towards the end of the winter. It got to be the end of January, and I felt like all right, my three months were up and I was supposed to go back to spring training again, but you forget you had that extra month off in October, and that's why the winter seemed so long. Playing in the postseason is great and there's nothing like it. I came here to New York thinking this was an organization that had a chance to do it. I still feel that way and hopefully before it's all said and done, I'll have that opportunity again.

Nobody expected the Marlins to play in the postseason in 2003. Is it possible they were lucky?
    I don't think they were lucky. When a team wins a World Series, I don't think you can say they were lucky. They had a bunch of unselfish players and did what they had to do, and most importantly, they played great defense, they pitched well and they just got enough offense when they had to. If you play good defense and pitch well, you give yourself a chance to win every night.

Realistically, do many teams have a legitimate chance to win their division?
    No, but I think many teams have a chance to get into the playoffs. I think that's a great thing about the wild card. You may not necessarily be a division contender, but if you look at the end of the summer [last year], it couldn't be any better. We had so many teams vying for those last couple of playoff spots. You had so many teams in the hunt right into September, and that's a good thing. I don't think you can necessarily look at every single team and say they have a chance to win their division or they even have a chance to make the playoffs, but every year we have surprises. Nobody picked the Marlins last year, so that's why you play.

When you came to the Mets in 2003, did players on the team ask you how the Braves sustain and get to the postseason year after year?
    Yeah. When you come from an organization like that, there is always people picking your brains, and certainly when you come over to another organization, that goes on when you see other players in other settings or in other ballparks, they always ask me, "Hey, what's going on there or what are you guys doing, or what makes you guys successful," so yeah. When you have a model of consistency like that, [sure] everybody wants to tap into that and see what's different, see what they're doing that other teams aren't doing or what their players are doing that other players aren't doing, and honestly in the end, I don't really think there was a magic potion or a magic answer over there.

I think the two biggest things that the Atlanta Braves had going for them all those years was they had very strong starting pitching and they stayed away from injuries for the most part. When you can do that, you have a chance to be successful. If you look at that team over the course of their success, they've always had two or three guys in the middle of that lineup that play 150 to 160 games a year. When you can pencil the middle of your lineup in for that many games a year, you have a chance to be successful.

From your postseason experience, what do you tell many of your teammates who haven't played in the postseason?
When you talk about it, you preach the patience side of it. When you get into a situation where you're vying for a championship, it can get tense and you can get very emotional about it. You can get caught up in each day's activities, good and bad, and in this game you can't do that. It is such a long season, and even now as excited as we are to be in the position we're in, we still have half a season left. So, there's going to be good days and bad days, and there's going to be other days in between. You can find a way to make a difference and that's what you have to focus on— just kind of steady the course and come to the park every day ready to play.

How do you keep loose as you're making a run toward the postseason?
I remember those years in Atlanta and we had those personalities of guys that just like to goof around. And that was so important, particularly coming down the stretch because you wanted to maintain the level of looseness that you need. You need that relaxation to go out there and play.
Smoltz was a good example of a goofy guy by telling a joke or goofing around, or making fun of himself, and stuff like that. It's important to have that element in your clubhouse because you have to have some sense of relaxation, and get rid of some of the jitters that go along with being in a pennant race. I think that helped us and the good teams know how to keep loose.

Do you feel your team can make a run at the postseason?
I think we're as good as anybody in our division. I really don't see anybody in our division that has been head and shoulders better than us. There might be a player here or a player there that makes them a little bit stronger than us, but I think we're the kind of team that the Atlanta Braves were in 1991, where with each week that goes by, we gain more and more confidence, and more and more of a belief that we can win this thing, and

that's kind of the intangible. You just don't ever know how much you can tap into that.

When you came up with the Braves in 1988, who were some of the positive influences that guided you to a Hall of Fame career?
 I think one of my earliest, biggest influences in my career was Dale Murphy. Watching Dale go about his business on a daily basis on the baseball field was special. I thought he was fantastic the way he treated people both on and off the field. Some of the other guys along the way—I got a lot of help from Bruce Benedict and Leo Mazzone. Maddux and Smoltz have been positive influences in my career. You see certain guys and you're around certain guys that make you a better player because they're knowledgeable and you get good ideas from them, but I think so much of what you are comes from your parents, and as much as I want to give anybody else credit, I have to give my parents credit. They are the ones who've shaped me into the person that I am, and have given me determination [not to just be a good baseball player], but to be the best baseball player I can be, whatever that is.

When you leave the game and talk to your children about your most memorable World Series, what are you going to tell them?
 I still think everything gets back to the 1995 World Series. Everything evolves around winning and the feeling that comes with winning. All the other ones were exciting for their own reasons and great accomplishments, but in the end you want to win. So I would certainly start there and sit down, and talk to them about the feeling of being a championship team. I would talk about all the hard work that went into it. I would touch a little bit on my own personal experience and my own personal performance, and stuff like that. I think I would touch upon more the tremendous feeling of satisfaction that went into a group of guys setting out in February to achieve a goal. Then the feeling when it all came together and we got to enjoy it.

Burt Hooton

MR. HAPPY, 1981 CHAMPIONSHIP SEASON

*1981 NL All-Star and
Houston Astros Pitching Coach*

> *"It's no disgrace to give up a home run to Reggie Jackson—he only hit about 563 home runs. He was really an all-or-nothing hitter; he would hit a home run or strike out, so I gave up one of the home runs and, to my recollection that was the only home run I ever gave up to him. I keep telling Charlie Hough if he hadn't given up the third one, they wouldn't keep showing the one I gave up on ESPN all the time."* —Burt Hooton

Burt Carlton Hooton had a good major league career, beginning in 1971 with the Chicago Cubs and stretching 15 years, over which he compiled 151 wins and 29 shutouts. Following his junior year at the University of Texas he was drafted by the Cubs in 1971 and made his major-league debut nine days later, fanning his first batter—Lou Brock. On April 16, 1972, in only his fourth major-league start over two seasons, Hooton threw a no-hitter for the Cubs against the Phillies.

He pitched the majority of his games for the Dodgers but along the way made stops with the Cubs and Rangers. He was traded to the Dodgers in 1975 and had a magnificent season with 18 wins and a 2.82 earned run average. While pitching 10 seasons with the Dodgers, Hooton recorded 11 or more wins seven times and helped lead the Dodgers to postseason play in 1977, 1978 and 1981. He pitched in 11 postseason games with a 6–3 record and posted three World Series wins during his career.

In 1977, he had a great year with only 12 wins (15 no-decisions) and a 2.62 earned run average. The following season (1978) was outstanding as he accumulated 19 wins and a 2.71 earned run average. In the strike-shortened 1981 season, Hooton was selected to the National League All-Star Team, compiling an 11–6 record with a career-low 2.28 earned run average. He won two games in the 1981 league championship series and was named the Most Valuable Player. In the 1981 World Series, Hooton won Game 6 over the Yankees to clinch the title for the Dodgers. Overall, he was 4–1 with a 0.82 earned run average in the 1981 postseason.

Hooton completed his major-league career with the Texas Rangers in 1985. He began his coaching career in 1988 with the Single-A Salem team of the Northwest League. In 1990, he became pitching coach for the Texas League's San Antonio Missions in the Dodgers organization. After five seasons with San Antonio, Hooton was promoted to pitching coach of the Dodgers' Triple-A club at Albuquerque.

From 1996 to 1999, he worked at the University of Texas as a pitching coach and joined the Houston Astros coaching staff in 2000. He got his nickname "Happy" from his former manager, Tommy Lasorda, because he seldom looked as if he were happy.

I conducted an interview with the articulate Hooton in May 2004 in the Astros clubhouse at Pro Player Stadium in Miami, Florida. He was happy to discuss the addition of Roger Clemens and Andy Pettitte to his staff, and with these talented pitchers the team could possibly win their division. Hooton recalled his memorable 1981 World Championship season.

CONVERSATION WITH BURT HOOTON

Let's begin with your 15-year big-league career: You started pitching with the Cubs (1971–75), the Dodgers (1975–84) and the Rangers in 1985. Talk about your career and the players who helped you along the way.

Early in my career I was blessed with having other pitchers helping me. Some of them ended up in the Hall of Fame. When I first came to the Cubs, it was Ferguson Jenkins, and it's not so much talking to him, but watching how he went about his business. When I came to the Dodgers, they had Don Sutton; Andy Messersmith was there and he was a very good pitcher then. Tommy John was there at the time and he had a very good work ethic. You sit around and watch guys who pitched for quite a while and have been very successful, even after I came into contact with them; they pitched for several years more. And the blessing there is just being able to watch and talk to them about pitching. You observe how they go about their business and you hope some of that rubs off on you. I think some of it did and helped me out quite a bit.

You mentioned great pitchers like Jenkins and Sutton. Did they talk to you about pitching?

No. It was more observing. When they pitched their games I was more attentive. When they worked out, I was attentive. You watch and observe anybody who is successful, to see how they go about their business. When you see them in action—to me actions always speaks louder than words—you watch them as they go along, and they are being successful. You can pick up things they incorporate into their games and you try to put them into your own games.

On April 16, 1972, as a 22-year-old rookie and your fourth big-league start, you pitched a no-hitter for the Cubs against the Phillies. Talk about that unique experience, and some of the hitters you faced in the Phillies lineup.

It was a cold day in Chicago; it was the second game of the season after a 13-day strike to start the season. Ferguson Jenkins started the season the day before and I started the second game. The temperature was in the 40s, I was pitching against the Phillies and I ended up walking seven and struck out seven, and pitching a no-hitter. Some of the hitters in the lineup that day—I think Deron Johnson was in the lineup, Greg Luzinski, Larry Bowa, Willie Montanez—to name a few. Gosh, that was over 30 years ago; I can't remember that far back.

In 1975 you were traded to the Dodgers, winning 18 games with a 2.82 earned run average. Was that a turning point in your career?

I would say so. When I first came out of college into major league baseball, I was pretty much a two-pitch pitcher. I had pitching coaches—the Cubs were an unstable organization back then, and in three years, I had three managers and four pitching coaches, and I was 21 years old coming into the big leagues. All of my pitching coaches were sinker or slider pitching coaches and pitchers when they played. I was a straight four-seam fastball, straight four-seam curveball and occasional four-seam change-up pitcher, and they thought I needed a little bit more movement on my pitches. I started listening to them; never could throw a good sinker, never could throw a good slider, and in three years I was a whole lot worse pitcher than I was when I first got there. When I was traded to the Dodgers, it was a different organization; they had a real good pitching coach there named Red Adams. He perceived that I was frustrated throwing sinkers and sliders, and knew that I was basically a two-pitch pitcher—both of them were pretty good. He told me to can the sinker and slider, and go back and be the pitcher I was three years previous to that. When I did that, it was like finding an old friend ... everything became familiar again, and all of a sudden, I knew how to pitch again. Everything fell into place with the Dodgers.

In 15 big-league seasons you piled up 151 wins with a 3.38 earned run average. Over that same period you pitched in 11 postseason games and posted a 6–3 record. Talk about playing in the postseason, which began in 1977.

That's why we play the game, to get into the postseason. The goal is to get to the World Series and win the World Series. I know many, many great ballplayers who never even played in a World Series. They had long careers and never played in a World Series, let alone win one. Being able to be on teams that played in three World Series and winning one in 1981 was remarkable. You play baseball your whole life and look for that one opportunity to play in a World Series, and eventually win it. We had the opportunity to play in the World Series in 1977 and 1978 and we lost to the Yankees. And in 1981 we defeated the Yankees in the World Series and we were able to call ourselves world champions. So, nothing has changed, and that's why we play this game; we play this game to win the ring at the end of the season.

Burt Hooton in the dugout at Pro Player Stadium.

You were 3–3 in six World Series outings, pitching in 1977, 1978 and 1981, all against the Yankees. What was it like to pitch in the World Series?

Well, it's exciting, it's

something you look forward to your whole life; again, dream comes true. People want to know what it's like; I can't describe what it's like. The only way you know what it's like is to play in it. There's no way anyone who never played the game of baseball could ever imagine what something like that is like because it's just something you have to experience. In the 1977 World Series, I recall pitching a complete game and allowing the Yankees something like five hits in Game 2. Then in Game 6, you think you're capable of winning again, but unfortunately I was the losing pitcher that game, and the Yankees won the World Series.

It's a peak experience for the players?

It's something you look forward to your whole life; you play against the best all summer long to defeat them and you get to narrow it down to the two best teams in each league that year, and you have a best-of-seven series to find out who the world champion is. Ever since you're a kid, the World Series has been going on for over 100 years and growing up it was almost like a holiday when the World Series was played. Even the teachers in elementary school would bring TVs to school, so they could sit there and watch the World Series. That was a pretty big event and that's the way I grew up. Eventually, some 20 years later from when your teachers brought TVs to school, to be playing in one, that's pretty exciting.

In the 1977 World Series you played against a great Yankees team. Was Reggie Jackson's three-home-run performance the turning point in that series, and did you throw one?

Well, yeah. I was the starting pitcher that day [Game 6] and I threw the first one, but Reggie had a phenomenal series in 1977. People always ask me about that and it's no disgrace to give up a home run to Reggie Jackson—he only hit about 563 home runs in his career. He was really an all-or-nothing hitter; he would hit a home run or strike out. So I gave up one of the home runs and, to my recollection, that was the only home run I ever gave up to him. I keep telling Charlie Hough if he hadn't given up the third one, they wouldn't keep showing the one I gave up on ESPN all the time.

Nineteen seventy-eight was your most outstanding season with 19 wins, a 2.71 earned run average and pitching over 236 innings.

I felt like I pitched a lot better in 1977. I had 15 no-decisions, had a lower earned run average, I think I averaged about seven innings a start in 1977, had my career-high in strikeouts—wasn't a strikeout pitcher—but had a career-high of 153, and ended up pitching 223 innings, and only had 12 wins in 1977. I pitched well enough to win 19 games, 20 games, just didn't do it. So the following year, I didn't feel I pitched as well, but I still had a good solid season and ended up with 19 wins.

Why did you win more games in 1978?

I got the winning runs at the right time, where the year before I didn't. I still pitched as well in 1977 as I did in 1978. Well, a lot of it has to do with timing. In 1977, we won the National League championship and when you go seven innings, and you're tired, you come out of the game [many times] with a no-decision. I had 15 no-decisions in 1977. In 1978, I would go six innings and come out ahead, and we end up winning the game and I would get the win. Again, I didn't do anything different in 1978 and it's a matter of timing. I pitched well in both years, well enough to win 20 games.

In 1981 you get the Dodgers into the postseason and pitch in the World Series against the Yankees again. What do you recall about that championship season?

The biggest thing I recall, we had the extra playoff series because of the strike that year, and we had to play Houston. Back then we played the best three out of five series. This was a little bit more nerveracking than the best four out of seven. We lost the first two games in Houston and then went back to Los Angeles. I was pitching the first game in Los Angeles, so we're down 2–0 and all they have to do is win one more game, and we're out. I pitched well in Game 3 and we win the game 6–1. Valenzuela pitched the next game, [that] was a complete game and he wins. So it's 2–2, and then Jerry Reuss and Nolan Ryan hook up in a duel for the deciding game, and Reuss throws a shutout and we win the series.

Now we play the National League Championship Series against Montreal. Well, I was the starting pitcher in Game 1; we played in Los Angeles and we won the first game. We lost the second game, so now we have to go to Montreal to finish up the playoff. So we're 1 and 1, and well, we lose Game 3 in Montreal. Now we're down 2–1 and if we lose one more game we're out of it. I'm pitching Game 4 and we end up winning that game. Valenzuela pitches in Game 5 and that's the game Rick Monday hits the game-winning home run off Steve Rogers in the top of the ninth inning to center field, and we win the game 2–1 to carry us into the World Series.

We open up the World Series in Yankee Stadium and we lose the first game. I remember Jerry Reuss pitched that game and we lost 5–3. I was the starting pitcher in Game 2 and Tommy John shut us out 3–0, and we lose the game. So now we go back to Los Angeles and win the next three games there, and head back to New York for Game 6. I'm pitching in Game 6 and the one thing I still remember about that is Tommy John was pitching against me, and normally we didn't hit John well. I still remember the Yankees manager, Bob Lemon, taking Tommy John out of the game, and pinch-hitting Bobby Murcer. I'm still pitching; I'm standing on the mound and it's two outs, and they have a couple of runners on—all I'm thinking is I couldn't believe he took Tommy John out ... in the first place, in a 2–1 game in the fourth inning, and I looked over there in their dugout, I still remember seeing Tommy John at the end of their dugout with his jacket on and no hat on, just sitting there and shaking his head because he was thinking the same thing—like I can't believe it either. Well, I'm thinking if I get Bobby Murcer out, we win the World Series. And I think it was a 2–2 change-up that I threw him, and he hit a fly ball to the right field warning track for the third out. I got him out and we went on to win that game and the World Series.

You talk about the 1981 postseason like it happened yesterday.
Well, that was an unbelievable move to me and I couldn't believe that they took Tommy out so early because we really had difficulty hitting him. That was the World Series that George Frazier lost three games. He replaced Tommy John in the fifth inning and we tagged him pretty good for three runs. I forget what the final score was of that game; we ended up winning by six or seven runs.

When you look back at your career, you had the opportunity to play in not one, but in three World Series.
Well, again, as ballplayers ... it's a dream come true just to become a major-league ballplayer. I played baseball my whole life and that's just what I wanted to do, and I'm one of the few that gets to realize my dream of having such a long career and playing in three World Series. In that regard I was blessed and then we play the game to become champions. You want to win every year and the winning part is the tough part. And being consistent in winning—I tell guys even Hall of Fame pitchers have lost over 40 percent of their games; this is a pretty tough racket. So if you can pitch for 15 years and have a better-than .500 record, you're doing pretty well. That's the same thing for hitters. It's just phenomenal that hitters can play 15, 18, 20 years and end up with a .300 batting average. It's been said that baseball is a game about failure and it's who can handle the failure the best. We all believe we're pretty good and indeed at the major-league level. You're playing against the best in the world day-in

and day-out and it's still a game of failure, and even the best have their problems at times. It's not so much how you handle things when you're going good, but how you handle things when things aren't going so good. Can you still give a decent account of yourself to where your team has a chance to win ballgames as a hitter or a pitcher?

Shifting gears, talk about your role with the Astros as a pitching coach.
My role boils down to whether the pitchers are successful or not. Do they get better through the course of a season? Do they stay healthy throughout the course of a season? And we believe that some of the things that we do help them stay healthy, but basically my responsibilities are the 12 pitchers that I have, and to help them perform at the best of their capability when they're out there performing. Being a major-league coach is—do we have information stored in our head? Yes, we have a lot of information. Do you always need to dispense it? Rarely, because you have guys that basically have a pretty good idea of what they're doing. My job is to learn each one of them—learn what makes them tick, learn their delivery and basically do the best that we can together to keep them within themselves, so they can perform at a highly consistent level.

With the addition of Clemens and Pettitte, you have two experienced veterans. What can you say about Clemens and Pettitte?
I'm finding out why Roger Clemens is going into the Hall of Fame. He's a different breed. You have real good pitchers and you have the elites. Roger is one of the elites, just gifted in what his make up is and what his aptitude is, and what his abilities are. He's one of the rare breeds who have tremendous ability that can manage it, he knows how to manage it, and on top of that he's just a superior competitor.

What about Pettitte?
Pettitte's a great competitor; he has very good control of his pitches, he has a very good idea of what he is doing with them and he has a very good delivery. Having guys like that, for a pitching coach that's pretty easy work.

With the addition of Clemens and Pettitte, you have two experienced veterans with many world championships. Do you see the Astros making a run into the postseason and World Series?
Well, yeah. If I said no, I shouldn't be here. [Laughs.] Yes, we have a very good team that's every bit as capable of making it to the postseason and winning the World Series if everyone pulls their own weight. And

everybody does the things they're capable of on a consistent basis. We're very optimistic; we feel like we can win the World Series this year.

Why do you feel this team has all the ingredients to get into the postseason?

Well, we have a very good starting pitching staff and we have a very good bullpen, we have a very good offense, and our defense is adequate. We're very good competitors. Houston is starved for a World Series championship team. [Laughs.] And it's time for Houston to bring a world championship team in baseball.

Any piece of the puzzle that may be missing?

Well, it's probably a question that I'm not going to answer. It's for me to know and no one else to find out.

From your perspective, what did you notice about the 2003 Marlins young staff?

Well, the thing that impressed me—I saw Josh Beckett grow up in the playoffs. I actually saw Kerry Wood grow up in the playoffs too. Josh Beckett, to me, grew up as a major-league, championship-caliber pitcher in the postseason. And the whole country saw that. I think some of his teammates probably picked up on that as well.

As the pitching coach what do you hope to accomplish?

I want to win the World Series as a coach. I've done it as a player. I can't do it as a player anymore, but I can do it as a coach. It would be great for Houston; there's never been a World Series played in Texas.

What are some of the factors to get there?

The biggest factor to getting to the postseason is keeping your horses healthy and that's basically your pitchers. Pitching nowadays is so thin, and if one of your top pitchers goes down, it's hard to replace them, if you can at all. Same thing with the players you have out there on the field that you count on day-in and day-out. You have to take care of them and do the best you can to keep them healthy, and keep them on the field. Then it's a grind; you have to realize the importance of every game, and you can't take any game lightly because even last year, we lost by one game last year. So, if you lose by one game, you can look back and probably find seven or eight games that you should've won. It would probably be in your favor if you won all the games that you're supposed to win. There are some games you go back and look at, and you think gosh, if we just done this a little bit better and that a little bit better, hustled here or made a better pitch here; that makes a difference between going into the postseason and not.

Why did Tommy Lasorda call you "Happy" throughout your career?
    We were in the Dominican Republic, up in his apartment New Year's Eve and the clock struck 12. Everybody is rejoicing with Tommy Lasorda, Bobby Valentine, Charlie Hough, Joe Ferguson and a bunch of other guys. Those of us who had wives were there and then everybody else is jumping up and down, and I'm sitting there and playing solitaire, and Lasorda looked at me and said, "Isn't he happy," and it kind of stuck. New Year's Eve and Halloween aren't my favorite days.

Lou Piniella
SWEET LOU, CLUTCH WORLD SERIES PERFORMER AND MANAGER
1969 AL Rookie of the Year, 1972 AL All-Star, 1995, 2001 Manager of the Year

> *"Bob Welch was the pitcher for the Dodgers and they walked Reggie Jackson intentionally to get to me. With two outs in the 10th inning I came through with the game-winning hit. That's how I earned my money: being a clutch hitter. And the first pitch he threw me, I lined it to right-center field and the ballgame was over."* —Lou Piniella

Louis Victor Piniella was signed by the Cleveland Indians in 1962 and was drafted by the Washington Senators for the 1963 season. He was assigned to Peninsula, where he hit .310. He was traded to the Orioles on August 4, 1964, playing 20 games at Aberdeen, and was called up by the Orioles in September 1964. He spent the next four seasons in the minor leagues, most years with Portland, where he was hitting around .300 each season. He was traded back to Cleveland in 1966 and played in six games with the Indians that season.

Piniella was selected by the Seattle Pilots in the 1968 Expansion Draft, and traded to the Kansas City Royals on April 1, 1969. He collected the first hit and scored the first run in Royals history. In his rookie season in 1969, Piniella had a .282 batting average with 139 hits, 11 home runs and 68 runs batted in, and was selected American League Rookie of the Year. In 1970, he had an outstanding season with a .301 batting average, 163 hits, 11 home runs and 88 runs batted in.

Piniella had a breakout season in 1972 and was chosen for the American League All-Star Team, with a .312 batting average, 179 hits, league-leading 33 doubles, 11 home runs and 72 runs batted in. He was traded to the New York Yankees on December 7, 1973, and spent the next 11 seasons with the Yankees. He had an outstanding season with the Yankees in 1974 with a .305 batting average, with 158 hits and 70 runs batted in. He missed most of the 1975 season with inner ear problems that required surgery and returned in 1976 with a .281 batting average, and finished second in the American League for Comeback Player of the Year voting.

Piniella was an outstanding postseason clutch performer hitting .305 (43–141) and hit safely in all five American League Championship Series games in 1977. He had hits in all six games of the 1978 World Series and had hits in the first three games of the 1981 World Series. He had a game-winning single with two outs in the 10th inning of the 1978 World Series giving the Yankees a 4–3 win in pivotal Game 4. He contributed to World Series titles in 1977 and 1978 as a player, and won his first World Series as a manager in 1990 with the Cincinnati Reds. He led the Seattle club to the postseason in 1995, 1997, 2000 and 2001 and became the Tampa Bay manager in 2003.

Piniella had an excellent 16-year major-league career with a .291 batting average, 1,705 hits, 305 doubles, 41 triples and was considered a consistent clutch performer.

I met up with Piniella in his office at Pro Player Stadium in July 2004 and we discussed his outstanding postseason play in 1977, 1978 and 1981 as a player and experiencing Reggie Jackson's three-home-run performance in Game 6 in the 1977 World Series. He also talked about his accomplishment as a manager with the Cincinnati Reds in his first year (in the National League) in 1990, winning the World Series crown and sweeping Oakland in four games.

CONVERSATION WITH LOU PINIELLA

Signed by Cleveland in 1962 and traded to Baltimore in '64. Along the way, you made stops in Cleveland (1968), Kansas City (1969–73) and spent the next 11 seasons with the Yankees (1974–1984). Talk about the beginning of your career.

I signed in 1962 with Cleveland and I got to the big leagues for 30 days in September of 1964, and then I didn't get back to the big leagues until the last 30 days of the 1968 season. Finally in 1969 [expansion year], I played with the Kansas City Royals, where I was the rookie of the year.

I played in Kansas City five years and my last year there, I played for Jack McKeon, the manager of the Florida Marlins. I was traded to the Yankees in 1973, where I would spend 11 years as a player over there. It took me awhile to get to the big leagues. I think I signed when I was 18 years old and got to the big leagues when I was 24. I turned 25 that summer, so it was a long road, but I was fortunate in that I was fairly well prepared when I got there, and played until I was almost 41 ... so I had a long career.

What was it like playing for Jack McKeon?

I played for Jack one year and I didn't really have a particularly good season that year. It was probably the worst year I had in the big leagues. I hit .250 and had nine home runs and drove in 69 runs. So they shipped me over to New York after the season. [Laughs.] I found McKeon to be a pretty square shooter and I think we got off on the wrong foot because the previous year I was second in the league in hitting and Kansas City really didn't want to pay me what I thought I was worth, so I held out and they just renewed my contract ... sort of set things off on the wrong foot. McKeon was fair and gave me an opportunity—I just didn't hit as well as I had in prior years. Getting traded to the Yankees was the best thing that happened to me. I wasn't happy initially because I played five years in Kansas City. I lived in town and I had a lot of friends in the area. It was basically a young team that was growing up together, so a lot of my teammates were still there from the original expansion team, and Kansas City was a nice place to live. At the same time, coming to New York was the best thing that could've ever happened to me. If you can play in New York City, you can play anywhere.

When do you feel you matured as a ballplayer?

Probably in the mid–1970s; by that time in my career I was in the 30–31 age range and those are really the best years for a player—the mental and physical aspect of playing all come together. I had some real nice solid years for the Yankees teams of the 1970s and we were very successful Yankees teams that went on to win a couple of world championships, and I think we played in four World Series.

In 1976 you get to play in your first postseason in the league championship series against the team you were traded from [Royals]. What do you recall about that series?

I don't remember all that much about the 1976 league championship series. The thing I remember the most is Chris Chambliss hitting a game-winning home run in the bottom of the ninth inning in the fifth and decid-

Lou Piniella watching batting practice at Pro Player Stadium (courtesy of Oscar Huete).

ing game off Kansas City pitcher Mark Littell. I remember the ball going over the right field wall and Al Cowens jumping up, and trying to catch it. That got us into the World Series. I don't remember all that much about the rest of the series.

What do you remember about the 1976 World Series?
  I remember the '76 World Series and we were a little disadvantaged. First of all, Cincinnati had a great team—the Big Red Machine, and they had a star-studded lineup. We were forced to play five games against Kansas City and our pitching wasn't set up the way it should've been. Cincinnati swept us and they won four in a row. I remember I was a designated hitter in the first game in Cincinnati. It was a cold day and there were snowflakes during the game. I got the first at-bat, the first hit and scored the first run ever as a designated hitter in a World Series, but Cincinnati swept us in four games. We learned a lot from that experience and then we got back to the World Series in 1977 and 1978 and beat the Dodgers twice to become the world champions.

In 1977 you had an outstanding season with a .330 batting average and in the league championship series you hit .333 with seven hits and drove in two runs. You had a hit in all five league championship series games and were considered a clutch hitter.
  Well, I enjoyed hitting with men on base, I really did. I wasn't really a home-run hitter, so I used the whole field to hit with. That type of hitter should have some consistency, and what I had was consistency as a hitter. And what we had in New York basically was left-handed power and right-hand hitting that hit for average. Your better hitters were right-handed and your power hitters were left-handed. And that was perfect for Yankee Stadium because of the small dimensions to right field and the bigger dimensions in left field and left center, and a good way to set up a team. And we had some great players. You look at Chambliss, and you look at Willie Randolph, you look at Bucky Dent, at Nettles, and you had Reggie Jackson in the mix; Mickey Rivers, Roy White, Thurman Munson, and then your pitching—Sparky Lyle, Goose Gossage, Catfish Hunter, Don Gullett, Guidry and Figueroa, and it goes on and on. We had really good teams.

Talk about the 1977 World Series against the Dodgers and your first World Series win.
  I don't remember much about the 1977 World Series. I remember the Dodgers winning the first two games—no, that was in the '78 World

Series. I don't remember too much about the '77 World Series. I was playing left field in that series and I think Reggie Jackson hit three home runs in Game 6 to give us a World Series victory. We played Kansas City again to get to the World Series and I remember one time when we played Kansas City we were down in the ninth inning of the fifth game in their ballpark and we scored two runs to go ahead and win. I wish I could remember more about that series.

In 1978 you had another outstanding season with a .314 batting average and guided the Yankees to the postseason. Do you recall you had a walk-off game-winning single in the 10th inning in the '78 World Series, giving the Yankees a 4–3 win in Game 4?

I remember that and it took place in Yankee Stadium. Bob Welch was the pitcher for the Dodgers and they walked Reggie Jackson intentionally to get to me. With two outs in the 10th inning I came through with the game-winning hit. That's how I earned my money: being a clutch hitter. And the first pitch he threw me, I lined it to right-center field and the ballgame was over.

In the 1978 World Series you had a hit in all six games.

I was fairly consistent hitting-wise in all postseasons. I didn't try to hit home runs, so I could use the whole field to hit with. That type of player should have more consistency and get more hits, and be able to move guys over. I was able to do that and I was more of a line drive doubles hitter. Throughout my career I had good postseasons; however, when you look at my hitting, I never walked in the playoffs and the World Series — how about that? I never got a base on balls and that isn't good.

How would you compare the 1977 Yankees with the '78 team?

The 1978 team was a more confident team. We already had won in 1977 and the 1978 team was a good baseball team, but I'll tell you this, a real good baseball team was the Boston Red Sox. We had to beat them in a playoff game in Fenway Park to get to the postseason. Both teams won 99 games that season and we met in Fenway. In fact, one of my coaches here, Don Zimmer, was managing the Red Sox in 1978. I remember that game well; I remember the Red Sox jumped ahead by two runs; then I remember Bucky Dent hitting a three-run home run into the net in left field. I remember Reggie Jackson hitting one into the center field stands to give us a [little] bigger cushion. I remember Gossage coming in and relieving Guidry, and I remember the ninth inning, where I made a play out there in right field that proved to be a pretty decisive play. You look at my career and people would think this guy was a pretty good hitter, but actually, I became a pretty good outfielder also. When you play on world championship teams you need to be a good offensive and defensive player. I wasn't an all-star player by any stretch of the imagination, but I enjoyed playing, I played hard, I played with some passion, I knew how to play and could perform under pressure. Maybe that's the reason why I'm managing now.

You play in the league championship series in 1980 against Kansas City. What do you remember about that series?
   That postseason Kansas City beat us. We had a good team and I think our 1980 team won something like 103 games. I recall Willie Randolph was sent home by Mike Ferraro [third base coach] and was thrown out at the plate late in the game, and Dick Howser [manager] was fired after the World Series. That was Dick Howser's first year with the club. He won 103 games and he did a darn good job. Howser got fired and the irony was that he got hired by Kansas City, and won a world championship with the Royals.

In 1981, you play in your final World Series against the Dodgers. After winning the first two games were you surprised by the Dodgers taking the next four games to win the World Series?
   Yes. We thought we had a better team than the Dodgers that particular year. I really thought we had a better team. Again, we had good teams over there, and we won the first two games, and after winning in '77 and '78, you say to yourself—we've got these guys' numbers. Well, lo and behold, they win a couple of close games and all of a sudden get the momentum, and sweep four games in a row. [Laughs.] We were surprised. When we jumped ahead two games to zero, we felt pretty good about our chances.

That season you became a player/hitting instructor. Did you feel that role would lead to becoming a manager in the future?
   Well, towards the end of my career I had some decisions to make. I thought I would get into the business world, quite frankly, and get out of baseball. Mr. Steinbrenner called me up to his office and he said, "I see some skills in you that would be conducive to being a good coach and being a good manager. I would like for you to consider sticking around and see if those things materialize." So when he hired Billy Martin again (second time), part of Billy's job description was to prepare me to manage, and I became his player/hitting coach on August 24, 1981. I officially

retired in June of 1984 and became Billy's full-time coach. Then I served as the hitting instructor in 1985. Then Billy Martin got fired at the end of the 1985 season and here I was managing the Yankees, a year and a half removed from playing, with really no experience managing anywhere. Mr. Steinbrenner took a chance on me and I always appreciated that.

As a big-league manager, did you model yourself after Billy Martin?

Well, I think you remember the guys that you played for, the managers you played for and you try to remember the things that you liked about that particular manager, and you disregard the things that basically you didn't like. Billy was probably the guy that had the most influence on me. I played for Billy quite a few times in New York towards the end of my career. I liked his passion for the game, I liked his fire, he was a real heady manager [did the unexpected], and took some chances. He was good and I learned a lot from him.

From 1986 to 1988 you managed the Yankees without getting to the postseason. Did you feel like you were under the microscope with Steinbrenner?

No, not really. I wasn't under the microscope, but the guy wants to win. He didn't have the patience with me that he should've really had. I did a good job over there and we were in first place a lot of those years for most of the season, and just didn't hold on. Our pitching was a little older and caused us some problems in the hot summer month of August. I think I averaged around 90 wins a season over there for three seasons and it wasn't just good enough. After I was fired, I became the general manager of the club for about a year. I liked the feeling of being a general manager better than being in the front office, although I came to recognize that the general manager's job was a more professional job. You wear a coat and tie and it's more businesslike, and I enjoyed that part of it. I wanted to go down on the field and try it again. I went down to manage the Yankees one more time in 1988 and we got eliminated the next to last day against Detroit, and George fired me for the second time. He tried subsequently to hire me for the third time, but since it didn't work twice why get into that again? I've always been appreciative of Mr. Steinbrenner and he gave me my first opportunity.

How did you feel when you replaced a legend like Billy Martin in 1988?

Not easy, not easy to replace a guy like Billy. Billy and George had a love-hate relationship and I think George fired Billy six times. It wasn't easy, but Billy Martin was a great manager. He should be in the Hall of

Tony Perez and Lou Piniella guided the 1990 Reds championship team (courtesy of Oscar Huete).

Fame, and he probably never will be. I liked Billy Martin; I really liked him. He had a nice disposition; he was a player's type manager, he let guys play and I enjoyed playing and coaching for him. I got replaced over there and I think if I had stayed over there in New York, which I didn't, Steinbrenner intended for me to be the new Billy, as far as Lou 3, Lou 4 or whatever, and I didn't want that. [Laughs.] I went over to Cincinnati in 1990 to manage the Reds.

Named manager of the Reds in 1990 and in you first campaign with the Reds, you win your first World Series as a manager. Talk about the postseason, playing Pittsburgh in the league championship series. Oakland in the World Series.

You talk about replacing a legend; I replaced Pete Rose over there in Cincinnati. I didn't realize that because I was in the big leagues with the Yankees and Kansas City my whole career—I didn't realize how big the Reds were in Cincinnati and how popular they were. I went there and had Tony Perez as one of my coaches; Billy Hatcher, a coach here with Tampa Bay, was one of my players in Cincinnati and hit .750 in the 1990 World Series. He had nine hits in 12 at-bats in that series; that's pretty amazing. We had a good season, went wire-to-wire, something that hadn't been done for a long time. We played the Pirates in an exciting, extremely well-played playoff and defeated them in six games, and then we faced Oakland, who was a prohibitive favorite. My good friend who I grew up with in Tampa and played American Legion with and high school baseball against was Tony LaRussa, who managed Oakland. I told my coaches, you know, we're being underestimated here, we have pretty good talent, we have good power, good pitching in our rotation and bullpen, and we're going to give Oakland all they can handle. That's exactly what happened; our kids went out there and really, really played well and we swept Oakland in the World Series.

Don Baylor
Manager,
1987 Championship Season
1979 NL Most Valuable Player, 1979 NL All-Star,
1995 NL Manager of the Year

> *"After Game 6, I don't think you can get any lower than that. That was the lowest point the team had been the entire season. Even losing Game 7 wasn't as disappointing as losing Game 6."* —Don Baylor

Donald Edward Baylor had a good major-league career, beginning in 1970 with the Baltimore Orioles and stretching 19 years, batting .260 in 2,292 games with 338 home runs, 1,276 runs batted in and establishing a major-league record—was hit by pitches 267 times. He played the majority of his games with California, but along the way he made stops with Oakland, New York Yankees, Boston and Minnesota.

In 1979, Baylor had a breakout season, leading the American League with 120 runs scored and 139 runs batted in. That season he had 36 home runs (a career high), 186 hits and a .296 batting average and earned the 1979 American League Most Valuable Player Award. He was named to the *Sporting News*' American League All-Star Team in 1978, 1985 and 1986.

Baylor hit 13 grand slam home runs during his career, including one in the postseason in the 1982 American League Championship Series against Milwaukee. He's been to the postseason nine times during his professional career, seven times as a player and once each as a manager and a coach. He managed a young Colorado Rockies team (third year in the National League) into the division series in 1995 and was eliminated by

Atlanta. Baylor was a member of Minnesota's world championship team in 1987 and had a postseason career .273 batting average with 33 hits in 38 games, four home runs and 21 runs batted in.

I conducted an interview with the articulate Baylor in the Mets clubhouse at Pro Player Stadium in July 2004, and he discussed the disappointments in postseason play with different teams during his career. Most disappointing was the 1986 World Series, the Game 6 meltdown, when the Red Sox were one out away from winning the World Series.

CONVERSATION WITH DON BAYLOR

Talk about your career beginnings with the Orioles and playing in your first postseason with the Orioles in the 1973 league championship series.

As a young player I began my career with the Orioles and they were pretty much a dominant force in '69, '70, and '71. In my first full season with the Orioles in 1972, it was kind of disappointing not playing in the postseason. After playing in the World Series for three years in a row, we got beat out by Detroit and it was kind of a bummer for the young guys that were just starting on the team. In 1973 we came back and made it to the postseason. Jim Palmer had an outstanding year and I believe he won the Cy Young Award that year. I remember we were defeated by Oakland in the playoffs and I had three hits in that series. In '73, '74 and '75 we were right there again, but in '73 and '74, it just kind of gave me an appreciation of what the playoffs were about. It was different levels now that you had to win to get to the World Series. The American League East was probably the best division in baseball.

In 1973 and 1974 you face Oakland in the postseason. Was it disappointing to not play in the World Series? What was it like facing the Oakland pitching staff with guys like Hunter, Blue and Holtzman?

Hunter, Vida Blue and Kenny Holtzman were on that team, and I recall Hunter beat us twice in the playoff. They had so many professionals on that club—Bando, Joe Rudi, Campaneris, Tenace—matched up against some Orioles players that had been in a World Series. It was difficult to lose, but it was fun as a young player. You think this is what it is supposed to be like. Is it always going to be this way? Being in the playoffs is one thing, but getting to the World Series is another.

Who were some of the players on the '74 Orioles that you played with?

In '74, Brooks Robinson was still there, Paul Blair, Boog Powell, Bob Grich was there, Al Bumbry, Richie Coggins, Andy Etchebarren, Elrod Hendricks, McNally was there and Cuellar was on that team. We had a real good team that year and I remember we beat Oakland in the first game of the playoff, but got swept in the next three games and Blue and Holtzman shut us out in Games 2 and 3.

In 1979 you play in the postseason with the Angels. What was that team like?

The Angels were a fun team to be on. Offensively

Don Baylor, Mets hitting instructor at Pro Player Stadium.

we had so many different weapons on that team. As far as our pitching, we relied so much on Nolan Ryan and Frank Tanana all the time. So it was pretty much an offensive club and we could just kind of pound our way into the playoffs, but you also need pitching. The Orioles beat us three games to one in that playoff.

In the 1982 league championship series against Milwaukee you win the first two games in the series and had an excellent postseason.

That was probably my most disappointing postseason. We won the first two games in Anaheim. We go to Milwaukee and lost three consecutive games [that was when the playoff was the best of five]. So it was difficult to swallow. We had Reggie Jackson on that club, Fred Lynn was there, Carew, myself and we had four former MVPs on that team. I remember I hit well in that postseason and drove in 10 runs. We really felt like we should've represented the American League at that time. There was no doubt in our mind that we should've beat Milwaukee. Milwaukee just clawed and clawed, and they won, but that was probably the most disappointing postseason for me in my entire career.

From 1983 to 1985, you play with the Yankees, a team destined to play in the postseason. What was it like playing on those Yankees teams?

    I enjoyed my time there; I played for Yogi [Berra] for a brief time; I played for Billy Martin for two years and I played with Piniella, Roy White, Bobby Murcer, Winfield, Griffey and Mattingly. We had an array of players, but we could not get past Toronto. Toronto was our Achilles heel, really—we played good baseball all the time. The 1985 team had Rickey Henderson on that club and was the best team overall from 1-8 [that] didn't win. I don't know what really kept us from winning. Maybe all the fights between George and Billy kind of affected our club from time to time. So they didn't win in the '80s. They won the strike-shortened '81 season, but they went through a long stretch where they didn't win.

Did you feel added pressure by Steinbrenner by not playing in the postseason?

    I didn't feel any pressure there; it was really not like it is today. I think the players really feel that pressure because the payroll is completely different than it was back then. So there wasn't pressure on the players by not playing in the postseason, but I think playing in New York City brought on enough pressure from people expecting us to win every year.

What would you say was the reason the Yankees didn't get to the postseason the years you played there?

    We still had Guidry in his prime; Righetti was a good pitcher and we just couldn't put the pieces together. We had small distractions like Andre Robertson, our shortstop, was in a huge car accident and he's out for the season. We had the pine tar game where that really distracted players for about a month. There were a lot of distractions and not like it is today. Billy Martin was still a TV star and trying to manage, and I think that affected our play. We had talented teams in 1983 through 1985, but we didn't make it to the postseason.

You go to Boston in 1986 and put up good numbers with 31 home runs and drive in 94 runs. Talk about the Red Sox team and playing in your first World Series.

    I got traded over to Boston with maybe 10 days left in spring training. Being an outsider looking in the Red Sox, you can never see any closeness at all. It was like what everybody always said, "25 players, 25 different cabs." So you never saw any closeness. So I went there and talked to these guys about winning. A lot of the writers kind of scoffed at what I told the players—sure, you don't know what you're talking about. But we started the kangaroo court and started to bring guys closer to each other, and the guys had fun playing. We had a great time and [that] team came together in '86, and made it to the World Series.

The 1986 World Series was exciting, but the mood changed from celebration to disappointment.

We had that one chance to win and we won the first two games at Shea Stadium. We returned to Boston and lost two out of three games there. We had Game 6 won, we had Game 7 won, and so, we knew we were the best club that didn't win. And the bounce of the ball that got away from Buckner; the same thing that eluded the Angels for along time and they got their championship eventually, but the Red Sox will probably get theirs one day.

In Game 6, with the Red Sox one out away from winning the World Series, what was the feeling in the dugout when the Mets started a comeback with timely hits and when Buckner booted Wilson's slowly hit ground ball?

I'm standing with Tom Seaver in the dugout because he was on the disabled list and we're about ready to run out on the field. Buckner misses the ground ball and you suddenly feel guys being deflated. But we knew we could come back; we had a rain out, I believe, so now you have to wait, wait more, so the intensity just kind of builds, but we felt like we're going to win Game 7, without a doubt.

What was the mood like in the clubhouse prior to Game 7, after what happened the previous game? Did you feel a letdown in Game 7?

You don't feel a letdown until the game is over. So there was no letdown; there was fight in guys because in prior weeks the way we won Game 5 in Anaheim, we still had that memory, you know. After Game 6, I don't think you can get any lower than that. That was the lowest point the team had been the entire season. Even losing Game 7 wasn't as disappointing as losing Game 6.

In 1987 you play with the Twins for 20 games and help them make it to the World Series. What was it like playing in your second World Series and winning a world championship?

That was quite an experience to go to, maybe, a nonbaseball town.

Everybody thinks of Minnesota and that part of the country as not being a baseball town like New York, Boston or Chicago. I believe when they rolled out the "home run hankies" that entire region became Twins believers. Sitting in the dugout where you couldn't hear your own emotions was deafening. It was tough to concentrate because we had crowds so-so, but not like that in the playoffs and World Series. We had players like Puckett, Hrbek, Brunansky, Gaetti and Lombardozzi. We had Jeff Reardon and a close bunch of guys that wanted to win. They didn't care who was going to be the hero that day; it didn't matter who contributed a game-winning hit or whatever. It was a close-knit team that won every game at home, but lost games in St. Louis.

In the 1987 World Series you hit .385 with five hits and knock in three runs. You feel you made a contribution in the series?

I do. Game 6 we needed to win—I got a base hit and Puckett scored. I remember the pitching coach going out to talk to John Tutor. I don't know what he told him, but by the time he got to the dugout, I hit a two-run home run off of him, which got us one run closer, and we ended up winning that game. That home run was pretty special because my mom was still alive at the time, my dad was there, my brother, my sister, everybody was there—my son, my wife, and as a kid you always dream about hitting a home run in the World Series, so that was pretty special.

You end your playing career with Oakland in 1988 and play in the World Series for the third time. Oakland is the favorite to beat the Dodgers in the World Series and runs into a hot pitcher named Orel Hershiser. What do you recall about that series?

Oakland was the Goliath of baseball in 1988, and Eckersley had a great year, as well as Canseco, McGwire, Dave Stewart and Bob Welch. We were the overwhelming favorites, but they had a bunch of scrappers that got base hits at the right time. Gibson's home run really convinced them that they could win the World Series. He only gets one at-bat that turned the World Series around. It was probably as disappointing as all the others because we did have the best club and sometimes that doesn't work out. Hershiser was the hottest pitcher in baseball and he continued in the playoffs and in the World Series. He was dominant in that series and nobody on Oakland could hit him.

Who would you say were the toughest pitchers you faced in the postseason?

Toughest pitchers—Mike Witt, who pitched with the Angels, was tough. When his breaking ball was going good, he was unhittable. We knocked him around in the 1986 League Championship Series. In Game 5, the Angels were three outs away from winning the pennant and had a 5–2 lead in the ninth inning. And with one out and one on, I hit a two-run home run off Witt that made it 5–4, and we ended up beating the Angels 7–6 in 11 innings. That home run helped to save our season. When I was younger, Catfish Hunter was a tough pitcher. He didn't make too many mistakes; he knew where he wanted to throw the ball all the time — in, out, up, down; that's how he pitched.

Toughest closer?

Gossage was pretty much like Mariano Rivera. He threw 96, 97 and as a hitter you tried to give yourself a little more time by standing on the back line of the batter's box. You tried to give yourself more room to look at his fastball. So we always had some battles all the time.

You became the Rockies' first manager in their inaugural season in 1993. From 1993 to 1998, the years you managed the Rockies, did you ever believe you would get to the postseason?

Well, we ended up as a wild-card team in 1995. We had a bunch of good hitters and playing at Coors Field was an offensive ballpark. In '95 we had the replacement players and we had to go back to spring training. That was a distraction and we had to play 144 games that year. And just to be a part of the playoffs — many of the players were never involved in anything like that before. So I had to kind of share my experiences with them about being in the playoffs. And some of the players experienced the pressure of playing in the postseason and they enjoyed it.

How did you get there?

It's a hard road to get there. Everybody would like to be in that spot; some guys would have to give up their tee times or fishing obligations and all those other things, but here we are playing in the postseason for the first time. I knew it was a young club [just starting] three years old and trying to get to the World Series. It was long odds because we were playing the Atlanta Braves and a base hit here and there would've given us a win. I remember Chipper Jones made a great play down the line against Galarraga — we could've won Game 1. Game 2 was the same thing, but we were outmanned and were playing against a great experienced team, with outstanding pitching and hitting and Atlanta won their only world championship in 1995. So we can always say that we got beat by the world champs.

In 1999, you worked as the hitting coach with the Braves. What was it like working with a low-maintenance type of team?

The Braves weren't a low-maintenance type of team. There were guys there that took instruction very well. Being around Chipper Jones and building his confidence, and working with Andruw Jones, Klesko and all those guys to make them better players was a great experience. So the relationship I had with the Braves was tremendous. Chipper Jones was the 1999 MVP and he was a dominant from the right side and had struggled in the past, and had a great year hitting 45 home runs. Well, you could say low maintenance, but the ability was there and all I'm trying to do is get all that ability to the surface. I had Bret Boone and Randall Simon was on that club, and as a hitting coach I provided these guys with lots of encouragement. The 1999 club was a dominant offensive team and probably as a good or better than the '95 team that won the World Series.

Steve Blass
1971 Pirates World Series Hero
1972 NL All-Star Team

"Game 3 was a great game. I pitched a three-hitter and I remember Bob Robertson hit a three-run homer in the seventh inning to give me a 5–1 win. Bob Robertson missed a bunt sign and hit a three-run home run, and it was just incredible. In those days a complete game would take two hours and 10 minutes. It was phenomenal; it was a wonderful experience." —Steve Blass

Stephen Robert Blass has been involved in Major League Baseball for the past 44 seasons as a player and broadcaster, and associated with the Pittsburgh Pirates since signing his first professional contract on June 27, 1960. The former right-handed pitcher spent 10 seasons (1964–1974) with the Pirates, accumulating 103 wins and 16 shutouts in 282 games.

From 1964 through 1972, Blass had six seasons with double digits in wins and in 1967, he had an 18–6 record with a 2.12 earned run average, and league-leading .750 winning percentage. In 1971 he piled up 15 wins with a 2.85 earned run average and was the World Series hero as he pitched complete-games wins against the Orioles in Game 3 and Game 7.

In 1972, he led the Pirates into the postseason winning 19 games (a career high) with a 2.49 earned run average. He was a member of the 1972 National League All-Star Team and won 78 games during a five-year span from 1968 through 1972. In 1983 he joined the Pirates in broadcasting and presently works as a color analyst.

Blass and I met up in the press box at Pro Player Stadium in 2004, and we talked about the postseason challenges in the early 1970s with the competition among the Reds, Giants and the Pirates. The greatest accomplishment for him was winning two games in the 1971 World Series and playing with Roberto Clemente, Willie Stargell and Bill Mazeroski.

Conversation with Steve Blass

You spent 10 seasons (1964–1974) with the Pirates, winning 103 games. What do you recall about your rookie season in 1964?

I can probably tell you everything that happened from the day I got there. [Laughs.] That was the realization of a dream. Every kid that plays baseball wants to play in the big leagues and I had never quit playing all the way up since Little League, and I finally got the call after we had driven all night from Syracuse, New York, back to Columbus. I was playing for Columbus (Triple-A) and we got in at six o'clock in the morning after driving all night. And I was sleeping when Joe Brown, the general manager, called and it was "the call." Every player refers to it as "the call." And my wife answered the phone and Brown said, "I would like to talk to Steve," and she told him I was sleeping. He said, "Can you wake him up?" She said, "No." He said, "This is Joe Brown. I want him to come to the big leagues. You can wake him up now." She said, "Yes," and woke me up. [Laughs.] It was the fulfillment of a dream; I can remember everything that happened when I arrived and it was raining at Forbes Field that day. [Laughs.]

What was the makeup of the team in the 1960s?

In the early '60s the team was in transition; it had won the World Series in 1960 by beating the Yankees and then it slipped away for a while. We had a good year in '65 where we came fairly close. Then in the late '60s, we started really getting the fruit of a really good minor-league system—we had Oliver, Cash, Sanguillen, Hebner, Robertson, Doc Ellis—all those guys seemed to get ready to come to the big leagues in the late '60s and that's when we started assembling a real good team that led to the division championships and the great decade of the '70s.

In 1968, you win 18 games and in 1969, 16 games. With those outstanding seasons, did you see the Pirates getting into the postseason?

Not really. That team was starting to form and those youngsters that I mentioned were just coming up. I was too preoccupied probably getting into my own career. [Laughs.] And on June 1, 1968, I had a 1–2 record and ended up 18–6. We were starting to form and that group would win in the '70s.

Beginning in 1970, the Pirates emerged as a formidable championship team.

Oh, yeah, yeah. You could see it coming with the young players coming out of the farm system. In 1970, we won the division and got beat by the Reds in the playoffs. In 1971, we became real good, a solid team, and we beat the Giants in the playoffs, and beat the Orioles in the World Series. In 1972, I think we had a better team than the '71 championship team because we had gone through that experience and still remained pretty much intact. The '72 team was managed by Bill Virdon and was the best team he ever saw. He played with the Pirates for many years and became the Pirates' new manager in 1972.

In 1971 you had another outstanding season with 15 wins and pitch in the postseason. What do you remember about the '71 season?

Well, that was a good season. We were confident; we knew we were good; we were good the year before in '70, but got beat in the playoffs. In 1971, we knew what we had and we knew it was a real good baseball team. We had Clemente, Mazeroski, Stargell, Oliver, Hebner, Cash, Robertson, Ellis, Sanguillen, May and Kison. We had a talented bunch of guys that provided clutch hitting and good pitching throughout the season.

What was most memorable about the 1971 World Series?

First of all, before the World Series, I had a real good year, so I started a couple of games in the playoffs and I had not pitched in the '70 playoffs—that's critical to this point I'm trying to make. I watched the '70 playoffs and when I first got my chance in '71, it was my first experience in postseason play. I thought I had to be better than I was in the regular season and I tried to do more, and I got my brains beat in by the Giants. Fortunately, everybody else played well and we made it to the World Series. But I had to learn that lesson after the playoffs—hey, you got to be yourself. I think the realization that I tried to do too much in the playoffs really helped me in the World Series. The World Series was just an incredible experience. It's everything you think it's going to be times 10. And because I got beat up in the playoffs, I didn't start until the third game of the World Series, and during the course of that series, in the first six games, we used six different starting pitchers. I was the only one who had two starts and that was because it went seven games (I started Game 7). It was an unbelievable experience; you dream about playing in a World Series and it is as simple as that—it's every kid's dream and there's only a few of us that get a chance to live it.

You fulfilled a dream in that you won two games in that World Series. Talk about Game 3.

Game 3 was a great game; I pitched a three-hitter and I remember Bob Robertson hit a three-run homer in the seventh inning to give me a 5–1 win. Robertson missed a bunt sign and hit a three-run home run, and it was just incredible. In those days a complete game would take two hours and 10 minutes. It was phenomenal; it was a wonderful experience.

How did you feel about pitching in Game 7?

I didn't know I was going to pitch until the morning of the sixth game. Murtaugh told me that if we didn't win today, I would start tomorrow. So, I woke up the day I was going to pitch the seventh game—I just wanted it to be five o'clock because the waiting is the worst part. And we got out there and it was an overcast day. Clemente had a great series with a hit in all seven games and hit a home run in the fourth inning. I pitched a four-hit complete game for a 2–1 win and the title. Again, it was a phenomenal experience.

Earl Weaver came out in the first inning and told the umpire that I was pitching illegally off the mound. I was so nervous; I think he helped me without realizing it. Whenever I see Earl, I thank him for getting me so distracted from being so nervous, and I was so mad at him that I forgot how excited I was. He stopped the game for about 20 minutes and after that I was fine. Thanks again, Earl.

Steve Blass, Pirates television analyst, in the broadcast booth.

What do you recall about getting the final out in Game 7?

It was bedlam; I remember when I was eight years old ... you're playing in your back yard a hypothetical World Series game as a kid and you're pretending what are you going to do after the last out? And I got to live that and I jumped straight up, and ran over to first base where the out was made—I jumped up and onto Bob Robertson—he weighed about 220 and is 6'4" tall, and he could handle that jump. I weighed less then than I do now, and it was insane out there on the field after we won the World Series. It was 10 dreams come true and there's nothing like it.

Who were some of the leaders on that championship team?

Well, I'm not crazy about the word leaders; I like examples. We had guys who were wonderful examples of how to go about your profession and your craft. I came up in 1964 with those kinds of people—Bob Friend, Vernon Law, Gerry Lynch, Bill Mazeroski, Willie Stargell and Clemente, and I walked into a baseball university. The leaders on that '71 team—we had a unique mix because we had white guys, black guys and Latin guys, and at the head of each of those groups, examples of how to work your profession, how to apply your trade—Clemente was a Latin guy, Stargell was a black guy and Mazeroski was a white guy, and we had it all covered.

Your recollection of Roberto Clemente and what he meant to the team?

How much time you got? [Laughs.] Clemente was the best baseball player I ever saw and he carried himself, I think, unlike other players. He had a presence; I thought he was several notches above the rest of us. He had a presence and dignity, and it was like a beacon. We were the soldiers, he was the general. I pitched in the big leagues 10 years and he would turn 10-year major-league veterans into 10-year-old kids the way he played. He was phenomenal.

Who were the toughest hitters in the Oriole lineup in the 1971 World Series?

The Orioles World Series team was one of the best assembled and I mean that very sincerely. I was very concerned about Boog Powell because he had so much power as a left-handed hitter. I was very concerned about Frank Robinson because I pitched to him briefly as a rookie [when] he played for Cincinnati, and Merv Rettenmund was a great contact hitter. Davey Johnson was dangerous; Buford could run. They had such a well-balanced team, but I was most concerned with Powell and Frank Robinson.

In 1972 you had another outstanding year with 19 wins and a 2.49 earned run average. What was it like pitching in the league championship series against the Reds?

The decade of the '70s featured the Reds and the Pirates, and a decade of great head-to-head baseball. Besides the Giants in their heyday, that was the toughest lineup I ever faced. The Big Red Machine with Bench, Perez, Rose, and up and down the lineup, Joe Morgan and all of them. The ironic thing about that is that my last start of the regular season, I had one chance to win 20 games, and John Milner hit a ball off my elbow. I didn't know if I would pitch in the playoffs, but I started the first game and Joe Morgan hit my second pitch over the right field wall. It was a low, sinking fastball, which I thought was a pretty good pitch. And I said to myself, that's it, no more fastballs and I don't think I threw them four more fastballs the rest of the game. Morgan hit that home run in the first inning and we won the game 5–1. And then I got to pitch the last game and pitched well. I left with a 3–2 lead and they came back. Bench hit a home run and then a wild pitch sent us home, and sent the Reds to the World Series. Either team that was going to represent the National League would've been terrific representatives. We wanted to obviously, but the Reds team was absolutely terrific also.

Toughest hitters you had to face in the Reds lineup in the 1972 LCS?

All of them—Morgan, Bench, Perez, Rose, Concepcion, Cesar Geronimo—up and down the lineup, they were all tough. When I compare them to other lineups, the Giants come to mind because they had Mays, McCovey, Cepeda, Bonds, Jim Ray Hart and all those guys. But the Reds lineup might've been top to bottom tougher.

Look at how many players who never had an opportunity to play in the postseason. What can you say about your postseason experience?

Well, I got pounded by the Giants in the 1971 league championship series, but I was happy with my work. To pitch a seventh game of a World Series, there's nothing that compares to that for a pitcher, absolutely nothing, and I won a complete-game four-hitter. I'm very proud of my postseason.

Talk about the last two seasons of your career in 1973 and 1974.

Well, they weren't good. I went from winning 19 games in 1972, to winning three games in '73 and no games in '74. I just lost my control; it's been discussed chapter and verse, and I really don't care to get into that—a lot of detail; I'm not uncomfortable with it, but it's old news. I did try everything for two years that I possibly could to get the control back. It didn't come back, so I felt satisfied that I'm not looking back and saying, "What if I tried that?" because I tried it all and believe me, I tried more bizarre things than you can think of. So I'm satisfied with my career. I achieved more than I ever dreamed of; I'm well ahead of the game. I had a chance to participate with a bunch of guys and you can't do it yourself. You have to be part of a team that went through 30 games of spring training, 162 regular season games, playoff and World Series games and we got the rings. Nobody can take that away and for one brief, shining moment, we were the best.

Sitting in the booth as a broadcaster, any memorable Pirate postseasons?
We won three divisions in '90, '91 and '92. I thoroughly enjoyed that—the excitement and the energy that comes with it. Seeing it from a different perspective than I did as a player is terrific. I remember the throw in the '92 playoff by Bonds that didn't get there in time to get Sid Bream. Now all of a sudden the Braves go to the World Series and the Pirates go home. Similar to the wild pitch that Bob Moose threw in '72—in '92, 20 years later another play at the plate results in the Pirates going home and somebody else going to the World Series. I've experienced many postseasons and this is my 43rd year with the Pirates, and being with one organization my entire career. So I've had a chance to watch it from a lot of different viewpoints.

With the changes in baseball today, it's interesting to note that you played your entire career with the Pirates. Do you see it becoming more difficult for teams other than the Yankees to repeat a championship season?
Yeah, because the economics of it have become a big part of baseball. You hope that changes to some degree; they have revenue sharing, but I don't think it's to the degree that's going to make a significant difference. Baseball is a unique game and there are so many more games than there are in other sports, so the cream comes to the top in baseball. And it can take awhile, but the people with the most, deepest pockets are going to have the highest percentage of chance that they can win and repeat. You're going to have exceptions—the Marlins won last year with a low payroll and that doesn't help the system because, now the big boys can say, "See, it can be done." And it can be done, but the higher percentages are with the deeper pockets.

Do you see a team like the Pirates (with a small payroll) competing with the other National League teams and making a postseason run?

Yes. Because other teams with our circumstances financially have done it. So we have to make good decisions; we have to be very strong evaluating talent and developing talent. We can't make mistakes because we have to live with them. Teams like the Yankees and some of the other teams, if they make a mistake, they just go out and get somebody else. Before we even talk about talent on the field, we have to make sure we maintain and acquire talented scouts, evaluators and developers. We can compete because other teams have done it.

In the last three postseasons, unexpected teams like the Diamondbacks, Angels and Marlins won the World Series and defeated tough Yankees teams. Do the experiences of these teams provide hope and confidence that the Pirates can get to the postseason one day and win a World Series?

Yes, yes. You see that example and you have a chance to get to the postseason. The thing about the postseason too, if you get there—the best teams in baseball get to the postseason. Does the best team win the World Series? Not necessarily; it's a crapshoot once you get into postseason play. Anybody can get some hot pitcher once you get there and you have to work your tail off to get there. But once you get there, a couple of hot pitchers and a couple of hot hitters, and you can run the table. The trick and the real value of a team is getting to postseason play. That's the real benchmark of a team, getting there. After that, anything can happen. Pitching, pitching, pitching is what it will take to get to the postseason. Because during the course of a season, you play so many games, you wear the hitters out—they have to play catch-up baseball every night; there's a lot of pressure on them and they're trying to do too much. Personally, they're trying to make things happen, they're trying to hit home runs when they shouldn't. If you have good starting pitching, your hitters are relaxed and relaxed hitters in my mind are better hitters. And if your starting pitchers keep the other team down, you have a bunch of loosey-goosey hitters up there on your team that I think are going to be more comfortable, more relaxed and more effective.

Jeff Bagwell
Superstar, Future Hall of Famer
1991 NL Rookie of the Year, 1994 NL Most Valuable Player; 4-Time NL All-Star

"I just want to win; I've never had a chance to win a World Series; I've never been to a World Series and that's the ultimate goal. Having good statistics will help us get to the postseason, but I really don't think about putting up big numbers and things like that. I just want to win a World Series." —Jeff Bagwell

Jeffrey Robert Bagwell was selected by Boston in the fourth round of the June 1989 draft. After signing with the Red Sox, he spent time in the Gulf Coast and Florida State Leagues where he played at Winter Haven and had a .333 batting average with 65 hits in 64 games. In 1990, he was selected Most Valuable Player of the Eastern League at Double-A New Britain and hit .333 with 160 hits and league-leading 34 doubles.

Bagwell was acquired by Houston on August 31, 1990, in exchange for Larry Andersen. In 1991 he had an outstanding rookie season with a .294 batting average, 163 hits, 26 doubles and driving in 82 runs, and was the first Houston player to win the National League Rookie of the Year award. The following season he played in 162 games with 160 hits, 18 home runs and 96 runs batted in. In 1993 he had his breakout season with a .320 batting average, 171 hits and 20 home runs.

The 1994 season brought with it the most impressive stats of Bagwell's young career: 39 home runs, 116 runs batted in, 104 runs scored, 147 hits, career-high .368 batting average and 110 games played. He broke the fourth metacarpal bone in his left hand on August 10th and missed

52 games that season. He was the unanimous selection by the Baseball Writers Association of America as the National League Most Valuable Player in 1994 and the first player in the Houston franchise to win the award.

From 1995 through 2000 he continued to post MVP–type statistics, and in 2000 he had another career year with a .310 batting average, league-leading 152 runs scored, 183 hits, 47 home runs and 132 runs batted in. During the 2001 campaign Bagwell had a .288 batting average, 173 hits, 43 doubles, 39 home runs, 130 runs batted in and 126 runs scored. He was selected to the National League All-Star Team in 1994, 1996, 1997 and 1999.

Bagwell has played his entire career with Houston and has compiled a .297 lifetime batting average. At the end of the 2004 campaign, he had 2,289 career hits, 446 home runs, 1,510 runs batted in and 1,506 runs scored. Bagwell should finish out his career becoming a member of the 500 home run club, accumulating over 1,600 runs scored and driven in, and, barring injury, he could reach these milestones in a couple of seasons. He's the only first baseman to hit 30 or more home runs and steal 30 or more bases in the same season, a feat he accomplished in both 1997 and 1999. His outstanding career statistics should provide him a place in the Hall of Fame within the five-year requirement after his retirement.

I interviewed Bagwell in the Houston clubhouse at Pro Player Stadium during the 2004 season. He expressed his disappointment at not being able to play in the World Series, and his biggest goal is not just getting there, but to win one. That would be an appropriate ending to his outstanding career.

CONVERSATION WITH JEFF BAGWELL

You've had a magnificent 13-year career, been a four-time all-star with a lifetime .300 batting average and closing in on 500 home runs and 1,500 runs driven in and runs scored. What do you hope to accomplish this season?

I just want to win; I've never had a chance to win a World Series; I've never been to a World Series and that's the ultimate goal. Having good statistics will help us get to the postseason, but I really don't think about putting up big numbers and things like that. I just want to win a World Series.

Would you give up those great statistics to get the opportunity to play and win a World Series?

I would love to, but part of those statistics is getting us to the World Series. [Laughs.] I guess my numbers on paper look good, but it would look better with a World Series ring. At this point in my career, my goal is to win a World Series and that's all I'm looking for.

With the addition of Roger Clemens and Andy Pettitte, is there more pressure and is it expected that the team will compete in the postseason?

I think there are more expectations; I don't think there's any pressure. The fact that we feel we have a good ballclub and we have an opportunity to win, that's a good feeling.

Is this season different from previous ones?

Yes. We never had this type of talent to start the season. We had a great team in '98 when we added Randy Johnson, but we never started with the expectations that we have this year. We have a good offensive club and have some outstanding pitchers.

What do you hope to accomplish before you leave the game?

We just talked about it; I want to win a World Series. If I can do that and I feel like we have the best team in baseball, then my career will be complete. Not just getting there, but to win it. I think that would be the appropriate ending to my career.

Jeff Bagwell in the dugout at Pro Player Stadium.

You played in the postseason in 1997 through 1999 and 2001, and were eliminated in the division series. Would that be a big disappointment in your career?

I think it's a big disappointment and when I look back on all the years that we played in the postseason, I was disappointed that we were eliminated in '98 because I thought we had a great team. My career would not be diminished if we don't end up winning again. I want to have another chance to play in the World Series and I'm excited about the team we have this year. I know there aren't many chances left.

What happened in the '98 postseason?

We had a great team that season. I think we won something like 102 games; our offense was outstanding and I thought that club would play in the World Series. We acquired Randy Johnson at the end of July and he was a big addition to our pitching staff. We played a hot San Diego club in the postseason and they shut our offense down. We didn't score many runs in the playoffs and San Diego took the series in four games. It was very disappointing.

Did you do anything different in your preparation in spring training and early in the season to get ready to make a run at postseason play?

No, not at all. It's a long season, it's not 16 games, it's not 82 games, it's 162 games; that's a long time. So I try to keep my body in shape and get ready to roll.

When did you start thinking that the team had a chance to play in the postseason?

I thought about it when we signed Roger Clemens and Andy Pettitte, but the bottom line is, you have a long time to play. It's a long season with a lot of ups and downs, and you have to remain healthy and all those kinds of things. But we have the talent here and other than that, we have to concentrate on one game at a time.

You indicated that you want to win a World Series before you leave the game. What do you need to do to get to the next level?

I work hard to continue to improve my hitting; I work out and I try to get my body right for the season. It's a long season, it's a grind and you have to maintain a level of consistency throughout the season.

What is it going to take for the 2004 Astros to get to the postseason with players like Kent, Biggio, Berkman, Bagwell and your improved pitching staff?

First of all, we all need to be healthy and stay healthy, and be able to play to our abilities. If we can remain healthy and play good baseball, I think we have a chance.

Looking back at the 2003 Marlins World Series win, what did you see as the reason for their accomplishment?
They got hot at the right time. They're a good ballclub; they're a very solid ballclub. I don't know if they were the best team, but they put it together at the right time. Josh Beckett really got hot at the right time; he started pitching real well. Their offense was a very good offense with a lot of speed and was able to manufacture some runs. You need to do some of those things when you're in the postseason.

Do you see the Astros having similar or more ingredients to play in the postseason?
I don't think we're that similar to them. They had a lot more speed than we do; they play a little different game than we do. That being said, we can win with our group too.

Do you look at this season as a challenge and is the clubhouse environment different from previous years?
No difference at all. It's the same clubhouse and we've added some guys, but nothing has changed in here except we have an expectation to win. That's a good thing.

Are you hungrier to play in the postseason this year?
Oh, yeah. I'm hungry to get to the postseason every year. But this year with the ability that we have, I think it will be a great opportunity for us.

How do good teams keep loose in the pursuit of making it to the playoffs?
Because it's such a long season you can't concentrate on one game. You have to learn how to relax during the season and there are going to be ups and downs that you have to get through. It's when you get to the postseason, and then you concentrate on one game again. There's nothing that you can get nervous about and all that kind of stuff; you just have to go out and play.

Describe the team chemistry, how players interact with each other.
Twenty-five guys have 25 different personalities ... trust me. Throughout the course of a season all those personalities interact and

come together. The chemistry here is great; we don't have any problems and guys always succeed here when they come here. We have a good bunch of guys here.

For players like you, Biggio, Clemens and other veterans, this may be your final opportunity to play in the postseason.
    I think many of the players understand that. This is a veteran club and many guys will have their contracts come up after this season. Many organizations, except the Yankees, have a turnover of players and have to retool. And with the kind of talent we have on this club, we have an opportunity to play in the postseason.

Why do you think the Astros have a chance to play in the postseason?
    We have great starting pitching, we have a great offense and our bullpen is rounding into shape. And if we continue with all those guys and everybody stays healthy, we have a chance.

Any teams you see that have the qualities to make it to the postseason?
    There are a lot of teams that have the qualities to make it to the postseason. The Marlins are pretty much the same team they had last year—they have speed, pitching, defense; the Cubs with their pitching staff—they have a great opportunity; the Phillies have a lot of power in their lineup and good pitching; the Braves always manage to play in the postseason and despite losing some of their pitchers will be competitive.

Jim Thome
PHILLIES' WINNING SLUGGER
2004 NL All-Star, 3-Time AL All-Star

> *"Getting back to playing in the postseason and to contribute, and do something special, especially in those types of situations, is why I think we all play. In Game 3, I remember hitting a two-run home run off Tim Wakefield in the second inning that gave us a 2–0 lead."* —Jim Thome

James Howard Thome was selected by the Cleveland Indians in the 13th round of the June 1989 draft. He began his professional career in 1989 with the Gulf Coast Indians, hitting .237 in 55 games. He split the 1990 season between Single-A Burlington and Single-A Kinston and hit a combined .340. He was tied for third in the Appalachian League in home runs (12), despite playing only 34 games due to being promoted to Kinston.

In 1991 he began the season at Double-A Canton-Akron and was leading the league with a .337 batting average when he was promoted to Triple-A Colorado Springs. Thome hit .285 in 41 games for Colorado Springs before being promoted to Cleveland on September 4. He made his major-league debut on September 4th and collected his first big-league hit; he hit his first major-league home run, a game-winning two-run shot, on October 4 off Yankees pitcher Steve Farr.

Thome began the 1992 season on the disabled list after suffering a strained right wrist in spring training. He hit .336 in 30 games while rehabbing with Double-A Canton-Akron and played 30 games with Cleveland that season. In 1993 he started the season with Triple-A Charlotte and led the International League with a .332 batting average and 102 runs batted in, and hit 25 home runs. He was recalled by Cleveland on August 13 and hit a home run that night against Texas. He hit .266 in 47 games with Cleveland in '93 and had seven home runs.

In his first full season in 1994 Thome led all American League third basemen with 20 home runs. In 1995 he had an outstanding season with a .314 batting average, 142 hits, 25 home runs and 73 runs batted in. In 1996, he had a breakout season with a .311 batting average, 157 hits, 38 home runs, 116 runs batted in and 122 runs scored. In 1997 he was moved from third base to first base with the acquisition of Matt Williams and hit 40 home runs, knocked in 102 runs and was named to his first American League All-Star Team.

From 1998 through 2000 he continued to be a dominant slugger and hit 30 or more home runs in three consecutive seasons and was selected to the American League All-Star Team in 1998 and 1999. In the 1998 league championship series, Thome had an outstanding postseason performance against the Yankees, hitting four home runs and driving in eight runs, and in Game 6 hit his first postseason grand slam.

In 2001 Thome had a great season with a .291 batting average, 49 home runs and 124 runs batted in. During the 2002 campaign he had a .304 batting average, 146 hits, career-high 52 home runs (a Cleveland franchise record) and 118 runs batted in. Thome was signed by the Phillies as a free agent on December 3, 2002. In his first season in the National League in 2003, he had an outstanding season and tied for the major-league lead with 47 home runs and career-high 131 runs batted. On June 21, 2004, he hit his 400th career home run against the Cincinnati Reds for a total of 42 on the season. He has 423 career home runs and should become a member of the 500 Home Run Club. Barring injury, he could reach this milestone by 2006. Thome has hit 30 or more home runs in nine consecutive seasons through 2004.

I conducted an interview with the outgoing Thome in the Phillies dugout during his visit at the end of July 2004. He looked at the pennant stretch and getting to the postseason as a challenge—fun and exciting. He talked about postseasons past and playing with Cleveland in the 1995 and 1997 World Series.

Conversation with Jim Thome

Manager Tony LaRussa believes the game becomes easier in a pennant stretch because the finish line is in sight to provide a tangible goal. You've been in the chase many times; how do you see it?

Jim Thome interviewed in the dugout at Pro Player Stadium.

Obviously, I think the finish line is out there. I think once you get into the second half of the season, I would definitely agree. Once you see the end approaching, you know the goal is to get there. Especially when you're blessed and fortunate to be in a pennant race, and you're on a good club; that's the reason why we all play. That's the reason it becomes fun and exciting because you know you have a chance to play in the postseason. When we start in spring training, it is a long haul to get to the end and once you get near the end, it kind of makes everything more worthwhile, and what you've done all year that much more gratifying.

How do you react to the pennant race pressure?
Well, I think you don't. The best way to describe it is you don't and you just play every day. You understand that each game is very important and you go out and try to do the best you can. And when you get everybody together, and you try to make that puzzle into the big picture—make that one piece fit here, one piece fit there; that's when you know you reached the ultimate at the end.

What is the mood like in the clubhouse as you make a postseason run?
I think it's very exciting and when you're in a pennant race it seems

like you're always at the ballpark because you're having fun. You get there early and do the important things you need to do to make your club better, and to make yourself a better player. I've always said, it's the most exciting time there is when you're competing to get to the postseason.

In 1995 you had an outstanding season with a .314 batting average and 25 home runs. What was it like playing in your first postseason against Boston?

It was a dream come true; I just think it was a dream come true every time you watch the postseason on TV and you get that opportunity to play in the postseason. It was a tremendous feeling; there's no better feeling.

Do you remember Game 3 at Boston when you swept the series with an 8–2 win?

Yes, yes. Getting back to playing in the postseason and to contribute, and do something special, especially in those types of situations is why I think we all play. In Game 3, I remember hitting a two-run home run off Tim Wakefield in the second inning that gave us a 2–0 lead. It was just awesome taking the series in three games and beating Boston at their ballpark.

Toughest Boston pitcher you faced in that series?

Back then probably Tim Wakefield. His knuckleball was a tough pitch and I remember when I hit that home run off him, I actually got a knuckleball that was up. I just remember him being really tough.

Talk about the 1995 League Championship Series against Seattle.

They had just come off that great series with the Yankees and their emotions were high. The fans out in Seattle were pumped up and I had never seen them that noisy and into it. I just remember going into the Kingdome and the fans were loud, they were excited and what a good series. I remember Kenny Lofton scoring on that wild pitch from second base that put us ahead in Game 6 and then we put the game away by scoring three runs in the eighth inning. We beat Seattle that game 4–0 to play in the World Series. All around, great pitching and great defense won that series.

In Game 5, Cleveland was trailing 2–1 when you hit a two-run home run off Chris Bosio that turned into a game-winner.

That was awesome; I think emotions were high, you know, and usually in situations like that one big hit can kind of put you ahead. And I think that happened. Hitting that home run was awesome, tremendous and the best feeling you could have. We had a great team and it was a special time for sure.

Describe the experience of playing in your first World Series against Atlanta in 1995.

The best, I mean, when you get the opportunity to go to a World Series, it's like you always dream about as a kid and when you finally get there, your emotions are high and everything is so tremendous.

Having to face pitchers like Glavine, Maddux, Avery and Smoltz in the '95 World Series, who was the most difficult to hit against?

Well, I think in that series I would say both Glavine and Maddux were very tough on us. I think good pitching is what helped them win the series. They were both tough on me personally. I think I got a base hit off Maddux up the middle. I might've scored either the tying run or the go-ahead run. In Game 6, Glavine pitched a shutout, so he was just as tough as Maddux. I would say both of them were right there.

What was it like facing their closer, Mark Wohlers?

Wohlers threw very hard; he had great stuff and was very tough. I think their pitching really took over in that series.

Was Game 6 a disappointment when Glavine threw a one-hitter and ended the series with a 1–0 win?

Well, I think it was a disappointment from the emotions, but I wasn't disappointed because we got there. We were fortunate to be in that situation, to get into the World Series and made it to Game 6. I don't look at the experience as a disappointment; it was just the fact of disappointment from not winning.

In describing your first World Series experience you said, "You always dream about it as a kid." In those dreams what was the outcome of the World Series?

Obviously to win. Your dream is to win the World Series and maybe get the game-winning hit in the ninth inning or make a great defensive play. I grew up a Cubs fan, but had dreamed about playing in the World Series with the Indians. We had gone to the postseason a couple of times, so the dream was there; we just didn't complete it.

Do you recall Game 5, when Cleveland beat the Braves and Maddux 5–4, and you broke a 2–2 tie in the sixth inning?

I remember that game and Maddux threw me a pretty good pitch [a change-up] that I hit up through the middle, and it actually was a pretty big hit in the game. I felt good about being able to contribute and help us win that game.

In 1996 you play in the division series and get eliminated by the Orioles. Did you expect to play in the World Series that year?

I think you always expect to play in the World Series when you play in the postseason. After being there in '95, we kind of expected that we would play in the World Series again. We just didn't get the opportunity that year. I broke my hamate bone in that series, so I really didn't do a whole lot. I was hurt and kept playing, but I was really a nonfactor because I was playing hurt.

What was it like beating the Yankees in the '97 division series?

It was awesome defeating the Yankees in the best of five series. It was probably one of the biggest accomplishments we made, because it was against the Yankees. It was just a great series and it went to five games. It was a tremendous feeling and our emotions were high coming into that series.

Do you recall the grand slam you hit off David Cone in Game 6?

That was awesome. I remember everything just seemed to stop and Yankee Stadium became so quiet. I had never seen the fans that silent and it was a great feeling.

Toughest Yankees pitchers you faced in that series?

Rivera and Stanton. Rivera was especially tough with that hard cutter. He's hard to face because he has that good cutter. As a lefty, he handles left-handed hitters pretty well. We battled and we battled, and I had some good at-bats against him. I think we played good defense and had really good pitching in that series, and that helped us win.

Which was a better club—the '97 or the '95 team?

Both were very different. One team wasn't expected to play in the postseason, the other club was. The '95 club was magical; the '97 club didn't know it was going to the playoffs. I think both years were very special and very unique for sure. The '95 season was magical; it was like a dream, a magical moment and we knew we would play in the World Series. Our '97 club wasn't expected to go to the World Series and it just worked out for us. We had better hitting in '95 and better defense in '97.

In the '97 league championship series, Cleveland defeated the Orioles in six games. Was that a tough series?

That was a tough series because all of the games that we won were decided by one run and it could've gone either way. I remember I didn't hit well against Baltimore, but we had great pitching and our defense was outstanding.

In the 1997 World Series, Cleveland had a one-run lead in the bottom of the ninth in Game 7. What do you recall as you headed out to first base to begin the inning?

I was thinking that everyone in the world was watching the World Series, and we needed only three more outs to become the world champions. This is what you've dreamed about ever since you were a kid.

Game 7 was decided in the 11th inning as the Marlins win the title.

Well, that was an exciting World Series and we got to Game 7, and once you get to Game 7, anything can happen. They got a couple of big hits, a couple of breaks and we weren't fortunate enough to get the breaks—they did. And we went seven games, you know; flip a coin and anybody can win at that point.

Did the cold weather and snow in Cleveland favor the Indians?

No, no because you never play baseball in that kind of weather during the World Series. Nobody had the advantage. When you get to the World Series anybody can win it. It's a short series and everybody is pumped up, and either team can get hot at that moment.

Do you feel you contributed in the '97 World Series?

Definitely. I had the opportunity to play and I hit well in that series. I hit a couple of home runs that helped our club, and that's always a plus.

Most memorable postseason?

I don't think any particular postseason stands out; they're all unique. I've had the opportunity to play in many postseasons, you know, and all of them for sure have been memorable.

Craig Biggio
ASTROS LEADER AND GOLD GLOVE WINNER
7-Time NL All-Star, 4-Time Gold Glove Winner

> "The '98 team was probably the biggest disappointment. We had a team that could've beat the Yankees. Obviously, we didn't get there; we ran into Kevin Brown and he pretty much dominated us, but that's the way it goes in the postseason. The 1998 postseason was probably the biggest disappointment in my career." —Craig Biggio

Craig Allen Biggio was Houston's first-round selection in the June 1987 draft. He joined Single-A Asheville of the South Atlantic League in the summer of 1987 and hit .375 with nine home runs and 49 runs batted in, and played 64 games for the Tourists. He began the 1988 campaign at Triple-A Tucson and was hitting .320 with 90 hits in 77 games when his contract was purchased by Houston on June 26. His first big-league hit came on June 29 off Orel Hershiser.

Biggio completed his first full season with a .257 batting average with 114 hits, 13 home runs and 60 runs batted in, and he led all major-league catchers with 21 stolen bases. In 1990, he became the first Astros catcher ever to lead the team in batting, finishing with a .276 average, 153 hits and 25 stolen bases. In 1991, he became the first Astros catcher selected to the All-Star team, and led the club in hitting for the second consecutive season with a .295 average.

Biggio played 162 games in 1992 with a .277 batting average, 170 hits, scored 96 runs and became the first player in major-league history to make the All-Star team at both catcher (1991) and second base (1992). In 1993 he had another outstanding season with a .287 batting average, 175 hits, scored 98 runs and set a club record for home runs by a second baseman with 21. He was selected to the National League All-Star Team for the third time in 1994 and led the league with a career-high 39 stolen bases. He had a .318 batting average with 44 doubles and earned his first Gold Glove Award with a .988 fielding percentage.

From 1995 through 1998 he continued to post MVP–type statistics, and in 1998 had his most outstanding season with a .325 batting average (his career-high), 210 hits, scored 123 runs and drove in 88 runs. That season he combined power and speed, and joined Hall of Famer Tris Speaker as the only players in the 20th century to collect 50 or more doubles and 50 or more stolen bases—Biggio finished 1998 with a club record 51 doubles and a career-high 50 stolen bases. He was voted the club's Most Valuable Player for the second consecutive year and the third time in his career (1995), and finished fifth in the Baseball Writers voting for the league MVP.

Biggio became only the sixth player in major-league history to have back-to-back seasons with 50 or more doubles, breaking his own club record with 56 (a major-league record) in 1999. That season he had a .294 batting average with 188 hits and scored 123 runs. In 2000 he was on the disabled list for the first time in his 17-year career. From 2001 through 2004, Biggio has had consistent batting statistics, averaging 160 or more hits each season and has played three positions during his career—catcher, second base and center field.

Biggio has had a magnificent 17-year career with the Houston Astros with a career .286 batting average, scoring 1,603 runs and approaching 3,000 hits (2,639 hits through 2004). Barring injuries or retirement, he could reach this milestone in three full seasons.

I met up with Biggio in the Astros clubhouse at Pro Player Stadium during the 2004 season. He talked about his disappointment in Houston's postseason play. He reflected on the 1998 club as being a real talented team that should've gone to the World Series. That loss to San Diego in the division series in '98 was his biggest disappointment.

CONVERSATION WITH CRAIG BIGGIO

You've played your entire 17-year big-league career with Houston as a catcher, second baseman and in center field. Will you play any position to help your team make it to the postseason?

The big leagues are a little different, I mean, obviously, you get here by playing a certain position and I've been a little different from the standpoint that I started out as a catcher, and made the adjustment to second base and now at center field. When the organization asks me to do some things, I go out there and do it. And I take a lot of pride from that standpoint alone. I guess you do what you got to do for your team and what you got to do to stay here.

As a 7-time all-star and in 1998 you became only the second player (joining Tris Speaker) to collect 50 or more doubles and 50 or more stolen bases in the same season. With all your great statistics, would you rather have the opportunity to win the World Series?

Yes. That's the ultimate goal; that's why you put a uniform on every day. The goal is to play in the World Series and hopefully get what the Marlins got in 2003, and that's a World Series ring.

What did you see in the Marlins' unexpected championship season?

They had a good team; they had good pitching and good defense, and it took them a long way. Obviously, they play the game the right way and they got some good arms. If you have a good team and you stay healthy, and things go your way, anything can happen. They had a good team.

During the off-season, when you heard Houston obtained Clemens and Pettitte, what were you thinking?

Well, that just solidified our staff. I mean, it takes our staff from three horses to five and it's kind of like the Cubs or Marlins—what they had. You get five quality starters, you get a chance to win every time you go out there and play.

Do you see this talented and experienced team playing in the postseason?

Well, I mean, you got to stay healthy and injury-free, and go out there and play well. We have to get there first; we haven't accomplished anything yet. We have to go out there and play good baseball, and hopefully we'll get there. Then if we do, hopefully get a little luck on our side, we'll get to the postseason.

With Houston being a favorite in many polls, would you be disappointed to not compete in the postseason?

That's the ultimate goal and obviously we believe in our team. We believe we have a good team, but like I've said, it's not going to be for a lack of effort that guys are going to go out there and play, and battle and hopefully we'll get there. Once we get there, the goal is to play in the World Series.

You've been to the postseason in 1997–1999 and in 2001. Did you expect a better outcome with any team in those years?

The '98 team was probably the biggest disappointment. We had a team that could've beat the Yankees. Obviously, we didn't get there; we ran into Kevin Brown and he pretty much dominated us, but that's the way it goes in the postseason. The 1998 postseason was probably the biggest disappointment in my career.

Why do you think the '98 club should've done better?

Because we had a great team. Offensively we had a dominant lineup and had Randy Johnson, and a couple of good starting pitchers. We had a chance to win, but unfortunately we didn't get it done.

Craig Biggio warming up at Pro Player Stadium.

What was the makeup of the 1998 team?

We had Randy Johnson; Billy Wagner was the closer. A lot of guys had some great years: Carl Everett was there; Bagwell had a huge year, and Caminiti and Alou contributed. We had a great team and weren't able to get it done in the postseason.

You still feel the team should've done better in the 1998 postseason?

Well, once again, the best team doesn't always win. You got to go out there and play, and unfortunately for us, Kevin Brown had two great games against us. He was tremendous and you have to tip your hat to him. In a best-of-five-games series anything can happen. We couldn't beat Kevin Brown twice and we had a nasty shadow game in San Diego for our other loss, but that's the way it goes, and there's nothing you can do about it.

You find Kevin Brown tough to hit against?

He's pretty good; he's one of the dominant right-handers and our team was pretty much a dominant right-handed hitting lineup, and that didn't help our cause.

Talk about your team. Some of your strengths and weaknesses you've observed.

Every team has a weakness. You go to spring training and there were only two jobs available, and that was in the bullpen. Well, we have good starting pitchers, we have a good offense, and we'll need good defense and a closer to have a pretty good team. It's up to the organization to find out what we really need.

Was losing Billy Wagner a huge loss?

Well, he's done a great job. The thing you miss about Wagner is he had 77 shutout innings, and a guy like [that], as nasty as he is, those innings are hard to replace. Hopefully your starters can go out there and the other guys can contribute as well.

What is it going to take to get to the postseason again?

Everybody on this team knows their role, they know their responsibility, they know their job and just going out there, and hopefully executing and getting it done. We don't have a lot of speed, where guys are going to steal bases, but we have a good offense, good power and good pitching.

With the addition of Clemens and Pettitte, do you think it's a lock that Houston will play in the postseason?

No. Nothing is a lock; there are no guarantees on anything. Baseball is a humbling game; it will knock you down when you think you're on top of the mountain and crumble you in a heartbeat. [Laughs.]

Describe the mood in the clubhouse this season and how do you keep loose during a long season?

You have to focus on the main goal and that is to go out there and win games. You have to prepare yourself for a marathon. That's the way it is, a marathon for eight months. We have a good assortment of older guys and younger guys in here, and I think if you look at the guys on the staff, you know who they are. They know what's expected of them and what they need to do. And your everyday players know what their job is and their responsibility, and we all help each other out. If something needs to be said, I go out and say it, and it is as simple as that. Sometimes you have to pull someone on the side and help him out a little bit when they're having a hard time. You do the little things to keep the team together and encourage each other in the clubhouse. As a veteran you've learned to respect the game. You have to play hard, you run every ground ball out, every fly ball out, you don't show anybody up and that's what it's all about. And fortunately we have a good clubhouse and the guys respect each other.

What does Houston need to do to play in the postseason?

We got to just play well and understand that it's about a team; it's about everybody picking each other up and when pitchers aren't doing well, the offense got to pick them up, and when the offense isn't doing well, the pitchers got to pick them up. You have to catch the ball; throw to the right bases, run the bases right and hopefully get a couple of breaks your way, and maybe get lucky and get there.

Any other National League teams you've observed that have the characteristics to play in the postseason?

I've observed a lot of good teams. The Marlins have a good team and they're the team to beat because they won the World Series in 2003. There are a lot of good teams that are out there. The Cubs have great starting pitching, a closer and a good lineup. The Braves are a great team— 12 straight pennants say something for that team. They've lost some pitchers, but somehow manage to replace them with other good players. The Cardinals are very good; they have a dominant lineup, good pitching and play good defense.

You've played 17 years with Houston. What do you hope to accomplish before you leave the game?

I play the greatest game in the world against the greatest athletes and I dream about getting a World Series ring. A World Series ring is what it's all about. I've played 17 years in the big leagues and to get a ring would be the ultimate goal.

Larry Bowa
THE PHILLIES FANATIC—MANAGER, 1980 CHAMPIONSHIP SEASON
5-Time NL All-Star and 2 Gold Gloves

> *"My dream was always that I would get the last out. 'A ground ball to Larry Bowa, he picks it up, throws to first base and they win the World Series.' It didn't come out that way, but we did win the World Series."* —Larry Bowa

Lawrence Robert Bowa has demonstrated consistency in his major-league career, both as a solid player and as a successful manager. He played 20 years professionally, including 16 in the major leagues with the Phillies, but along the way he made stops with the Cubs and the Mets.

He spent four years in the minor leagues and jumped from Triple-A ball to the major leagues in 1970. In his first season with the Phillies he hit .250 with 137 hits. In 1971, he hit .249 with 162 hits and had the best fielding percentage in the major leagues (.987, 11 errors). In 1972 he broke his own major-league record for fielding (.9874 fielding percentage) with just nine errors and won his first Gold Glove, and led the major leagues with 13 triples. He was on the disabled list in 1973 with a broken left leg and missed 40 games.

Bowa was selected as the starting shortstop on the 1974 National League All-Star team and had a .275 batting average, 184 hits, scored 97 runs and played 162 games that season. In 1975 he had a career-high .305 batting average with 178 hits and was selected to the National League All-Star Team for the second time. In 1976 he was selected to the National League All-Star Team and led National League shortstops in fielding with a .975 fielding percentage. In 1977 and 1978, Bowa's batting average improved from .280 (1977) to .294 (1978) and he led the Phillies with a career-high 192 hits and won his second Gold Glove, leading National League shortstops with a .986 fielding percentage (10 errors) in 1978.

Bowa set a major-league record for highest fielding percentage for a shortstop, .991 (six errors) in 1979. He tied the National League record for most seasons leading the league in fielding percentage—five—and was selected starting shortstop for the National League All-Star Team for the third time. In 1980, he was the starting shortstop on the world champion Phillies, hitting .375 with nine hits and starting a World Series-record seven double plays.

Bowa played his final season with the Phillies in 1981 and had a .283 batting average with the fewest errors by a starting shortstop (11 errors). He was traded to the Cubs in 1982 and he played 14 games for the Mets in 1985. He completed his career with a .260 batting average and a .980 fielding percentage.

Bowa began his major-league managerial career with San Diego from 1987 through 1988 and posted an 81–127 record. He was named the manager of the Phillies on November 1, 2000, and he accumulated 252 wins in his first three seasons (most by a Phillies manager in his first 3 seasons since 1915–17). He was named 2001 National League Manager of the Year by the Baseball Writers Association of America. In 2003, the Phillies made a wild-card run throughout the season and into the last week of September, finishing in third place with an 86–76 record.

I conducted an interview with the articulate Bowa in the manager's office at Pro Player Stadium in late July 2004. He spoke about his most memorable postseason as a player in the 1980 league championship series when he started an eighth-inning rally in Game 5 off Nolan Ryan. And winning the 1980 World Series and earning a ring was the pinnacle moment in his career. Bowa was dismissed by the Phillies at the end of the 2004 season.

CONVERSATION WITH LARRY BOWA

You played 20 years professionally, most years with the Phillies, and you made stops along the way with the Cubs and Mets. What was the feeling of being part of a pennant race?

That's what you live for during the season. You want games that are meaningful in August, September and October; you'd much rather play games that mean something than just playing out the string.

Most exciting pennant race?

I would say in 1980 with Montreal and us. Schmidt hit a big home run in Montreal and we had to win two out of three up there to get in. We were able to defeat Montreal to get to the postseason.

Have you observed any heroes born in a pennant race?

Well, that's a good question. We might've had one in Philadelphia in Marty Bystrom. We called him up and he went 5–0 in the month of September. So here's a guy that was in the minor leagues all year. He got an opportunity to help us out and rattled off five quick wins.

Have you seen the same type of player in the postseason?

I think a guy like Doyle for the Yankees. I think Denny Doyle played for Boston and Brian Doyle played with the Yankees. I remember Brian Doyle hitting .500 in the '78 World Series with the Yankees and that was amazing.

As a player, what was your most exciting postseason?

The Houston series in 1980 without a doubt. All of the games except one went into extra innings, and then we played in the World Series against Kansas City. We were even with Houston [two games to two] in a best of five series. Nolan Ryan had a 5–2 lead in the fifth game and the percentage of him blowing a lead in the eighth inning was unbelievable. I remember I was the leadoff hitter and Pete Rose came up to me and he said, "If you get on, we're going to win this game." And I remember starting the inning off with a base hit, and we ended up scoring three runs to tie that game up. Once we got past Ryan, we knew we would win that game and we ended up beating Houston to advance to the World Series.

Most memorable game?

That game was memorable because of the fact that if we beat Nolan Ryan, I felt the momentum would carry over and we would take it in the World Series.

As a player, how did you deal with the pressure of getting to play in the postseason?

You know what? I didn't look at it as pressure; I looked at it as I was having fun. I think all the teams in baseball want to be where you're at. So the pressure, especially for me in '80, was the battle in the playoffs with Houston. I found the World Series to be a piece of cake; the pressure was getting to the World Series.

In 1976 you played against the Big Red Machine in the league championship series. What was it like playing in your first postseason?

Well, I think we were a little bit in awe of that team. So we had never been there and the first time you're there, you're just happy to be there. I think we were happy to be there. And then the Big Red Machine sort of kicked our rear ends. The first time you're there it's a different kind of feeling because you dream about stuff like that, and to see that come true is the greatest feeling. You always dream about playing in the postseason. This is what it's all about; it's about spring training, all the extra hitting and all the extra ground balls, and then once you're there, it's like wow. But sometimes you get caught up in the moment and you're just glad you're there. You forget what you're supposed to do.

Larry Bowa in the dugout at Pro Player Stadium.

You talk about dreams a couple of times. What was the outcome of your dreams?

My dream was always that I would get the last out: "A ground ball to Larry Bowa, he picks it up, throws to first base and they win the World Series." Tug McGraw struck out the center fielder for Kansas City [Willie Wilson] and then to relive that, it wasn't a ground ball to me, but to feel that, [everything stops in slow motion] when he was swinging through the ball, and you look up and it's over. It's like oh my god; this is what every athlete wants ... to get that ring. And everything sort of just slowed down for a moment. You're jumping up and down, and you can hear the fans, but for that moment of time it just like freezes and it's unbelievable.

What do you recall about the '76 Reds club?

That club had everything—power, speed, pitching, defense, and they had Pete Rose, Joe Morgan, Johnny Bench, Davey Concepcion, Griffey and Tony Perez. They had it all; there was no weakness on that team.

Do you remember Game 4 of the 1977 league championship series with the Dodgers leading two games to one, and the Phillies leading by two runs with two outs in the ninth inning? How did the outcome of that game affect you?

It was disappointing because the play that hurt us happened when Danny Ozark didn't make his defensive move late in that game. Greg [Luzinski] was never in the game in the ninth inning. Jerry Martin was always in there for defense. And I remember Danny Ozark saying, "I'm going to leave Greg in and maybe he can celebrate with the team." It never did come to that; we didn't celebrate. But the ball that Greg almost caught—I had nothing against Greg; he was a great player, but Jerry Martin was a very good defensive player. He probably would've caught the ball.

Do you recall the events that followed after Luzinski missed the fly ball?

Oh, yeah. Davey Lopes hit a hard ground ball off of Schmidt's glove which came to me and I caught the ball bare-handed, and threw in one motion to first base. Davey Lopes was out, but the umpire called him safe and it was a huge play. Bruce Froemming was the umpire and I think he just automatically figured—and if I was the umpire, I probably would too—that Lopes, as quick as he is, if he hits a ball off an infielder's glove, there's no way anybody else can throw him out. Everything worked perfect, like I was coming to the bag, I caught the ball bare-handed and threw in one motion. And to this day, I still believe he was out. Bruce still thinks he was safe. That game would have changed the outcome of that series.

Was the 1980 season exciting and magical?

That was the ultimate for me—winning the World Series the way we did it. We sort of floundered around through August and all of a sudden we got hot. We just took off and really played together as a team down the stretch. It was an unbelievable season.

What was that club like?

That was a very veteran-oriented club, which was pushed by Dallas Green. Dallas could care less about egos and I remember him benching Garry Maddox; I remember him benching Boone and Luzinski. You're talking about veterans that were super players and they were mad. But what I think it did, it elevated them when they did get back in there. It was like, I'll show you; you made a mistake. But we had guys like Keith Moreland and Lonnie Smith that took their place and they did a great job.

What was the mood of the clubhouse during the pennant stretch?

It was a pretty loose team; it really was. We had a bunch of veteran guys that knew what it took, plus we also knew as a team that was probably going to be our last year together. We read oracles all year that if we don't do it this year in '80, they're going to break that team up because we came close the previous three years. So we knew what was at stake.

In 1980, you had an outstanding postseason hitting .316 against Houston in the LCS. Do you recall Game 5 and hitting against Nolan Ryan in the eighth inning?

Yes, and that was the key at-bat. The thing about it is, it happened so fast. I can remember it. I think I hit the second or third pitch for a single. Bob Boone hit a one-hopper to Nolan Ryan, it went off his glove and just trickled, because Boone didn't run well, and Ryan couldn't make a play. And then Greg Gross dropped a perfect bunt down. So we had the bases loaded within eight pitches. So people ask why they kept Ryan in there? It happened so quickly and then he walked Pete Rose, and we got a big hit from Manny Trillo. But it happened so quickly that Ryan couldn't get anybody out.

In the 1980 World Series you hit .375 with nine hits and scored three runs. Talk about playing in your first World Series and winning the title.

Well, you know, I used to like to play big games and nobody really expected me [on that team] to be the offensive threat. I would hit .260, .270, .280, but I guess because of the lineup we had, I had a pretty good series and stole some bases, and did it all. It was a lot of fun playing in the World Series. People talk about pressure and I thought the pressure was in the Houston series, not the World Series. That was the best World Series.

In 1982 you were traded to the Cubs and you played in your final postseason in the 1984 League Championship Series against San Diego. What do you recall about that series?

It was disappointing because we were up two games to zero. I remember winning the first two games at Wrigley Field and we were on the airplane, and I remember talking to Gary Matthews. We had some young guys on that team—they weren't celebrating, but they were feeling pretty good about themselves. I remember Gary and I were talking and Sarge says, "I hope these guys realize that we still have to win another game." We went to San Diego and they beat us three straight.

You became a major-league manager with San Diego (1987–88) and returned to Philadelphia in 2001. What is it about making a run to the post-season that is exciting or nerveracking?

It's exciting that you got your team in a position to be successful going down the stretch. It was nerveracking as a player if you weren't hitting or not making plays. You could go out and work on it, and you would eventually get up with the bases loaded or make a play that mattered. As a manager, when the umpire says, "Play ball," with the exception of a move or two, it's out of your hands. You got to hope your players are prepared and they go out and do the best they can. It's sort of a helpless feeling that as a manager you have to watch it, but as a player, you could do something about it.

As a manager, is winning and having the opportunity to play in the World Series the essence of baseball?

Yes. It will never be as exciting as a player, but it will be right up there. As a player that's the ultimate. As a manager, I'm sure you feel good about it; it has never happened to me, but I can't imagine it being better than it is for a player.

When you're sitting in the dugout, what are you looking at during the game?

I'm looking at how my pitcher is throwing and whether he's up in the zone. I'm looking at how the other pitcher is throwing. Do you need to get an early run? Do you think your team is going to hit this guy, where you don't have to sacrifice early? When do you make a pitching change? What kind of matchups do you have in the eighth or ninth inning? Who do you have on the bench to come in and hit off certain guys as a pinch hitter? There are a lot of things you look for—the strategy, do you play for a big inning or do you play for a one or two-run inning? If your pitcher is throwing real good, you could win 2–1.

Do you use the same strategy in the postseason?

I would think there would be more of a sense of urgency in the post-season. You have the luxury during the season to stay with your starter, but because it's such a short series, I think you might have to make some moves that you might not make during the regular season.

Having an intense personality and a fierce determination to win, was not playing in the 2003 postseason a big disappointment?

I was very disappointed. I'm always disappointed when I don't win or get to where I want to go. But you know what? Everybody can't get to where you want to go every year. That's why there's only one World Series winner. And that's why you respect it when it happens, because it doesn't happen that much. The team wasn't really ready then and we surprised a lot of people. You know sometimes when you sneak up on people they don't think you're really good, and the next couple of years they think you're pretty good, and you got to win. There's a difference there, but the key to me to get to the postseason—not only do you have to have a good team, you have to be healthy, you can't have a lot of injuries and that takes luck. That takes luck, determination and being good, and you need those three ingredients.

How do you see the 2004 club?

We've been banged up all year and we're still banged up. We're hanging in, but we're banged up. We need our players back—Padilla, Wolf, Wagner and now Madson went on the disabled list. It's hard to play with your second string sometimes, but you know what? That's just the way it is and you got to deal with it.

As you approach the final two months do you see the finish line ahead of you?

Oh yeah. If you get in that position it's right there in front of you and you got to go for it. But getting there sometimes is a little difficult because of the fact that you have a lot of injuries and some guys have subpar years. In spring training when you sit down you say, "This guy is going to do this, this guy is going to do that," and you have an idea. Sometimes those plans don't work out. A guy might hit 30 home runs one year and the next year he hits five. So last year we had four pitchers win 14 games. Four starters, they all pitched over 200 innings. I might have only one pitcher throw 200 innings this year, because of injuries.

What do you love about postseason play?

Competition. The fact that two teams are going after the same prize and only one is going to prevail. And you respect the opponent and you hope they respect you, and may the best team win. That's what it's all about.

Alfonso Soriano
ALL-STAR, SUPERSTAR AND FUTURE HALL OF FAMER
3-Time AL All-Star, 2004 All-Star Most Valuable Player

> *"In the 2001 postseason, in Game 4, when I hit a home run off Sasaki [Seattle's closer], that was the best moment for me and I'll never forget that I hit a home run off Sasaki to win the game."* —Alfonso Soriano

Alfonso Soriano was signed with the Yankees on September 29, 1998, after playing the 1996–97 seasons in Japan. He made his United States debut in the Arizona Fall League, hitting .254 with six home runs and 28 runs batted in while playing 34 games for Grand Canyon. He spent most of the 1999 season at Double-A Norwich where he hit .305 with 110 hits, 15 home runs, and played 20 games at Triple-A Columbus. He was a September call-up with the Yankees.

Soriano played the majority of the 2000 season at Triple-A Columbus, hitting .290 with 133 hits and scored 90 runs. That season he played 22 games with the Yankees and hit a solo home run in his first start of the season on April 8 at Seattle. In his first full season in the big leagues in 2001, he batted .268 with 18 home runs, 73 runs batted in and 43 stolen bases.

In 2002, he had an impressive sophomore campaign, hitting .300 with a league leading 209 hits and scoring 128 runs. That season Soriano hit 39 home runs, drove in 102 runs and collected 41 stolen bases in 156 games. He continued to have another outstanding season in 2003, hitting .290 with 198 hits, 38 home runs, 91 runs batted in, 114 runs scored and

35 steals in 156 games. He became only the third player in major-league history to put together consecutive seasons with at least 35 home runs and 35 stolen bases.

In Game 4 of the 2001 league championship series against Seattle, Soriano hit a two-run ninth-inning walk-off home run and became the first rookie to hit a game-ending home run in postseason history. He had his second game-winning hit of the postseason with his 12th inning single that knocked in the winning run in Game 5 of the 2001 World Series against Arizona.

On February 16, 2004, Soriano was traded to Texas for Alex Rodriguez. He had a .280 batting average with 28 home runs and 170 hits during his first season with the Rangers in 2004. He was selected to the American League All-Star Team for the third time in 2004, hitting a home run off Roger Clemens and was named the All-Star Most Valuable Player.

I conducted an interview with the lanky Soriano in the Rangers clubhouse at Pro Player Stadium during the 2004 season. He talked about his opportunity to learn how to play the game with help from Joe Torre and his teammates. And in his first three seasons in the big leagues, it was an unbelievable experience to play in the postseason each year with the Yankees.

CONVERSATION WITH ALFONSO SORIANO

In 2001, you played your first full season with the Yankees. What did you learn that season?

I learned a lot in my first year in the big leagues and I learned a lot from my teammates and from Joe Torre. I need to work hard every day and I've been working on my pitch selection to improve my hitting.

How did Joe Torre help you when you came to the Yankees?

He taught me how to play the game; he talked to me about different situations in the game. He always told me to focus on the game and play hard every day.

In 2001, you play in your first postseason with 16 hits and two home runs. Talk about the two-run ninth-inning walk-off home run in Game 4 of the ALCS against Seattle?

That was a great moment in my career. Being in that situation in the playoff and to be able to hit a home run off Sasaki was exciting. He was difficult to hit against and hitting that home run was good for me.

What was it like playing in your first postseason?
It was exciting because it was my first time playing in the postseason, and my teammates told me to have fun and enjoy the playoffs.

Who were some of the players on that Yankees team that helped you at the beginning of your career?
Jeter always talked to me and helped me during my first year. He told me to play hard and focus on improving myself every game. He would help me improve my game by pointing out things that he did to make himself a better player.

What do you recall about playing Arizona in the 2001 World Series?
That was an exciting World Series because that was my first one, too, and I was so excited that so much happened in my first year in the big leagues. To be able to help my team and play in the World Series was a very good moment for me.

Toughest pitcher you faced in that World Series?
Randy Johnson was tough and very intimidating. He's a tall guy who throws very hard (97 or 98 mph) and has a very good slider. He keeps the ball close to the plate and that is why it was difficult for me. Schilling is another tough pitcher, but not as tough as Johnson.

In 2002, you had a breakout season with a .300 batting average, league-leading 209 hits and 128 runs scored, and 39 home runs. What contributed to that outstanding season?
I don't know. I just worked hard and played hard all the time. I was very focused and like I've said before, I had a very good season and everything worked for me that year. I think that was my best season.

In the 2002 postseason the Angels eliminated the Yankees in the division series. What happened to you and the team in that playoff series?
I was surprised a little bit when they beat us in the postseason, but the Angels were a good team, with good pitching, and everybody in that lineup got hot during the playoffs. We had never been in that position before, where we were always behind, and it was difficult to come back in that series.

Alfonso Soriano in the dugout at Pro Player Stadium.

In 2003, you have another outstanding season with a .290 batting average, 198 hits, 38 home runs and score 114 runs. You get to play in your third consecutive postseason and second World Series. Did you think you would have an easy time against the Marlins?

That World Series against the Marlins was a little difficult because they had better pitching and better pitch command. That pitching staff was very young and they had a lot of emotion. Beckett was tough because he had a good fastball and breaking ball too. That team was very emotional and had breaks at the right time. That is probably the reason they won the World Series. You want to have fun when you play in the World Series. The focus is to play hard during the regular season so we can be in the World Series. When you get to the World Series, you want to win, but you want it to be fun.

You have the opportunity to see Mariano Rivera pitch throughout the season and postseason. What can you say about Rivera?

I think Mariano Rivera is the best closer that I've seen. He has a good fastball and a good cutter. I think he's the best in baseball. He knows how to keep the ball close to the plate and he's the best.

Do you miss playing for the Yankees?
No, no. I feel comfortable here with Texas.

When you learned you were traded to Texas on February 16, 2004, how did you feel?
I felt like that situation was part of the game. I felt bad because I didn't have my teammates, my friends or my apartment, and there were many things in New York that I wouldn't be able to see anymore. Guys that helped me like Jeter, Rivera, Posada, Bernie Williams, Clemens and Pettitte. Those guys always talked to me about offensive situations of the game and helped me become a good player. They told me it was a hard game; it's a long season, like six months. I should concentrate on my offense and keep my mind on the game. I learned to work hard and focus on getting better.

Why do you think the Yankees are a successful team and get to the postseason every year?
I think it's expected that you're better than the other teams and the owner is only focused on winning. The owner wants the best players, guys that only want to win. I think that is why the Yankees always go to the postseason. They have a great team, they have great pitching, they have a great offense, they have everything. Mr. Steinbrenner is good because he spends money to win. He's not satisfied unless he wins. Joe Torre is a great manager and got me focused on the game when I came to the Yankees. I feel like he's my father in baseball; he always talks to me and tries to make me better.

Texas is making a run to the postseason in 2004. Talk about the make-up of the team.
I feel so comfortable right here and we have a lot of young talent—a lot of the guys who are good players and play like a team. We have a nice group of players—guys like Michael Young and Blalock, and all my Dominican people. I'm close to everybody on this team.

What is it going to take to get to the postseason this year?
To get to the postseason, this team will have to be consistent all year long. We have to work very hard, play good baseball as a team and we have to be consistent to get into the playoffs. We have good pitching, good

defense and offense, and we have to keep everything together so we can maybe win the division or get in as a wild card.

Many players never get an opportunity to play in the postseason. You've been there the first three years of your career. What can you say about that experience?

It has been important and a great experience to play in the postseason. A lot of players will play their entire career in baseball and never get the opportunity to play in the World Series. In my first three years I was able to go to the playoffs and twice to the World Series. So I thank God that I had the opportunity to play with the Yankees and to play in the World Series. That is something I will always remember.

Most memorable postseason experience?

I will always remember the 2001 postseason when we played Seattle. In the ninth inning at Yankee Stadium, in Game 4, when I hit a game-winning home run off Sasaki [Seattle's closer], Yankee Stadium became so loud and everybody was happy. That was the best moment for me and I'll never forget that I hit a home run off Sasaki to win the game.

Jeff Nelson
THE SET-UP MAN IN PINSTRIPES
2001 AL All-Star

> *"I always enjoyed going to Yankee Stadium and pitching there. We played the Yankees five games and lost the first two. Then we returned home and swept them in the next three games. That had to be the most memorable postseason that I've played in."* —Jeff Nelson

Jeff Nelson was selected by Los Angeles in the 22nd round of the June 1984 free-agent draft. He pitched at Great Falls and Bradenton, making 10 relief appearances with a 0–0 record and a 1.35 earned run average in nine games at Bradenton. He struggled with his control in 1985–86 and had a combined 0–12 record in those two seasons.

In 1987, Nelson was 3–7 with a 5.74 earned run average in 17 appearances (16 starts) at Single-A Salinas. He led San Bernardino in games started (27) and was second in innings pitched (149.1) while picking up eight wins in 1988. He spent the entire 1989 season at Double-A Williamsport, going 7–5 with a 3.31 earned run average in 15 starts. In 1990, Nelson was converted to a reliever and began to dominate the Carolina League, holding opponents to a .214 batting average and had six saves in just 11 relief appearances.

Nelson split the 1991 season between Double-A Jacksonville and Triple-A Calgary, earning seven wins with an overall 2.67 earned run average. He led the entire Mariners minor league system with a combined 19 saves. In his rookie season with the Mariners in 1992, he pitched in relief in 66 games with a 3.44 earned run average and six saves. In 1993, Nelson was tied for third in the American League with 71 appearances and had a 5–3 record. He split the 1994 season between Calgary and Seattle and held his opponents to a 2.26 batting average (right-handed hitters had a .168 batting average).

Nelson had a breakout season in 1995 with a 7-3 record with an outstanding 2.17 earned run average and two saves in 62 relief appearances. He allowed runs in just 12 of 62 games. In 1996 he had a 4–4 record in his first season with the Yankees and appeared in a team-high 73 games. He appeared in a team-high 77 games in 1997, holding opponents to a .191 batting average and prevented 42 of 53 inherited runners from scoring (the best in the American League).

Nelson became the premier set-up man in the American League from 1998 through 2001. In 1998 he prevented 18 of 24 inherited runners from scoring; he made two trips to the disabled list in 1999 and in 2000, and he had a single-season career-high eight wins (2.45 earned run average in 73 appearances). In 2001, Nelson returned to Seattle and held opposing batters to a .136 batting average, which was the lowest among all major-league relievers. He had four wins, a 2.76 earned run average in 69 games and guided Seattle to the postseason for the second time in his career.

Nelson has appeared in the postseason eight years (1995–2003), winning four World Series championships. He has a 0.79 earned run average in the division series and a career 2.65 earned run average in the postseason. In the 1996 postseason, he tossed three shutout innings in Game 3 of the division series at Texas for his first career postseason win. He became the first pitcher in major-league history to pitch in every game of a four-game World Series in 1999. He pitched in nine games in the 1999 postseason and did not allow a run. In the 2000 postseason, he was 1-0, but was scored on in just two of eight appearances.

Nelson and I met up in the Texas dugout in June 2004. We talked about his postseason experiences with the Mariners and winning four World Series championships with the Yankees.

CONVERSATION WITH JEFF NELSON

Talk about your 12-year career beginning with Seattle in 1992?

I played in the minor leagues for seven years, so it was a long time coming. I was 24, so I was still young, but it was a dream come true. Obviously, ever since you were little, you always dream about playing in the big leagues and it finally happened. In some ways it was a good situation

Jeff Nelson is interviewed in the dugout at Pro Player Stadium (courtesy of Oscar Huete).

or a bad situation—a good situation because we didn't have a good team. I made the team out of spring training and really stayed because we weren't very good. And I think we wound up losing 98 games that year. And I think for guys that are coming up and down, usually it's tough because the teams either need a guy because of an injury or teams are pretty good. So you wind up having a lot of guys like on a so-called elevator. I got lucky that our team wasn't really that great and I was able to stay up the whole year.

Was that a good learning experience?

It was because I got in some great situations as a set-up guy. I even closed in the second half of the year and it was a great experience. I got to play against a lot of guys that I grew up watching and it was exciting.

Who were some of the players you grew up watching that you faced?

Well, I played against Cal Ripken, Jr.; I played against Steve Sax, Bo Jackson, Harold Baines, Mark McGwire and Robin Yount. I played with Goose Gossage and Lance Parrish, and a lot of guys who are Hall of Famers, managers or coaches. And in some ways it's good that I'm still around and in other cases, now I'm getting older because these guys are managers now. [Laughs.]

What was it like pitching for Seattle from 1992 to 1995?

Well, like you've said, it was a learning experience and you're excited about being in the big leagues. Bill Plummer was my manager for the first year in '92. Then the next season it was Lou Piniella with his experience and his career as a manager, and leading the Reds to the World Series in 1990. And it was almost another learning experience, as he wanted to turn the organization around. In 1993, it was a better year as the club won more games than the previous year. In 1994, it was another good year, but then we went on strike, and I think we were a game or two out of first place when we went on strike. Then, of course, the magical season was in 1995 — something nobody thought we could do and that was the first postseason in Seattle history. We were 14 or 15 games out of first place at the beginning of August and the next thing you know, we wind up playing a one-game playoff against Anaheim to see who goes to the first division series. And the last two months in Seattle in '95 was just unbelievable.

Talk about your first division series in 1995.

Well, you finally get to the playoffs with Seattle and it was something the whole city was looking forward to ... it was incredible. And then you're playing the Yankees, the first time they've been back since maybe 1982. So it was two organizations that one finally made it to their first playoff and the other one finally got back in probably 13 years, so it was great. I always enjoyed going to Yankee Stadium and pitching there. We played the Yankees five games and lost the first two and then we came home, and swept them in the next three games. That had to be the most memorable postseason that I've played in.

Who were some of the toughest Yankees hitters you face in the '95 post-season?

Don Mattingly, Wade Boggs and Bernie Williams were pretty tough hitters. I pitched a lot in that series and one time I pitched four innings, and went out for the fifth inning in Game 4, but it was just incredible. I can remember how the fans got into it and how loud they were. I think the Kingdome was probably the loudest and most intimidating place in all of baseball. It was probably by far the loudest indoor stadium that ever was. And then you go to New York and I thought Seattle was loud, and they even got louder for an outside stadium. So your first playoff experience you will always remember.

Then in 1996–2000 you play with the Yankees.
You never expected it because you get to the playoffs for the first time with Seattle in '95 and you figure okay, we're going around, maybe even get further—we got to the LCS that year and the next thing you know, I was on a Mariner caravan, promoting the Mariners for the 1996 season. I was getting the fans ready for the new season and I was in Alaska with Dan Wilson. The next thing you know, I get a call that I was traded along with Tino Martinez to the Yankees. In a lot of ways, my home was there in Seattle. My wife and I had our first child there in 1995 during those playoffs, and we figured I would come back and help the organization, maybe get a step further to the World Series. The next thing you know, you're going to the Yankees, which wound up being not such a bad place to get traded to. So it was exciting, I mean, you're going to another organization, the same dreams you had with Seattle, new aspirations to get that step further and then we wind up going to the World Series in '96. So it was an exciting place, for all the places you could've been traded to, New York by far was the best one.

When you received that phone call that you were traded to the Yankees in '96, how did you react?
I was shocked because I was on a Mariner caravan and I didn't think at all that I would be traded. I made my home in Seattle and I came up through the Mariner organization, and then I wind up getting traded to the most historical organization in all of sports in New York. So I wasn't too disappointed and it was an easy transition, I guess.

What was it like pitching for the Yankees in 1996?
It took a good month for me to get used to everything. The media is such a high level; the team, the fans expect a lot out of you and it took me a month to get used to everything, and finally settle in. And you're around superstars all the time; you're around Yankees Hall of Famers all

the time, even when you come to spring training. And you have Don Mattingly, who missed the World Series by one year when he retired after the '95 season, and the next thing you know, in '96 we go to the World Series. It was just incredible to put on those pinstripes and report to Tampa—first year at the Yankees new spring training complex. It was just a great experience. You definitely felt the awe of being a Yankee. I remember playing against those guys in the minor leagues; they teach a certain attitude and a winning attitude—something that you don't see in a lot of organizations. And I think playing against them, guys always hated them so much because they expect to win, and they walk out on the field all the time with an attitude that they're going to win. It's like an attitude that has been brought and put onto them when they were first signed as a minor leaguer, or out of high school or college. I never had any experience with an owner like Mr. Steinbrenner and you wind up respecting this guy even more for the job that he does for the organization, and for the fans in New York. And it was great playing for him.

It seems like the Yankees play in the postseason every year.
Well, Mr. Steinbrenner has a desire to win and I think you would love an owner like that; he wants to win and keep up that historic presence that the Yankees bring—23 championships before we won in '96, and he wanted to bring it back for the fans and the City of New York. And when you have a guy that is probably in the highest sports city in all of sports and the most notable, that he could go out and spend that money, and build a championship team, it's something that he loves doing.

Talk about your first championship season in 1996.
That was Joe Torre's first year there and the first year for all of their coaches, except Willie Randolph. And I think everybody was getting used to each other. David Cone was in his second year with the club and Andy Pettitte was finally coming up. We had John Wetteland there and Mariano Rivera was in his second year with the team. We made a lot of changes that year and it was like getting used to each other again—everybody was getting used to the coaches. So we're all going through a learning experience and it probably took us a little time to adjust. You look at Tino Martinez and it took him a good month because he was replacing a legend in Don Mattingly. And he heard it from the fans for probably a good month and he had a terrific year, and wound up being a terrific Yankee. But I think that season was a big learning experience for everyone.

In the 1996 postseason you pitched in three games in your first World Series against Atlanta. What was it like facing the Braves?

Well, it was incredible [to get] to the World Series for the first time. And to see how much media was around and how the fans got into it was exciting. We got beat pretty bad the first two games and we go to Atlanta, and they were writing us off. They were saying that we shouldn't have been in the World Series, that the Yankees don't deserve to be there. And the next thing you know, we win four in a row. So that was exciting and then you get to face three of the best starters in the game—in Maddux, Smoltz and Glavine. And how they can just dominate a game. They were incredible to watch and it was definitely fun. It was a lot easier pitching than it was watching all throughout my playoff career. You're sitting on the edge of your seat and then you finally get up, and at least you have some control when you're out there. And when you're on the bench watching or out in the bullpen watching, it's pretty tough and pretty tense.

Who do you recall facing in the '96 World Series?

I remember facing Andruw Jones. He was young then and that might've been his first year in the big leagues. I can remember the times and when I pitched, but it's hard to remember who I faced. I remember I pitched in that game when Jim Leyritz hit that big home run. I pitched two innings in that game and gave us a chance to come back. I remember pitching in the first two games and it was actually Game 4 that I pitched the two innings that we came back on them. Some of the guys you remember facing, but a lot of them you don't remember too much. You just remember the experience.

What was the '97 postseason like?

We get to the division series and Cleveland beat us in five games and that was something we never thought would happen. [Laughs.] We were winning in Game 4, and we felt we had it. Mariano Rivera was in his first year as a closer and did an outstanding job the whole year, and he gave up that home run to Alomar and it kind of broke our back. And we came out the next day and lost. It was one of those things that we felt we were going to the LCS and we felt we were going to win the World Series again. Like I've said, they teach you all through the minor leagues and the big leagues that you don't expect to fail as a Yankee. That's why they're so tough to beat and never rattled. You go through experiences in New York during the season that most people don't even see until you get to the playoffs, as far as the media, as far as the fans—the expectations of winning all the time. So when it's time for the playoffs, you're almost used to that. And in '97, we thought we're going again. And after coming back and winning four in a row from Atlanta in '96, we made a few more changes and bring in some other players, and you figure you're going to the World Series again. And the next thing you know, you're humbled and you realize that when you get to the playoffs anything can happen, and that's what happened.

How did you pitch in the '97 division series?

I pitched well. I pitched in I think two or three games that playoff and had a good year throughout the season, and I pitched in that Game 4. I was in the locker room just watching and Rivera was in, and he was automatic then. At the time, I was putting my tennis shoes on and getting ready to go out to the dugout to watch the final out. And you're sitting there and you can remember the home run going to the opposite field. They tie it up and go ahead and win. It was humbling and I can guarantee you that.

When you look at your success as a set-up man, it seems you could've been a successful closer in the postseason.

[Laughs.] A lot of set-up guys could be closers, but it was great setting up for Rivera and he probably is the greatest closer in the game, and the guy you want in the postseason. And I had a good time setting up for him.

After losing the division series in '97, were you hungry in '98?

We were hungry in '98 and the funny thing of it is, we started out 0-4 and we go out to the West Coast, and we lose our first four games. We didn't get our first win until the second game in Oakland. We got swept in Anaheim; we go to Oakland and lose the first game, and we finally win that fifth game. All the papers back in New York are saying that Joe Torre could be on his way out and the next thing you know, we won 114 games. That was a memorable year; that was one of those years that you go out and again you knew you were going to win, and it was fun. We stepped on the field, no matter what we did, and if we were behind, we knew we were coming back. If we were ahead, we knew they weren't coming back. And it was just an exciting year. You win 114 games and there's not too many times that you lose.

Was that your best year with the Yankees?

That was the best team year that I've had. And when I was in Seattle in 2001, we won 116 games. But that year in '98 we finished it off. We went right through the playoffs and we ended up sweeping San Diego in four games in the World Series. When we played Cleveland that year, I think they had the feeling that, okay, we were going to get them back for what they did to us in '97. But you know what? The good part about that season in '97, when Cleveland went to the World Series and took it to seven games—I think as a player when you get beat by someone, and they go to the World Series, you feel you got beat by a better team. When you get beat by a team that goes to the LCS and loses out, it's probably a little tougher loss because then you feel like we should've been there; we would've had a better chance to go to the World Series.

What was the make-up of that '98 team?

We had David Wells, David Cone, Graeme Lloyd; it was just a fun team in the clubhouse. It was a great feeling that we knew we would win all the time. We had a team picture at the end of the year and they printed the picture before the last game, and they assumed we're going to lose the last game. So they just put 113 wins and 48 losses. We ended up winning that last game, so they had to go ahead and change that team picture because they compared us to the 1927 Yankees or something like that. But it was fun; every single year with the Yankees they added another two, three or four players that had never been to the World Series. David Justice came to us and when he came to us, he was a spark. He was like our MVP that year. Chili Davis was another guy that was there in '98 and was a great guy to play with. You play with Tim Raines, Darryl Strawberry and Dwight Gooden. You're playing with guys that you grew up watching and you always wondered what it was like to be their teammate. You get to be their teammate and it was exciting.

What was it like pitching against San Diego in the '98 World Series?

In the '98 World Series I became the only pitcher in the history of baseball to pitch in all four games and that was some record that I was the only pitcher to pitch in a four-game sweep in the World Series. But you're pitching against a guy like Tony Gwynn [another Hall of Famer] who you never played in interleague play and you realize this guy is a great hitter. This guy hits anything you threw and it seemed like he knew what the pitchers were doing. He had a great approach at the plate and it was just fun watching him.

How did you pitch to Gwynn?

You have to be lucky and hope he hits the ball to one of your fielders. He's pretty tough to strike out and he makes a lot of contact. As a pitcher, you just hope he hits it at somebody.

In the 1999 World Series you pitch in four games without allowing a hitter to reach base and with three strikeouts. Your performance provided the Yankees with another championship.

It was easier going out there and pitching, and I knew I never wanted to be the goat. I never wanted to be the guy that gives up the key hits or be taken out of a game. And it's tougher sitting in that locker room or on the bench, or in the bullpen watching it, because you have no control and it's really tense. The fans are going at it, and it's easier when you have that ball in your hands. You have a little bit of control of what is going on when you come in to pitch.

After the '98 season we had 114 wins and you're coming into spring training with the exact same team. Next thing you know, the first day in camp, we get Roger Clemens and we give Toronto David Wells, Graeme Lloyd and Homer Bush, and like wow, this is unbelievable. So Roger Clemens agrees to come to New York in 1999 [during spring training] and he's looking for his first World Series. We had a great season in '99 and win the World Series again. It was exciting to see him get his first ring and playing with one of the greatest pitchers in the game.

Which team was better—the '98 or '99 team?

The '98 team won 114 games and we finished it off. I think that team was definitely better. But we won the World Series again in '99 and we swept Atlanta. We swept Texas in the division series. We played Boston in the LCS—what everybody loves, a Yankees–Red Sox postseason series, and we beat those guys. Only because we won 114 games in '98 that you would probably consider them better than the '99 team.

Talk about the 2000 Subway Series.

That was my favorite World Series because it was against the Mets. It was something I think maybe the rest of the world didn't care too much about, but as far as the state of New York, it was a lot of fun to see. I collected lots of memorabilia from the 2000 Subway Series. It was always a big deal when we played the Mets during interleague play. The 2000 World Series had the Clemens and Piazza deal.

What about Clemens hitting Piazza in his head during the season?

Obviously as players, we really don't get into all the media hoopla that everybody else does. When you think about it a little bit, I think the media made a lot more of it than what it really was. And TV and everybody just fed off of that. As players, I don't think any hitter wants to be thrown at, as far as headwise. I don't think he really meant to do that.

That's part of his intimidation factor and that's what makes him such a great pitcher. He throws inside and if you watch him pitch, he comes after the biggest and best guys. He doesn't pick out a number eight or nine hitter, or a number one or two hitter, he's coming after the number three or four guy that I think sets the tone to the game [other team's lineup], and he's going to knock them down. He doesn't mean to hit a player in his head, but he's going to throw inside and knock him off. In that way he sends a message to the whole team that this is my mound, this is my plate and you're going to have to respect that. That works, and I remember him facing Seattle in the 2000 LCS, and he did the same thing to Alex Rodriguez and ended up throwing a one-hitter. He did the same thing with Piazza because he's a big hitter and it's an intimidation factor. And that works for him.

What did you make of Clemens throwing a piece of Piazza's cracked bat toward him in the 2000 World Series?
    It's funny because you see it on TV a bunch of times and when Piazza hit the ball, it wound up going in our dugout. He started running because he had no idea where the ball was going. The bat came flying out to Clemens—he's a very intense person on the mound. I don't think he realized that Piazza was running on that because he saw where the foul ball had gone. He picked up the cracked bat and threw it by the on-deck circle as Piazza was running down the line. And I don't think he intended to hurt Piazza. Because the media makes this a big rivalry, the fans love it and that incident was made into a big deal.

In 2001 you returned to Seattle.
    Seattle was always my home since 1992. I wanted to go back there because of what we accomplished there in '95. I remembered we played in the postseason and I would like to go to the World Series with these guys. It was different because I just spent five years in New York and four out of five years you win a World Series, and I thought I could bring that winning attitude to Seattle. If we would've finished it off and won the World Series, maybe that team would've been the greatest team in baseball. You win 116 games and you're going out and winning just about every day. We didn't lose one series, maybe until the end of the year. And toward the end of the year, we lost two out of three for like the first time all season. We were sweeping teams and the clubhouse was unbelievable. Because the media is different here, the fans are not into their sports teams like the East Coast fans in New York, Boston and Baltimore. The media had three or four guys covering us and that year was just a great year.

Was that Seattle team in 2001 as good as the '98 Yankees?

It can't be as good because we didn't go to the World Series and win. And the Yankees wound up beating us in the league championship series. I don't know, but I think we had a lot of guys that year that really stepped up and had career years. That team had great chemistry. We had Jay Buhner and Edgar Martinez, and those kind of guys kept the core together. We had myself, who was a good guy in the clubhouse. We had Mike Cameron who was funny; we had Mark McLemore, Stan Javier, Al Martin and Norm Charlton. They were great guys in our clubhouse. We had guys that really made it fun in the clubhouse and it just carried over onto the field. And we had guys that had career years. I remember making the All-Star team in 2001, where it was at Safeco Field. Lou Piniella was the manager and we had eight guys on the All-Star team. That was a real memorable year.

The Yankees are built for the playoffs; they're not intimidated and they know what to expect when they get there. They're used to that all year, and the other teams that go to the playoffs aren't.

You return to the Yankees on August 6, 2003, and made another postseason run.

That was another great experience. Everybody says the Yankees are built for the postseason. The regular season they just used as practice and get ready for the postseason. And in some instances it is in a way, but it's not easy to get to the playoffs all the time. But when you're with the Yankees you know they're going to give you every chance you can to get to the playoffs, as far as Mr. Steinbrenner is going to go out and get all the possible pieces that go, and do it again. We played in the division series and that was a fun time. We played the Boston Red Sox and that went to seven games. And in the seventh game you thought that was it—the Red Sox are finally going to win the World Series. They're up by five runs and the next thing you know, those statues in Yankee Stadium come alive and do something. It's a mystery of the times the Yankees come back and beat the teams they're playing in the postseason, and nobody knows how it happens. It seems that the statues come alive and push the ball over the fence when we need a home run.

Were the Yankees surprised by the Marlins winning the 2003 World Series?

We were surprised because we didn't expect them to get through the Giants or anybody expected them to get through the Cubs. They went through the division series and the league championship series, and they weren't expected to win at all. And then they got to the World Series and they weren't expected to beat the Yankees. And we didn't think they would beat us either. Once we beat Boston we thought that was our toughest opponent to get to the World Series. I don't think we took the Marlins lightly, but it was one of those things that we're going to win this World Series. We were thinking how many games will it take to win it. And the next thing you know, they beat us and win the World Series.

Jim Edmonds
CLUTCH HITTING SLUGGER AND DEFENSIVE ANCHOR
3-Time All-Star and 6 Gold Gloves

> *"In the postseason everything is magnified a thousand times over. Every pitch is exhausting and when you come home from a postseason game, you don't even think about eating dinner. You think about lying down and relaxing, and your mind is racing. You're exhausted because every pitch is important and every situation is important."* —Jim Edmonds

James Patrick Edmonds was selected by the Angels in the seventh round of the June draft and appeared in 35 games for Rookie-level Bend in his first professional season in 1988. He played 39 games in 1989, the result of a season-ending shoulder injury that forced him onto the disabled list from June 19 to the end of the season. He played 91 games at Single-A Palm Springs in 1990, hitting .293 with 56 runs batted in. In 1991, he played his second season at Palm Springs, batting .294 in 60 games.

Edmonds began the 1992 campaign at Double-A Midland, hitting .313 with 77 hits and eight home runs in just 70 games. He was promoted to Triple-A Edmonton on July 14 and finished the season with a .299 batting average and six home runs in 50 games. He spent his final season in the minor leagues at Triple-A Vancouver in 1993, where he hit .315 with 112 hits, nine home runs and 74 runs batted in. He was called up in September and made his major league debut on September 9. He collected his first big-league hit, a pinch-hit double, on September 10.

In 1994, Edmonds was the only Angels rookie to spend the entire season on the major-league roster and appeared in 94 games, hitting .273 with 79 hits and 37 runs batted in. He had his breakout season in 1995, hitting

.290 with 162 hits, 33 home runs, 120 runs scored and 107 runs batted in. In 1996, he was on the disabled list twice during the season, however, had an outstanding season with a .304 batting average, with 131 hits, 27 home runs and 66 runs batted in, while appearing in only 114 games.

From 1997 through 1998, Edmonds's hitting continued to improve and he made spectacular defensive plays in both seasons to earn Gold Gloves. In 1998, he hit .307 with 184 hits (career-high) and 25 home runs. He played his final season with the Angels in 1999 and spent the majority of the season on the disabled list, playing 55 games that season.

Edmonds was acquired by St. Louis on March 23, 2000, and in his first year with the Cardinals he established a club-leading 42 home runs (a career high), hitting .295 with 155 hits, 108 runs batted in, 129 runs scored and his third Gold Glove. He finished fourth in voting for the National League's Most Valuable Player. In 2001 and 2002 he hit above .300 in both seasons, and in 2001, he had 30 home runs and 110 runs batted in. In 2002, he had 28 home runs and knocked in 83 runs.

Edmonds had an incredible first half of the 2003 season with 28 home runs and ended the season with 39 home runs, and he earned his sixth Gold Glove Award. In 2004, he had a .301 batting average with 42 home runs.

I met up with Edmonds during spring training and during the 2004 season. I conducted an interview with him in the Cardinals dugout at Pro Player Stadium in mid–August while St. Louis was enjoying a 13½ game division lead. He was very cautious to discuss the upcoming postseason and indicated that the postseason is a special time for special teams and it's something all its own.

CONVERSATION WITH JIM EDMONDS

Coming up with the Angels in '93 and playing there through 1999, were you ever involved in a run to the postseason?

Not really. We finished second a couple of times and we had a one-game playoff that we lost. We never really had a good team. We never played well enough to get to the postseason.

In your first year with St. Louis, you had an outstanding season with a .295 batting average, career highs with 42 home runs and 108 runs batted in. What was that season like?

For me, every season I go out there and do my job, and I don't put too much thought into numbers. I just go out there and play. Every season can be up or down, and I remember we had a good team as a group. When you have a good team as a group or a good clubhouse, that's what separates the good years from the bad years.

Who were some of the players on that 2000 team?

Most of the players that we had on that team are still here. We had Shawon Dunston, Eric Davis, Thomas Howard—the main core of the guys that we have out here now with the addition of Matheny, Renteria, J. D. Drew, Fernando Vina and myself. So we had some different guys, but pretty much the core.

In the 2000 division series, you hit .571 with eight hits and two home runs. Would you agree that you were instrumental in leading the Cardinals to a three-game sweep over the Braves?

I think our whole team played well and I was happy to be hot at the time, but I think our whole team played well. That's the only way to win in this game—when everybody plays well.

Talk about playing in your first postseason.

It was exciting to play in the postseason and I would rather have played and lost than never played, I guess. Now that I think about it, it's definitely something that is a different level of the game and the intensity level is different. It teaches you how to really be focused and not to try to do anything different than just play your game. If you try too hard or try to do too much, you usually end up failing.

Do you recall any memorable games?

No, I really don't. I think everything has been a blur—my whole career now and it seems like it has gone by pretty fast, so I'm trying to enjoy it while I got it and when it's over, it's over.

Prior to playing in the league championship series against the Mets, did you see your team in the World Series?

Well, you never know what it's going to take and being in the postseason for the first time, you don't really know what it's actually going to take to get there. So it's hard to say. I would like to think that we were good enough to play and compete at that level, and we just fell short.

What do you remember about the 2000 LCS?

We just didn't play well. It was disappointing because we played

Jim Edmonds completes a spring training workout at Roger Dean Stadium in Jupiter, Florida.

pretty well against Atlanta and then we just didn't show up in New York. The Mets beat us and it was one of those things that happen in a short series.

After what you experienced in the 2000 postseason, were you disappointed that you didn't get to the World Series in 2001?

No. I wasn't disappointed—well, let's say I was disappointed, but I'm also a realist and I know that only two teams get there each year, out of the 30 [teams]. I feel that it's not as easy as everybody thinks it is. And you have to accept the fact that when you don't play well enough in the end, you're not going to make it.

In 2002, you had a career-high .311 batting average with 28 home runs. Did you see the postseason finish line ahead of you and the Cardinals finally playing in the World Series?

I just don't really know. I think even right now, you try to get to the playoffs and you try to play your best baseball. It's one of those things; you just never know what's going to happen. I really thought we had a good team in 2000 and we played terrible against the Mets. So it's one of those things you can never figure out.

In Game 1 of the 2002 division series, you hit a two-run home run off Randy Johnson and had three hits in that game. How would you describe your performance against the best pitcher in baseball?

It was great. Anytime you're playing in the postseason and facing a pitcher like Johnson, it brings all the attention and all the focus to right then and there, and there's no worry about tomorrow. In that game every at-bat and every pitch was important, and I think that's what makes the postseason so great.

The Cardinals sweep Arizona in three games. What was that like?

That was nice, but all those games come and go so quick that you truly play those three games and it's a relief to get by the first series. But you know how tough the second series is going to be and you really just try to focus in on playing the best baseball you can, and hopefully the luck is on your side.

You had a great performance in the league championship series with a .440 batting average and eight hits, and hit safely in five games. How would you describe that series against the Giants?

I think it was a good series. We played well and they played well, and they just beat us. They had a better team that year; they played better than we did and they got the key hits, and we didn't. That was frustrating because I thought that was the year we were going to win the World Series, and to watch them in the World Series, was unique. I felt we were so close and I knew if we won those games, I was going home and would play in Anaheim in the World Series. I thought that would be pretty special, but you win and you lose, and we lost. So you have to keep moving on.

Over your career you're batting .360 in postseason play. To what would you attribute your great success in the postseason?

I really don't know. You have to have the ability to know how to really slow down a little bit and get into the game, and not try to get overexcited. I think I have an ability, maybe, to focus a little bit more or just really not try to do too much and just keep playing the game the same way. Sometimes if you're hot at the end of the year, it carries over to the postseason and that's the way it goes. It's all timing and maybe the ability to not get carried away.

How is the postseason different from the regular season?

In the postseason everything is magnified a thousand times over.

Every pitch is exhausting and when you come home from a postseason game, you don't even think about eating dinner. You think about lying down and relaxing, and your mind is racing. You're exhausted because every pitch is important and every situation is important. Every time you get a chance to bunt, you got to get it down and move a guy over, and drive in a run. Your pitchers have to pitch well and keep you in the game. So every game is important; you don't get to play a hundred of them. The further you get into the postseason, the more exciting it gets and the more people are watching it.

Coming out of spring training in 2004, did you see this club running away in the division race?

No. I don't think any team saw anybody running away with the division race. I think everybody thought that Houston and Chicago were going to be the two teams to beat. We always felt that if we could play good baseball, we could stay right in the hunt. People were really down on us at the beginning of the season and I think that was the best thing about it.

With about six weeks left in the season and a 13-game lead, do you see the finish line ahead of you?

No. I don't think you ever see the finish line ahead of you, just because you know how tough it is to play the whole season and you keep your fingers crossed that your team can stay healthy. You have to keep on playing well and see what happens at the end.

The 2004 club has a powerful offense and good pitching. With the addition of Larry Walker, where do you see the Cardinals heading in the postseason?

No telling, really no telling. There are no predictions, there's no true way to put a mathematical situation into what happens in the playoffs. If you run into a team that's hot and you're cold, you're going to lose. And if you're hot and the other team is not ready to play against you, then you're going to win. So it's really about who's playing the best baseball in October. The team that wins the World Series is the team that gets hot in October. It doesn't matter how good you are — if you're the wild card or the best team in baseball. The Florida Marlins had proved that, the Anaheim Angels had proved that and if you watch baseball long enough, you know that's exactly how it works.

The Cardinals appear to be the favorite going into the 2004 postseason. Would not being able to play in the World Series be a big disappointment at this point in your career?

No, no it wouldn't. Like I've said, it's obvious that only two teams get to play each year and you do the best you can. I'm not going to be one of those guys that's going to say that my career wasn't complete because I didn't get to play in a World Series. There are many players out there that have played in cities that they don't even like to play in, but they've gotten stuck or played for the money, and I just think I've enjoyed my career. I've been lucky to go this far to play this long and I'm happy to be doing what I enjoy doing.

Which part of your career did you enjoy more—playing near your home with the Angels or with the Cardinals?

I like both. I like to just be able to go out there and play. It was great coming up with the Angels because I played at home. There was family and friends around all the time, and it was just like going to work like everybody else does. It was going to work at home and coming home to your family, and people you knew, and everything was very familiar. I think many players in this game don't get that experience or if they do, it's a little hectic. It was nice and I had the best of both worlds for a while.

Here's a situation that could play out in the World Series. It's Game 7 of the World Series, you're facing Mariano Rivera with the bases loaded, there's two outs and you're trailing by a run. What would you feel at that moment?

I would just try to put the ball in play. [Laughs.] I would try to have a good at-bat. Basically, what this game all comes down to is when you're a hitter, you go up there each time trying to have a good at-bat. And you're not always going to get a hit, but the more chances you give yourself to have good at-bats, the better chance you have to get a hit, and do something positive. I want to be in that situation every day. I would rather fail and be in that situation than never get that chance.

I know you don't want to speculate on the postseason, but any final thoughts concerning postseason play?

It's something you really can't talk about because not too many people get the privilege to play in it. Postseason play is a special thing that's its own thing and it's something you can't write about, talk about, and expect, because it's something all its own. And it's a special time for special teams and that's really the bottom line.

Craig Counsell
THE GRINDER AND WINNER

> *"Whenever I walk in this stadium, I remember Game 7 and seeing the stadium full. I scored the winning run in the '97 World Series and my shoes are in the Hall of Fame. I really look forward to the day when I can take my son to the Hall of Fame and show him my shoes."* —Craig Counsell

Craig John Counsell played a significant role in the Florida Marlins' 1997 storybook season, going from the minor leagues to scoring the winning run in the bottom of the 11th inning in the seventh game of the World Series. He spent the first half of the 1997 season on the disabled list for the Rockies' Triple-A Colorado Springs team. He was acquired by the Florida Marlins on July 27, 1997, however, and contributed significantly to their pennant-winning campaign while playing in 51 games. In the games he played with the Marlins he carried a .299 regular season batting average with 49 hits and .376 on-base percentage into the postseason, where he batted .293 and posted a .423 on-base percentage. Counsell's hard-nosed, blue-collar style of play quickly earned him the admiration and respect of manager Jim Leyland.

Counsell, a University of Notre Dame graduate and member of Colorado's first draft class in 1992, had been a shortstop in college. On September 15, 1995, he was called up to the Rockies, appearing in three big-league games and making his major-league debut as a pinch-hitter in his only official at-bat that season. During the 1996 and 1997 seasons, Counsell spent most of the time in the minor leagues and on the disabled list with an assortment of injuries.

Counsell started the 1998 season in the major leagues for the first time in his career, but his season was cut short after suffering a compound displaced fracture of his jawbone in early August. He had played in 107 games that season while contributing a .251 batting average. Joining the Dodgers in a mid–June 1999 trade, he was used primarily for defensive purposes.

During spring training in 2000, he reported to the Dodgers as a non-roster player and was released early before signing a minor-league contract with Arizona. He was hitting .348 with Triple-A Tucson when he was recalled by the parent club, where he played in 67 games and batted a robust .316. Counsell established career highs in almost every offensive category in 2001, including games (141), at-bats (458), runs (76) and hits (126). He finished the year strong with a .275 batting average.

Counsell made his second successful trip to the postseason in 2001 with an outstanding MVP performance in the league championship series, where he was hitting .381 (eight hits and four runs batted in). In his first at-bat in Game 1 of the 2001 World Series, he hit a home run to score Arizona's first run in the first inning. He was in the middle of the title-clinching heroics in the ninth inning of Game 7, getting hit by a Mariano Rivera pitch to load the bases just ahead of Luis Gonzalez's series-ending hit.

Counsell had another outstanding season in 2002, hitting .282 with 123 hits. He had only a month of play in the 2003 season when a dislocated right thumb sidelined him until early July after which he struggled to regain his hitting stroke. He was acquired by the Milwaukee Brewers on December 1, 2003, and has had a productive 2004 season, hitting .270 for most of the season until some injuries slowed him down.

I conducted an interview with the articulate Counsell in the Brewers' dugout at Pro Player Stadium late in the 2004 season. He indicated that winning two world championships was a great experience, a unique experience and he couldn't choose one series over the other as being more memorable.

CONVERSATION WITH CRAIG COUNSELL

Jim Leyland describes you as a ballplayer who is not talented, but a guy who grinds every day. What does he mean by that?

Well, I think what he means is that there are players with more physical gifts than I have, but you can find ways to be successful in this game and that's what I try to do. You can do it through consistent effort every day. You can use your head to find ways to succeed. There's tons of different ways to succeed and you just got to find that way, and you do it with the skills you have. The skills are what God gave you. You take those skills to the highest level you can and then you rely on everything else to try to still succeed.

You capped a storybook 1997 season by going from the minor league to the Marlins to help them make a postseason run. You had only one major-league at-bat at the time, and what did the Marlins see in you?

[Laughs.] Well, that's a question more for the Marlins—the people that traded for me. I think from what I remember, they wanted a second baseman who could play defense and get some hits. I was batting number eight in the lineup and my job was to draw some walks and drive in runs when I needed to. They weren't looking for me to be the star, but to be able to fill in a place and solidify the defense, and I think I did that.

You began the '97 season at Triple-A Colorado Springs. Did you ever imagine you would play an important role in the World Series?

Well, no. I don't think anybody that starts the year in Triple-A thinks they're going to be the starting player in the World Series. But it happened the way it happened. I was in the right place at the right time. I took advantage of an opportunity and you know, it was a storybook year, I guess. You don't think it's going to happen, but you don't eliminate it from your thought process. It's not something that's in your thought process while you're going through it. And I think maybe that's kind of what Jim Leyland is trying to say. You go about every day and do the best you can every day and then sometimes through fortunate results, you find yourself in those good spots.

How would you describe the 1997 World Series?

It was a great experience; it was a baseball player's dream. You spend the rest of your career trying to experience it again. That's kind of how it feels; that's why guys that haven't experienced it want to experience it because everybody who's been there knows how great it is. It's kind of like that elusive thing that you're always searching for, that feeling you want to feel again.

Talk about the '97 wild-card chase when you reported to Florida late in July. You hit .299 in 51 games.

Well, we were up a couple of games when I got here. We played really well the two months I was here during the regular season. And we were kind of in control of the thing the whole time along. I think when I came to the Marlins, we were a playoff team the whole time. We were pretty solid throughout; we were never behind in the wild-card race. I thought there were good points and bad points, but I was convinced that we were going to be in the playoffs.

What was it like playing in your first postseason in the division series against the Giants?

Well, it was exciting. It was my first postseason game and the postseason is such a build-up. It starts in the division series and I think you kind of get a taste of the intensity on the field. Then as the playoffs move on, I think the attention from outside starts to build, but we played it here in Florida and we won a game in the bottom of the ninth inning. So it was exciting.

In the '97 LCS, you had an outstanding .429 batting average with six hits, as you defeat the Braves and advance to the World Series. Did you ever think your experience was something you see in movies and stuff like that?

No. I think I'm a baseball player and maybe outsiders think of it as movie stuff, but I'm a baseball player, and that's what I do, and that's what I've always wanted to do. It's not something that was outside the realm of my thinking. It was stuff you think about; it's a place that you want to be. So I don't really consider it something you see in the movies. When you experience the success of winning a playoff series, I consider it the results of the effort I put in and then a little good luck along the way.

Talk about playing in your first World Series in 1997.

It's a great feeling and you realize how great it is. You hear about players that haven't played in it, that want to play in it so bad, and for the guys that played in it, they want to do it again because you never feel like that. It's those 10 days where you're on top of the world and you don't feel like that too often. That's why you want to do it so badly. It's the pinnacle of what we do and there's no higher level. There's nothing better than playing in the World Series. It's tough to achieve and that's what makes it great to be a part of.

Describe your contribution in Game 7 as the Marlins win their first World Series in the 11th inning?

Well, I was up in the bottom of the ninth and there was a runner on first and third with one out, and we're down a run. Jose Mesa was pitching and I hit a line drive to right field that was hit really well, and Manny Ramirez ended up catching it. I didn't think he was going to catch it at first, but he ended up catching it and we tied the game. The purpose of my at-bat was to get the game tied. That was really the only thing I wanted to do—somehow hit the ball to the outfield. So I was successful doing that and that's what I was really happy about. I wasn't thinking about winning the game or anything like that. I just wanted to tie the game up somehow and did that. We were able to win it in the 11th inning.

You were traded to the Dodgers in 1999 and released during spring training in 2000. Then you signed a minor-league contract with Arizona in 2000. What were you thinking at that time?

Well, it was a new start. You kind of feel like at that point when you get released that people have given up on you and there weren't a ton of teams knocking on your door that want you to play for them, but at the same time it was kind of like a new start. When I signed there, I knew I was going to play shortstop and third base. And I was really excited about that because I thought it was better for me in the long run that I play more positions and I knew I could play those positions. I thought I was re-creating myself as a player almost when I signed with Arizona because I was going to be a more versatile infielder.

You hit .348 at Triple-A Tucson when your contract was purchased in 2000 by Arizona. Did you expect to return to the big leagues soon?

It wasn't that big a deal, to be honest with you. I knew I would be back in the big leagues and it was just a matter of time. I wasn't shocked by it; I wasn't overly thrilled by it, because I knew I didn't want to just be in the big leagues. I wanted to be an everyday player in the big leagues. So I really thought of that as another step along the way.

Craig Counsell is interviewed in the dugout at Pro Player Stadium.

Was Arizona the right fit for you at that time?

It was a good fit for me because more that anything else, Joe Garagiola, Jr., and Buck Showalter [at the time]—they believed in me as a player and they wanted me to be a versatile player, and that fact was the biggest reason why I ended up going there and why I ended up being successful there.

In 2001, you made your second successful trip to the postseason. Talk about that postseason experience.

I think the best thing about that was playing New York in the World Series. It was shortly after September 11, so the whole country was really pulling together and it wasn't just a baseball thing. It was a great experience; I mean, we spent five days in New York and we lost all three games, but it was five days that I'll remember most in baseball. It was just an incredible experience being there at that time and how the city was healing. It was great that baseball was playing a part in the healing process and it was an incredible five days.

Prior to the World Series you had an MVP performance against the Braves in the league championship series.

Yep. I got on a hot streak and it was as simple as that. [Laughs.] I got on a hot streak at the right time. We played well and they made some mistakes. In that series we just played well.

You've always been a clutch player in the postseason. Are you one of those heroes that are born in the postseason?

Well, I don't consider myself a hero; I consider myself part of a winning team. On the team that wins the World Series, everybody is a hero. Everybody helps you win games in the postseason. But it's important if you're going to win, that at some point you have to make your contribution to the winning. So I see it as doing my job. At points during that postseason I helped us win games and I was an important factor in us winning games. But that's my job and if you're going to win, everybody had to do that on the team.

In Game 1, you start the World Series off by hitting a home run off Mike Mussina. Did that home run kind of give the team a feeling of confidence?

That was pretty special because we were playing against the New York Yankees and it was a special World Series. To do it in the first at-bat and the first inning, and the time of the game when they scored a run in the first inning—it was real important that we answer that run just to provide us confidence in our team. And I think more than anything that helped us in that game believe that we could play with them and score, and we ended up winning that game pretty easily.

Can you recall any other games in that World Series?
They all stick out in your mind. Game 7 was great, but the fourth game in New York when Tino Martinez hit the game-tying home run in the bottom of the ninth inning, and then Jeter hit a game-winning home run in the 10th inning. When Tino Martinez hit that home run, I had never seen anything like that in the stadium and that was pretty magical. It was incredible; you looked into the stands and it felt like the stadium was shaking. People were hugging each other, and it looked like they didn't even know each other. But everybody was hugging each other and it was pretty amazing.

Game 7 has to be special and one game that you will always remember?
It was remarkable and similar to Game 7, during the 1997 World Series here in Florida. The first seven innings just seemed to fly by and the game was tied, and nobody was scoring runs. The game just flies by and you get to the eighth inning and your like—what happened to the first seven innings? And that's the great thing about baseball—that for the last two innings, you're hanging on every pitch because it could be that pitch that changes the game. And it was obviously a great game, and to score two runs in the ninth inning off the greatest reliever in the history of post-season baseball was a tough task. But we managed to do it.

What were you thinking prior to stepping into the batter's box to face Rivera?
I was thinking, "get a hit." [Laughs.] I was in the same situation in the '97 World Series in the bottom of the ninth and it was the same situation again in the 2001 World Series. There was a runner on third base with less than two outs and I was thinking, "get the run in." It was the same exact situation and I had the same exact thoughts—just do something to get this run in. I wasn't thinking about a hit, but get the ball in the outfield; get a good pitch to hit and that's what you're trying to do.

What was it like facing Rivera with the game on the line?
Well, he's a great pitcher and he's challenging because he throws a cut fastball that's on your hands and you think it's on the barrel. You try to get a good pitch and he's like anybody else. You try to get a good pitch to hit and he's no different from any great closer.

What would be your most memorable postseason?

I don't have one that is more memorable than the other. It's like asking yourself, which one of your kids do you like better? Both were great experiences, unique experiences and you enjoy each one of them as much as the other.

How would you compare the 2001 Arizona team to the 1997 Florida team?

Well, I don't think any team is the same. It's one thing if you're on the Yankees and you're doing it every year with kind of the same guys. But this was a totally different team with 25 different guys. So it's completely different. There are similarities and obviously the path that you travel, and the things you feel individually, but it's a different team, so there's going to be different things that are going to happen. And you remember different things from each of them.

What do you recall about the '97 team?

It was a great team. We were a championship team, that's what we were. We had contributions from lots of guys and they helped us win games. I remember being here for Game 7; that's what I remember. Whenever I walk in this stadium, I remember Game 7 and seeing the stadium full. I scored the winning run in the '97 World Series and my shoes are in the Hall of Fame. I really look forward to the day when I can take my son to the Hall of Fame and show him my shoes. When I'm done playing, retired, maybe have a summer off, I'd look forward to that road trip to the Hall of Fame and where I could show him—here's Dad's shoes that he crossed home plate with and it's in the Hall of Fame. People remember what you do in the World Series forever. Any time I come to South Florida, I know people remember that and the same thing in Phoenix. When you play in a World Series, you become part of a community's memories forever and when you think about that, it's pretty special.

Bibliography

The Baseball Encyclopedia. 10th ed. New York: Macmillan, 1996.
Cohen, Stanley. *Dodgers!* New York: Birch Lane Press, 1990.
The Miami Herald Florida Marlins World Series Champions. Champaign, IL: Sports Publishing, 2003
McKelvey, G. Richard. *Fisk's Homer, Willie's Catch and the Shot Heard Round the World.* Jefferson, NC: McFarland, 1998.
Rosenthal, Ken. "Ahem! The Yankees Are Not Evil." *The Sporting News Magazine* (March 1, 2004).
Skipper, John C. *A Biographical Dictionary of the Baseball Hall of Fame.* Jefferson, NC: McFarland, 2000.
Smith, Ron. *The Sporting News Chronicle of Baseball.* New York: BDD Illustrated Books, 1993.
Zachofsky, Dan. *Idols of the Spring.* Jefferson, NC: McFarland, 2001.
2004 Major League Media Guides: Atlanta Braves, Baltimore Orioles, Cincinnati Reds, Cleveland Indians, Florida Marlins, Houston Astros, Milwaukee Brewers, New York Mets, New York Yankees, Philadelphia Phillies, Pittsburgh Pirates, St. Louis, Cardinals, Tampa Bay Devil Rays, Texas Rangers, Toronto Blue Jays.

Index

Numbers in **boldface** indicate pages with photographs.

Aaron, Hank 13
Adams, Red 160
Alexander, Doyle 132
Alomar, Roberto 109, 135, 153
Alomar, Sandy 232
Alou, Moises 30, 42, 110, 209
Andersen, Larry 193
Anderson, Sparky 75
Arnsberg, Brad 57
Avery, Steve 126–127, 134, 144, 203

Bagwell, Jeff 9, 14, 92, 112, 193–198, **195**, 209
Baines, Harold 229
Bando, Sal 178
Banks, Brian 61
Banks, Ernie 11, 77
Bautista, Danny 102
Baylor, Don 177–184, **179**
Beck, Rod 102
Beckett, Josh 2–4, 8, 10, 17–18, 21, 24, 31, 38, 47–53, **49**, 58–60, 62, 68–69, 97, 108, 127, 165, 197, 223
Beinfest, Larry 17, 19, 57
Bell, Jay 29, 95, 102
Belle, Albert 126, 153
Bench, Johnny 10, 70, 73, 75, 190, 216
Benedict, Bruce 156
Benitez, Armando 63
Berkman, Lance 112, 196
Berra, Yogi 36, 180
Biggio, Craig 14, 92, 112, 196, 198, 206–211, **209**
Billingham, Jack 73
Blair, Paul 179

Blalock, Hank 224
Blass, Steve 185–192, **188**
Blue, Vida 178–179
Boggs, Wade 153, 230
Bonds, Barry 13, 29, 118, 191
Bonds, Bobby 190
Bonilla, Bobby 31
Boone, Bob 105–106, 216–217
Boone, Bret 184
Borbon, Pedro 73
Bosio, Chris 202
Bowa, Larry 105, 107, 159, 212–219, **215**
Bream, Sid 135, 152, 191
Brecheen, Harry 5
Brenly, Bob 79, 96, 103
Brett, George 23, 86–87
Brock, Lou 5, 157
Brown, Joe 186
Brown, Kevin 6, 13, 31,65, 77, 129, 152, 206, 209–210
Brunansky, Tom 182
Buckner, Bill 181
Buford, Don 189
Buhner, Jay 237
Bumbry, Al 179
Burnett, A.J. 21, 25, 59, 63, 67, 112
Bush, George W. 7, 22, 35
Bush, Homer 235
Bystrom, Marty 214

Cabrera, Francisco 135, 152
Cabrera, Miguel 17, 24–25, 69, 76, 101
Cameron, Mike 237
Caminiti, Ken 92, 209

257

Campaneris, Bert 178
Canseco, Jose 182
Cardenas, Leo 71
Carew, Rod 179
Carlton, Steve 5, 105–106
Carroll, Clay 73
Carter, Joe 23, 109
Cash, Dave 186–187
Cashman, Brian 96
Castillo, Luis 6–7, 19, 25, 33, 63, 75–76, 97, 110, 118, 120
Castro, Ramon 21, 61–62
Catalinas, Ed 35
Cepeda, Orlando 5, 71, 77, 190
Chambliss, Chris 169, 171
Charlton, Norm 237
Clemens, Roger 113, 158, 164, 195–196, 198, 208, 210, 221, 224, 235–236
Clemente, Roberto 11, 186–189
Clinton, Bill 36
Coggins, Richie 179
Coleman, Vince 121
Concepcion, Dave 10, 70, 73, 75, 190, 216
Cone, David 128, 136, 204, 231, 234
Conine, Jeff 1, 19, 24–25, 31, 33–34, 41–42, 77, 112
Contreras, Jose 120
Coors Field 183
Counsell, Craig 29, 84, 93–94, 102, 110, 112, 246–253, **250**
Cowens, Al 171
Cox, Bobby 124, 145, 152
Cuellar, Mike 179

Daulton, Darren 31, 110, 112
Davalillo, Vic 107
Davis, Chili 45, 234
Davis, Eric 241
Dawson, Andre 100–101
Delpiano, Marc 57
Dempster, Ryan 52
Dent, Bucky 171–172
Devereaux, Mike 125
DiMaggio, Joe 3
Donnelly, Rich 34
Doyle, Brian 214
Doyle, Denny 214
Drabek, Doug 29
Drew, J.D. 241

Driessen, Dan 73
Dunston, Shawon 241

Eckersley, Dennis 182
Edmonds, Jim 9, 11, 27, 239–245, **242**
Ellis, Doc 186–187
Encarnacion, Juan 8
Etchebarren, Andy 179
Everett, Carl 209
Evers, Hoot 35

Farr, Steve 199
Fenway Park 13, 172
Ferguson, Joe 166
Fernandez, Alex 6, 45
Ferraro, Mike 173
Fielder, Cecil 153
Figueroa, Ed 171
Finley, Steve 92, 95, 102
Flood, Curt 5
Forbes Field 186
Foster, George 11, 70, 73, 75
Fox, Andy 61
Fox, Chad 60, 62–63
Frazier, George 163
Friend, Bob 189
Froemming, Bruce 216
Fulton County Stadium 126

Gaetti, Gary 182
Gagne, Eric 9, 12, 63, 133, 139
Galarraga, Andres 183
Garagiola, Joe 5
Garagiola, Joe, Jr. 251
Gehrig, Lou 3
Geronimo, Cesar 11, 70, 73, 75, 190
Giambi, Jason 13
Gibson, Bob 5, 77
Gibson, Kirk 182
Glavine, Tom 9–10, 126–127, 132, 136, 139, 142–144, 148–156, **151**, 203, 232
Gonzalez, Alex 19, 25, 33, 42, 75–76, 119
Gonzalez, Luis 9, 11, 84–86, 89–97, **91**, 102–103, 247
Gooden, Dwight 234
Gossage, Goose 171–172, 183, 229
Grace, Mark 84, 98–104, **100**
Green, Dallas 216
Grich, Bob 179

Griffey, Ken, Sr. 10, 70, 73, 75, 180, 216
Grissom, Marquis 124–125
Gross, Greg 217
Guidry, Ron 171–172, 180
Gullett, Don 73, 171
Guthrie, Mark 38
Gwynn, Tony 23, 234

Harris, Lenny 61
Hart, Jim Ray 190
Hatcher, Billy 176
Hebner, Richie 186–187
Helton, Todd 65
Hemond, Roland 35
Henderson, Rickey 10, 121, 180
Hendricks, Elrod 179
Henke, Tom 109
Hernandez, Livan 6, 30–31, 129
Hernandez, Orlando 103
Hernandez, Xavier 126
Hershiser, Orel 182, 206
Hitchcock, Sterling 129
Hollandsworth, Todd 61
Holtz, Lou 34
Holtzman, Ken 178–179
Hooton, Burt 157–166, **160**
Hough, Charlie 157, 161, 166
Howard, Thomas 241
Howser, Dick 173
Hrbek, Kent 182
Huizenga, Wayne 110
Hunter, Jim Catfish 171, 178, 183
Hutton, Tommy 105–113, **108**

Jackson, Bo 229
Jackson, Reggie 77, 157, 161, 167–168, 171–172, 179
Javier, Stan 237
Jenkins, Ferguson 158–159
Jeter, Derek 3, 11, 43, 153, 222, 224, 252
Jocketty, Walt 27
John, Tommy 106, 133, 158, 162–163
Johnson, Charles 30–31
Johnson, Davey 189
Johnson, Deron 71, 159
Johnson, Randy 13, 84–85, 95, 102, 152, 195–196, 209, 222, 243
Jones, Andruw 144, 184, 232
Jones, Chipper 9, 122–131, **124**, 183–184
Justice, David 124–125, 136, 234

Kaat, Jim 15, 23
Kaline, Al 77
Kent, Jeff 196
Killebrew, Harmon 23
Kim, Byung-Hyun 102
Kison, Bruce 187
Klesko, Ryan 125, 184
Kotsay, Mark 110–111
Koufax, Sandy 14
Kuenn, Harvey 79–81
Kuenster, John 134

Lamont, Gene 34
Lankford, Ray 11
LaRussa, Tony 26–27, 29, 35, 176, 200
Lasorda, Tom 158, 166
Law, Vernon 189
Lee, Derek 8, 42–43, 75, 77, 101, 116–117, 120
Leiter, Al 6, 31, 77
Lejoy, Bill 35
Lemon, Bob 163
Leyland, Jim 5–7, 9, 26–36, **28**, 110, 246–248
Leyritz, Jim 128, 152, 232
Lind, Jose 135
Littell, Mark 171
Lloyd, Graeme 234–235
Lofton, Kenny 13, 121, 153, 202
Lombardozzi, Steve 182
Looper, Braden 8, 60
Lopes, Davey 107, 216
Lopez, Javier 9–10, 139, 141–147, **144**, 150
Loria, Jeffrey 19, 57
Lowell, Mike 10–11, 19, 24–25, 33, 37–46, **40**, 100–101, 112
Luzinski, Greg 106–107, 159, 216
Lyle, Sparky 171
Lynch, Gerry 189
Lynn, Fred 179

Maddox, Garry 107, 216
Maddux, Greg 10, 13, 100, 126–127, 139, 142–144, 148, 156, 203–204, 232
Madson, Ryan 219
Mantle, Mickey 3
Marion, Marty 5
Maris, Roger 5
Martin, Al 237
Martin, Billy 173–174, 176, 180

Martin, Jerry 106, 216
Martinez, Dennis 141, 144
Martinez, Edgar 237
Martinez, Tino 230–231, 252
Matheny, Mike 241
Matthews, Gary 217–218
Mattingly, Don 180, 230–231
May, Milt 187
Mays, Willie 11, 77, 190
Mazeroski, Bill 186–187, 189
Mazzone, Leo 134, 143, 156
McCarver, Tim 5, 107
McCovey, Willie 190
McGraw, Tug 106, 215
McGriff, Fred 124–126
McGwire, Mark 182, 229
McKeon, Jack 3, 6–9, 15–25, **16**, 31, 33, 39, 44, 48, 50–52, 54, 57–60, 67–68, 76, 100, 108, 111, 116, 169
McLemore, Mark 237
McNally, Dave 179
Mesa, Jose 118, 249
Messersmith, Andy 158
Milner, John 190
Molitor, Paul 109
Monday, Rick 162
Montanez, Willie 159
Moore, Terry 5
Moose, Bob 191
Mordecai, Mike 69
Moreland, Keith 217
Morgan, Joe 10, 70,73, 75, 190, 216
Morris, Jack 135
Mota, Manny 107
Munson, Thurman 171
Murcer, Bobby 163, 180
Murphy, Dale 156
Murray, Eddie 126, 153
Murtaugh, Danny 188
Musial, Stan 5
Mussina, Mike 251

Nelson, Jeff 226–238, **228**
Nen, Robb 6, 112
Nettles, Graig 171
Nolan, Gary 73
Nomo, Hideo 123
Norman, Fred 73

Oliva, Tony 23
Oliver, Al 186–187

Oliver, Darren 21
O'Neill, Paul 152–153
Ozark, Danny 106, 216

Padilla, Vincente 219
Palmeiro, Rafael 71, 147
Palmer, Arnold 36
Palmer, Jim 178
Parrish, Lance 229
Pavano, Carl 8, 18, 21, 24, 51, 58–59, 127
Penny, Brad 8, 18, 21, 24, 42, 51, 58–59, 67, 69, 127
Perez, Tony 10, 70–77, **72**, **175**, 176, 190, 216
Perry, Gaylord 77
Pettitte, Andy 68, 93, 113, 137, 158, 164, 195–196, 208, 210, 224, 231
Piazza, Mike 235–236
Pierre, Juan 10, 23, 44, 61, 63, 67, 69, 97, 101, 112, 114–121, **117**
Piniella, Lou 167–176, **170**, **175**, 180, 229, 237
Pinson, Vada 71
Plummer, Bill 229
Posada, Jorge 2, 4, 69, 224
Powell, Boog 179, 189
Pratt, Todd 92
Prior, Mark 50, 119
Pro Player Stadium 60, 80, 91, 100, 124, 129, 134, 149, 151, 158, 160, 168, 170, 178–179, 185, 194–195, 201, 207, 209, 213, 215, 223, 228, 240, 247, 250, 253
Puckett, Kirby 182
Pujols, Albert 9

Raines, Tim 45, 234
Ramirez, Manny 126, 141, 144, 153, 249
Randolph, Willie 171, 173, 231
Reardon, Jeff 182
Redman, Mark 8, 38
Redman, Mike 45–46, 52, 61
Renteria, Edgar 6–7, 30, 77, 241
Rettenmund, Merv 189
Reuss, Jerry 162
Righetti, Dave 180
Ripken, Cal, Jr. 229
Rivera, Mariano 11, 42, 84, 93–94, 99, 103, 119, 183, 204, 223–224, 231–233, 245, 247, 252

Index 261

Rivers, Mickey 171
Robertson, Andre 180
Robertson, Bob 185–189
Robinson, Bill 45, 75
Robinson, Brooks 179
Robinson, Frank 11, 71, 77, 189
Rodriguez, Alex 9, 13, 221, 236
Rodriguez, Ivan 1, 8, 10, 19–21, 25, 51–52, 61–62, 67, 76–77, 118
Roger Dean Stadium 4, 16–17, 28, 38, 40, 48–49, 54, 56, 71–72, 115, 242
Rogers, Kenny 128
Rogers, Steve 162
Rolen, Scott 11
Rose, Pete 10, 70, 73, 75, 176, 190, 214, 216–217
Rosenthal, Wayne 8, 48, 54–63, **56**, 67
Rudi, Joe 178
Rumsfeld, Donald 7, 15, 22
Russell, Bill 107
Ruth, Babe 3, 42
Ryan, Nolan 162, 179, 213–214, 217

Sabo, Chris 99
Safeco Field 237
Sandberg, Ryne 100–101
Sanders, Reggie 11
Sandt, Tommy 34
Sanguillen, Manny 186–187
Sasaki, Kazuhiro 220, 222, 225
Sax, Steve 229
Schilling, Curt 84–85, 95–96, 102, 152, 222
Schmidt, Jason 118
Schmidt, Mike 105–107, 214, 216
Schoendienst, Red 5, **6**
Schourek, Pete 125
Scully, Vince 109
Seattle Kingdome 202, 230
Seaver, Tom 181
Selig, Bud 9
Shea Stadium 181
Sheffield, Gary 13, 29, 31, 34, 77, 110, 139
Showalter, Buck 251
Simon, Randall 184
Slaught, Don 29
Slaughter, Enos 5
Smiley, John 29
Smith, Lonnie 217

Smoltz, John 10, 12, 126–127, 132–140, **134**, 142–143, 155–156, 203, 232
Snow, J.T. 112
Sojo, Louie 45
Soriano, Alfonso 10, 220–225, **223**
Sosa, Sammy 102, 118
Speaker, Tris 207–208
Sprague, Ed 79
Stanton, Mike 204
Stargell, Willie 186–187, 189
Steinbrenner, George 96, 173–174, 176, 180, 224, 231, 237
Stewart, Dave 182
Strawberry, Darryl 234
Sutcliffe, Rick 100–101
Sutton, Don 158–159

Tanana, Frank 179
Tejada, Miguel 147
Tenace, Gene 178
Thome, Jim 126, 153, 199–205, **201**
Thorne, Gary 109
Torborg, Jeff 8, 16, 39, 57, 111
Torre, Joe 22, 96, 221, 224, 231, 233
Trillo, Manny 217
Tutor, John 182

Urbina, Ugueth 8, 44, 60, 112

Valentine, Bobby 166
Valenzuela, Fernando 162
Van Slyke, Andy 29
Vazquez, Javier 13
Vina, Fernando 241
Virdon, Bill 187
Vizquel, Omar 153

Wagner, Billy 209–210, 219
Wakefield, Tim 199, 202
Walker, Larry 65, 244
Walton, Jerome 100
Ward, Duane 109
Weaver, Earl 188
Welch, Bob 167, 172, 182
Wells, David 42, 234–235
Wetteland, John 231
White, Devon 77
White, Frank 23
White, Roy 171, 180
Williams, Bernie 153, 224, 230
Williams, Matt 95, 102, 200

Williams, Mitch 100, 136
Willis, Dontrelle 8, 10, 17–18, 21, 24–25, 38, 51, 54–55, 58–59, 63–69, **66**, 76, 108, 117
Wills, Maury 10
Wilson, Dan 230
Wilson, Mookie 181
Wilson, Preston 65
Wilson, Willie 121, 215
Winfield, Dave 135, 180
Witt, Mike 182
Wohlers, Mark 128, 203
Wolf, Randy 219

Womack, Tony 84–85, 102–103
Wood, Kerry 50, 119, 146, 165
Wrigley Field 1, 13, 41–42, 217

Yankee Stadium 1–3, 6, 9, 16, 41, 48, 50, 68, 81, 103, 108, 119–120, 144, 151, 162, 171, 204, 225–226, 229, 237, 252
Young, Michael 224
Yount, Robin 78–88, **80**, 229

Zimmer, Don 100–101, 172

www.ingramcontent.com/pod-product-compliance
Ingram Content Group UK Ltd.
Pitfield, Milton Keynes, MK11 3LW, UK
UKHW041932140426
5217IPUK00014B/434